# Muslim Identity and Social Change in Sub-Saharan Africa

# Muslim Identity and Social Change in Sub-Saharan Africa

*edited by*

LOUIS BRENNER



INDIANA UNIVERSITY PRESS

BLOOMINGTON AND INDIANAPOLIS

Manufactured in Hong Kong

**Library of Congress Cataloging-in-Publication Data**

Muslim identity and social change in Sub-Saharan Africa / edited by Louis Brenner.
p. cm.
Includes bibliographical references and index.
ISBN 0-253-31269-8. -- ISBN 0-253-31271-X (pbk.)
1. Islam and politics--Africa, Sub-Saharan. 2. Islam--Africa, Sub-Saharan. 3. Africa, Sub-Saharan--Politics and government.
I. Brenner, Louis.
BP64.A4S834 1993
306.6'97'0967--dc20 93-10131

1 2 3 4 5 97 96 95 94 93

# PREFACE

The contributions to this book were presented in April 1991 at an international conference on Islamic Identities in sub-Saharan Africa, co-organized by Professor Lamin Sanneh, now Professor at the Yale University Divinity School, and myself. Generous financial support from the School of Oriental and African Studies, University of London, the Center for the Study of World Religions, Harvard University, and the Nuffield Foundation in London, not only made this conference possible but also enabled a large number of participants to travel from Africa in order to attend.

The thirteen papers included here were selected from a total of thirty-two presented at the conference. Financial constraints made it impossible to publish the full proceedings in a single volume, although most of the papers which do not appear in this book have been, or are being, published elsewhere.

Several criteria were adopted in selecting contributions for this volume. Firstly, that the collection of articles should focus primarily on the evolution of Muslim societies in sub-Saharan Africa during the past several decades and represent the broad range of Muslim communities which exist, socially, doctrinally and politically. Examples range from the tiny minority communities of South Africa to regions where Islam, and now Islamism, enjoy an overwhelming influence, such as northern Nigeria and northern Sudan. An attempt was also made to provide broad geographical coverage, although inevitably there are imbalances. And finally, some priority was placed on including the work of younger scholars who are publishing the results of recent research for the first time.

A number of individuals assisted me in the preparation of this book, for which I would like to express my appreciation. Jackie Collis and Wangari Muoria typed portions of the manuscript onto disk, Catherine Lawrence prepared the map, Andrew Manley compiled the index, and Michael Mann and Renuka Madan provided invaluable technical advice for the preparation of camera-ready copy.

*London*
*May 1993*

LOUIS BRENNER

# PREFACE

# CONTENTS

# NOTES ON THE CO-AUTHORS

*Awad Al-Sid Al-Karsani* is Lecturer in Politics at the University of Khartoum, Republic of Sudan.

*Justo Lacunza Balda* is Lecturer in Arabic and Islamic Studies at the Pontificio Istituto di Studi Arabi e d'Islamistica, Rome, Italy.

*Bawuro M. Barkindo* is Professor of History at Bayero University, Kano, Nigeria. He is presently on secondment to the National Boundary Commission, Lagos, as Director of the Research and Documentation Centre.

*Louis Brenner* is Reader in the History of Religion in Africa at the School of Oriental and African Studies, University of London.

*François Constantin* is Professor of Political Science at the Université de Pau et des Pays de l'Adour, France.

*Emmanuel Grégoire* is Research Fellow at the Centre National de Recherche Scientifique in Paris, France.

*Muhammed Haron* is Lecturer in Arabic at the University of the Western Cape, Bellville, Republic of South Africa.

*Ahmed Rufai Mohammed* is Senior Lecturer in the History of Islam and Head of the History Department at Bayero University, Kano, Nigeria.

*R.S. O'Fahey* is Professor of Middle Eastern History at the University of Bergen, Norway.

*Stefan Reichmuth* is Heisenberg Lecturer in Islamic Studies at the University of Mainz, Germany.

*David C. Sperling* is Senior Lecturer in History at the University of Nairobi, Kenya.

*Alan Thorold* is Junior Lecturer in Anthropology at the University of Durban-Westville, Republic of South Africa.

*Muhammad Sani Umar* is Assistant Lecturer in Islamic Studies at the University of Jos, Nigeria, and is presently completing his Ph.D. at Northwestern University in the United States.

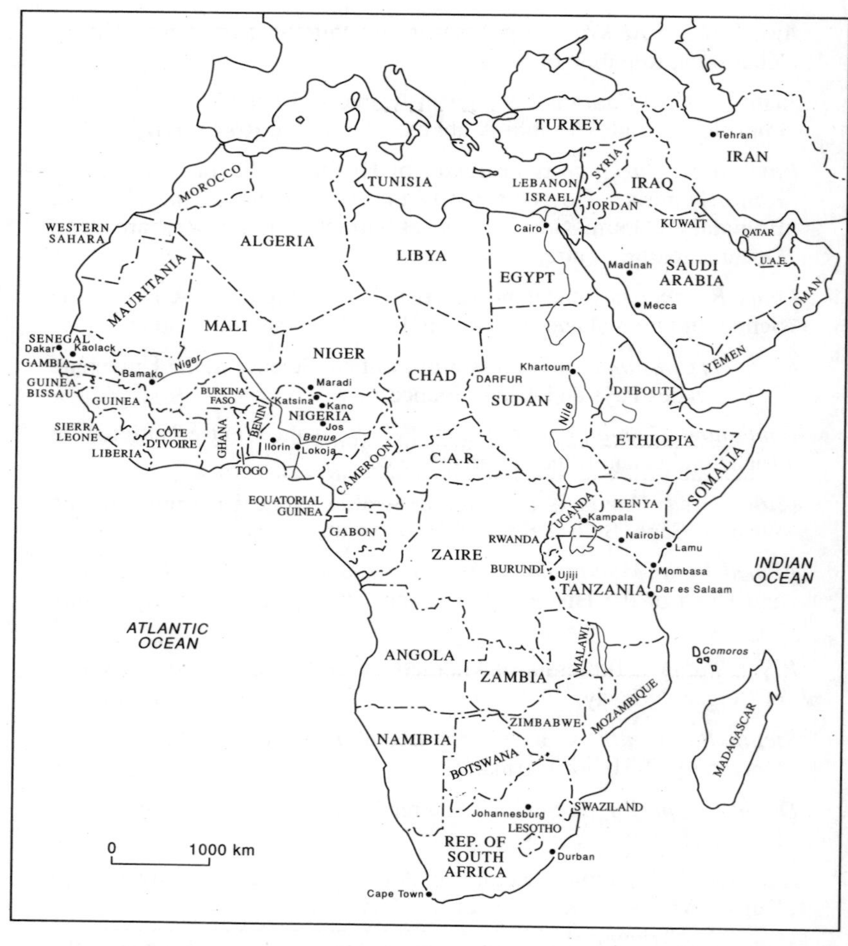


Political map of Africa showing locations mentioned in the text

INTRODUCTION

# MUSLIM REPRESENTATIONS OF UNITY AND DIFFERENCE IN THE AFRICAN DISCOURSE

*Louis Brenner*

In the mid 1960s, I.M. Lewis remarked in the final paragraphs of his comprehensive introduction to *Islam in Tropical Africa*, that

> ... if everywhere in tropical Africa Islam is today on the march, the wider political consequences of any great new expansion of Muslim influence and Pan-Islamic solidarity seem likely to be tempered by the increasing secularism of modern Muslim states and the general recognition that secular aims and politics are more important in the modern world than common religious interest. ... As with Christianity in the West, Islamic civilization is being gradually detached from its religious roots, and the gulf between the spiritual and the secular spheres of life is widening. While, as elsewhere in the Muslim world, continuing to influence deeply the private lives of individuals, it is thus at least questionable whether Islam can be expected in the future to exercise the profound political effect it has had in earlier periods of African history.
>
> Thus, although Islam may be regarded as a distinctive mode of life and religion, as a historical heritage, or as a general ideology of universal applicability, or, indeed, as all of these, it is increasingly on the first two, rather than on the last of these that the emphasis falls today. And the paradox is that Islam is gaining its greatest following in the history of tropical Africa at a time when its wider influence seems to be diminishing.[1]

It seems unlikely that an observer of Africa in 1992 would endorse this statement as it stands, so dramatically has the role of Islam in Africa, and in the world, changed within a few decades. Many of these changes were already underway by the mid-1960s, as the contributions to the present book demonstrate, although their impact and implications were not yet manifest. Today, Islam has become a major factor in world politics, and in consonance with this trend African Muslims have increasingly been turning to Islam for the resolution of their own social and political problems; they are injecting themselves into the political arena *as Muslims*.

Collectively, the studies in this book explore this process of how African Muslims are attempting to enhance their social status and to

[1]I.M. Lewis (ed.), *Islam in Tropical Africa* (London, 1966), p. 91.

assert their political objectives by adopting new strategies of self-presentation and political contestation. What seems clear is that the many challenges which colonization and secularization posed for African Muslims have in fact stimulated a new dynamic of Islamization on the continent. I.M. Lewis noted in the introduction to his book that the relative stability imposed in Africa by colonial rule had engendered an unprecedented expansion of Islam.[2] But he also concluded, in the excerpt quoted above, that "secular aims and politics are more important in the modern world than common religious interest." This statement requires reassessment, because present evidence suggests that the same social and political processes which were thought to undermine the influence of religion in public life have in fact served to strengthen it. The problematic which requires study is not how the secular comes to replace the religious, but how these two "world-views" have interacted in the lived experience of Africans.

Among the various themes which run through these essays, two seem to be particularly relevant to an analysis of this problematic. The first of these might be referred to as pressures toward the "rationalization" of African society, if this term can be understood in a neutral and non-pejorative sense. Under this rubric we include several trends, such as the politicization of public life, or what political scientists refer to as the emergence of the civil society in its various forms; here we are concerned primarily with the evolution of Muslim interest groups. There is also the increasing bureaucratization of religious organizations, what Weber referred to as the routinization of charisma; here the major example is the transformation of Sufi brotherhoods into political interest groups and even into political parties. And finally, there is the rise of mass education, both religious and secular, with the attendant increase in the incidence of literacy; modernized education may in fact be the most significant driving force of this entire process, because young educated persons have generally taken the lead in the formation of Muslim interest groups and in the politicization of Islam.

The second major theme is the role of "secularism" in post-colonial Africa. This term is necessarily ambiguous. The evolution of Muslim political consciousness is closely related to the resounding failure of what Muslims perceive as "secularism" to respond to the continuing and deepening social, economic and political crisis which grips the continent. "Secularism" in this view includes many notions: modernization, westernization, and materialism, to mention only a few. The ambiguity arises from the fact that, although many Muslims

[2]*Ibid.*, pp. 76-83.

claim to be firmly opposed to "secularism," the "rationalization" which is contributing to their own political dynamism brings in its train many secular attributes. Indeed, it is arguable that the single important ideological disagreement which distinguishes the Islamists from the secularists in Africa is over whether or not the laws which govern society should be based on God's revelations to Muhammad. When Islamists take power, as they are in the process of doing presently in the Sudan, the social and political implications of this difference are profound, especially for the secularists who formerly held power. But a question of deeper and longer-term significance poses itself: will their religious ideologies better equip the Islamists to resolve the crises which have contributed to their ascendancy, or have they simply contributed to the substitution of one dominant class by another, which once in power will quickly move to consolidate its own position in order to serve its own private interests? This question is not directly addressed in this book, but it is appropriate to raise it here in view of recent analyses of African politics which suggest that the Islamists are a counter-élite produced by the same processes and interests which produced the secularists.[3]

The distinction between "secularism" and Islam is particularly significant in public discourse, where some Muslims repeatedly refer to "secularism" and all its alleged detriments in order to reinforce their own Islamic identity. It is not unusual for social groups to define themselves in terms of the alleged attributes of an Other; for Muslims in Africa, the secularists provide a convenient Other, along with non-Muslims and Christians. But in the context of the social dynamics here under discussion, it is also common for some Muslims to distinguish themselves from other Muslims, that is to present themselves in public life as *particular kinds of Muslims*. One of the more frequent manifestations of this phenomenon, illustrated in this book, is the confrontation between Sufi and anti-Sufi factions, which is also widespread elsewhere in the Muslim world today. Several contributions to the book argue that such doctrinal distinctions are reflections of social and political divisions, for example between rich and poor, urban and rural, or youth and elders. Indeed, Awad Al-Karsani contends that in the Sudan, Islam is a vehicle for giving expression to "ideological, socio-economic and political cleavages." And if some Muslims have been generally critical of the secularists in power, they have also been critical of other Muslims in power, whom they have charged with using their positions for their own benefit.

[3]See J.F. Bayart, *L'Etat en Afrique. La politique du ventre* (Paris, 1989).

If this book is essentially about the "rationalization" of Muslim social and political strategies, and the blurring of religious and secular boundaries, it is also about the tensions which exist between the notion of Islam as a force for unification of all Muslims within the universal *umma*, and the powerful potential which Islamic ideologies provide for the expression of difference. This tension is manifest on all levels of the public discourse, and is indeed an integral part of the process of the politicization of Islam now underway. The discourse itself has been produced by those same forces of "rationalization," and the orientation of this introductory essay is to analyze the interplay of these notions of unity and difference in the context of both the local and continental discourses.

## *The "rationalization" of Islam*

Let us begin this discussion with a brief overview of recent events in South Africa, where Muslims constitute less than 2% of the population. Our purpose is to demonstrate how, even in the smallest of Muslim minority communities, Islam becomes politicized by the forces which we are here referring to as "rationalization." The specific process under examination is how Islam was recruited into the anti-apartheid struggle during the 1960s, '70s and '80s, a process which involved a transition from Muslims acting as individuals by joining various secular political organizations, to Muslims organizing themselves into *Muslim* anti-apartheid organizations.

We can begin in 1956, when, at the age of thirty-two years, 'Abdullah Haron was appointed Imam of the al-Jamia mosque in Claremont, Cape Town; thirteen years later, in 1969, he was murdered in detention.[4] He was allegedly arrested on suspicion that he was an agent of the Pan-Africanist Congress (PAC), and that he had been arranging for members of the PAC to receive military training abroad under the guise of recruiting students for the University of al-Azhar in Cairo. Regardless of the truth or falsehood of these suspicions, the Imam was certainly an activist who seems to have been politicized by the Sharpville massacre of 1960. In the repressive atmosphere of this period, he began to organize relief for the blacks in the townships surrounding Cape Town, and subsequently began to proselytize among them, the first move of this kind in South Africa. In 1961, he participated in the founding of a Muslim umbrella organization to oppose the Group Areas Act. He became increasingly associated with

[4]Information included here about Imam Haron is based upon B. Desai and C. Marney, *The Death of the Imam* (London, 1978), but also see Muhammad Haron's essay in this book.

the Coloured People's Congress, which was subsequently banned, and he began to speak out against apartheid in his Friday sermons.

In 1966, the Coloured People's Congress advised all its members to join the PAC, a party devoted to the overthrow of apartheid by any means possible, including violence. In December of the same year, Imam Abdullah departed for his fourth pilgrimage. First in Cairo, and then in London, he allegedly contacted PAC agents with whom he developed the scheme for which he was subsequently arrested.

'Abdullah Haron's brief public career suggests that he had placed Islam at the service of his political commitments. Not that he was any less religious, but he felt himself compelled to use his position as Imam to oppose the injustices which pervaded South African life. As Muhammed Haron argues in this book, the Imam's decision was based on his conviction that Islam was "a total way of life" and not simply a religion, a stance which distanced him from the more cautious *'ulama* of the Muslim Judicial Council of the Cape, as well as from other conservative Muslims. It was in this context that the *Muslim News*, for which he was a member of the editorial board during the 1960s, failed to speak out against his detention, claiming that he was being detained for his political rather than his religious views.

Imam Haron was not responsible for radicalizing Muslim politics in the Cape; events in South Africa had done this. But he has become a symbol of this transition for Cape Muslims, and his political radicalization seems to have been the result of his own experience of oppression within South Africa along with other South Africans of colour. The radicalization process continued after his death, giving rise to a spate of Muslim organizations, founded mostly by students and young persons and dedicated to the struggle against apartheid. In this process we see the interaction of external influences with the constraints imposed by social and political conditions in South Africa. The Muslim Youth Movement, founded in 1970, was much influenced by the books of Mawdudi and Qutb, and by the example of the Muslim Brotherhood. *Qibla*, an organization founded in 1980, was inspired by the Iranian revolution. It is a small but extremely radical group calling for armed *jihad* against the state and the establishment of the *shari'a* in South Africa. Some of its members even embraced Shi'ism, which earned them the vilification of the Sunni *'ulama*.

One of the actors in these events, Farid Esack, has argued in effect that the Muslim Youth Movement and *Qibla* have been ineffective in South Africa because they were not closely enough linked to local secular movements. As he put it, the Muslim organizations had embarked upon a "search for an outside model of Islam," whereas the Call of Islam (his own organization) was seeking what he called a

"South African Islam."[5] For him, a South African Islam would be one which could mobilize South African Muslims for an effective attack against apartheid.

However, *Qibla* was also linked with the PAC, and embraced the latter's orientation as a black consciousness movement. The 1970s saw the rise of the black consciousness movement and, in 1976, another major radicalizing event, the student uprisings in Soweto. The events in Soweto led to a small but significant number of conversions to Islam among black South Africans. One of these, who converted in 1977, is Abdurrahman Zwane, amir of the South African *al-Murabitun*. Zwane is a Zulu. He identifies his movement symbolically with the eleventh-century Almoravid movement in Morocco, and ideologically with the American black Muslim, Malcolm X. In his view, real political power cannot be removed from the whites in South Africa without the transfer to blacks of the control of the country's wealth.[6]

Muhammed Haron's essay about the *Muslim News* provides an insight into the kinds of tensions which built up in the Cape Town Muslim community as Imam Abdullah and others began to bring Islam into the struggle against apartheid. There was resistance from vested financial interests (the owners of the newspaper) and from more conservative religious elements within the community. But the trend took hold, and was subsequently radicalized by students and young educated persons who began to take an ideological lead from other Muslim and radical leaders abroad in order to confront their own problems in South Africa. Taken together, these Muslim movements in South Africa may resemble a bundle of ideological and doctrinal contradictions, but the process which has brought them into being is widespread in Africa: young, educated Muslims organizing themselves with the intention of bringing Islamic principles to bear in a political struggle.

The process can be examined in greater detail from the perspective of some of the essays contained in this book. Both Stefan Reichmuth and David Sperling write about the modernization and expansion of Islamic school systems (*madrasas*) in Nigeria and Kenya. The founders of these schools looked to Islamic models, of course, but both authors insist that the systematic and fundamental changes which evolved were stimulated by the existence and influence of secular and Christian

[5]Moulana Farid Esack, "Three Islamic strands in the South African struggle for justice," *Third World Quarterly*, vol. 10, no. 2 (1988), p. 492.

[6]Gamal Nkrumah, "Muslim Associations in South Africa," paper presented at the conference on "Islamic Identities in Africa," SOAS, London, 18-20 April 1991.

schools in these countries.[7] In the course of their evolution, these schools have taken many different forms. Some are simply reformed Qur'anic schools, but in Ilorin, for example, some have developed into a completely new form of Muslim institution in which secular and Islamic subjects are taught alongside one another. This process of integration has proceeded to the point in Ilorin where Islamic and secular education have become very closely interrelated with one another, even up to university level, with the result that persons educated in the Muslim schools have become fully integrated into public life in Ilorin.

Although the evolution of the rural *madrasas* of Kenya has been stimulated by the example of government schools, they have not been so fully integrated with the public system as in the Nigerian example. One reason for this is that parents have turned to the *madrasas* to resist the secularizing influences which are present in the state schools. But Sperling also demonstrates that in the rural Digo area where he has conducted his research, there is a strong resistance to any form of external intervention, whether in the form of secular technical advice or of Muslim financial assistance; the rural *madrasas* of the region serve, along with other religious practices, to reinforce the identity of Digo Muslims with respect to their coastal Swahili neighbours.

This tension between the Swahili coast and the Muslim interior is also discussed in the essays by Justo Lacunza Balda and François Constantin. Lacunza Balda describes the recent emergence of a "Swahili Islam" in East Africa, in reaction to the entrenched "Arab" hegemony of the coast. The terms "Swahili" and "Arab" require some explanation in this context. The East African coast is of course known as the Swahili coast. In the East African discourse, the term Swahili is a virtual synonym for Muslim, and in the interior African Muslims are often referred to as Swahili even if they have never been to the coast. But the coastal Swahili Muslims see themselves as the rightful guardians of the true Islamic heritage in East Africa, and they have consistently attempted to maintain their hegemony over all manifestations of Islam in the region, and look with disdain upon more recent Muslim converts from the interior.[8] But within this coastal group are those who perceive themselves as "Arabs" and as the true

[7]The same is true elsewhere in Africa. For Mali, see L. Brenner and B. Sanankoua, *L'enseignement islamique au Mali* (Bamako, 1991), and L. Brenner, *Controlling Knowledge: Religion, Education and Power in Muslim West Africa*, forthcoming. See also S. Reichmuth, "'Ilm und Adab. Islamische Bildung und soziale Integration in Ilorin, Nigeria, seit ca. 1800," unpublished Habilitation thesis, Universität Bayreuth, 1991.

[8]See Anne Kubai, "The Early Muslim Communities of Nairobi," *Islam et Sociétés au Sud du Sahara*, no. 6, 1992, pp. 33-44.

guardians of religious scholarship and knowledge in all of East Africa, including the coast. These "Arabs" have been recently challenged by two groups. The first consists of young men who have received a modernized religious training in Sudan, Egypt or Saudi Arabia, who are fluent in Arabic, and who are contesting the established leadership of the coast. And the second are the proponents of what Lacunza Balda calls "Swahili Islam," a movement based in the East African interior which is using the Kiswahili language, to the exclusion of Arabic, as the vector of proselytization among black Africans. This movement is well organized, having formed a number of associations designed not only to provide formal education but also to spread public preaching in Kiswahili. They are highly politicized, taking the Islamic Republic of Iran as a model, and strongly anti-Christian.

This East African example, like the South African one, demonstrates the current trend for educated Muslims to organize themselves into interest groups. In fact, this aspect of the "rationalizing" process is also stimulated simply by the founding of modernized Muslim schools. Sperling shows that the growth of the rural *madrasa* system of Kenya has been generated by a grassroots movement which necessitated a new level of local organization, because the new *madrasas* were managed by committees rather than by a single teacher, as was characteristic of most Qur'anic schools. In Ilorin, the pioneers of the modernized Islamic school system were the founders of the first modern Muslim voluntary association in Northern Nigeria, the *Ansaru 'l-Islam* Society. The *Ansaru 'l-Islam* Society promoted Muslim interests in general, and guided the expansion of the new school system in particular. There are those in Ilorin who claim that the *Jama'atu Nasril Islam*, founded in 1962 by the then Premier of Nigeria's Northern Region, Ahmadu Bello, was modelled on the *Ansaru l-Islam* Society. Whether this is true or not, the progression of institutional development and the evolution of Muslim political consciousness which it suggests is apt. There is a relationship between the emergence of modernized, mass education (whether secular or religious), the founding by educated persons of voluntary associations to represent and protect their own interests, and efforts by political leaders to coopt religion as a "political resource" (see the chapter by François Constantin).

The *Jama'atu Nasril Islam* was meant to promote Muslim unity in the north of Nigeria, although as one can see from Muhammad Sani Umar's essay, this project was compromised almost from the time of its inception by the emergence of so many conflicting interest groups in the region. Similar efforts by national leaders to organize Islam from the top down in order to control the fractiousness of Muslim groups and hopefully to build political unity on notions of *umma* are common throughout the continent. But as Constantin demonstrates for eastern Africa, these projects usually fail because they are rarely if ever built upon the real needs of the populations they are meant to serve. (See also the essays by Brenner for AMUPI in Mali, and by Lacunza Balda for criticisms of BAKWATA in Tanzania.) The existence of centralized state authority seems to give rise to a need to control the population, at least to the extent of maintaining a degree of stability consonant with the demands of executing policy decisions.

But any attempt to build such stability on the basis of a call to religious sensibilities seems a volatile strategy. The Republic of Sudan is a significant case in point, where an Islamic government is now in the process of establishing itself. Here there is presumably no need for a national Muslim organization, since the state itself will be Islamic. According to R.S. O'Fahey, in their attempts to establish a Muslim hegemony in the country, the Islamists are representing their policies as a return to Afro-Islamic "authenticity," a claim which has a particular appeal in a region which saw the appearance of the Mahdi in the nineteenth century. On the other hand, it is a contradictory appeal in a country which is deeply divided between a Muslim north and a non-Muslim south. Furthermore, if Awad Al-Karsani is correct in his assertion that religious protest is generated by social discontent, then given the conditions of social deprivation and instability from which the Sudan suffers, it seems unlikely that mere appeals to unity, on whatever grounds, will have much effect. In other words, the establishment of an Islamic government is unlikely in itself to put an end to Muslim protest. And indeed, recent events in the Sudan do not suggest that the government intends to rely simply on appeals.

As suggested above, the fundamental question for the Sudan is whether the policies and programmes of the Islamists will differ in any essential way from those of their predecessors, or whether they too will fall prey to the "politics of the belly."[9] The perquisites of power are extremely tempting, and the social and economic problems of the country are intractable. Can Islam make a substantive contribution to modern governance beyond the imposition of Shari'a law? Certainly, there is no other arena in which the boundaries of secularism and religion will be so thoroughly strained as in the field of contemporary government and politics. But of course, an assessment of this process must await future developments. These observations are also relevant to the situation in Kano, described by Bawuro Barkindo, where the

[9] J.F. Bayart, *L'Etat en Afrique. La politique du ventre.*

intense problems produced by rapid urbanization have led to a call for "Islamic solutions."

The history of the various Islamist groups which have gained such a predominant influence in the Sudan has followed the same general pattern described above: educated young persons, organizing themselves into Islamically-oriented interest groups which eventually manage to impose their weight on the evolution of national politics. Such Islamist groups define themselves not only in opposition to European and secular influences but also against Sufism, which they often castigate as a deviation from true Islam. This has been the case not only in the Sudan, but throughout Africa where Sufism has extended its influence in the past. The Sufi orders themselves have not resisted the pressures toward bureaucratization; in the Sudan, the Khatmiyya and the "neo-Mahdist" groups have been transformed into political parties.[10] But al-Karsani's description of the Niass branch of the Tijaniyya in the Sudan is particularly illustrative of this process: the evolution of a populist but highly centralized organization which stretches right across Sudanic Africa from Senegal to the Republic of Sudan. A comparison of his essay with that of Ahmed Rufai Mohammed demonstrates that the religious doctrines of the Niassiyya do not manifest themselves everywhere in the same manner, but once again the same process of social and political evolution is evident. In the Niger-Benue confluence region of Nigeria, the rise of the Niassiyya has been consonant with the emergence to positions of public leadership of a young, educated class of Muslim civil servants, integrated into public life through a process similar to that already described for Ilorin.[11]

The Sufi/anti-Sufi confrontation is discussed in a number of essays (O'Fahey, Brenner, Thorold, Al-Karsani, and Muhammad Sani Umar). Muhammad Sani Umar provides a fascinating analysis of the transformation of an anti-Sufi doctrinal initiative into a Muslim interest group. His analysis of the Nigerian situation is very similar to that of Al-Karsani for the Sudan. In his opinion, the anti-Sufi movement in Nigeria, though originating in a doctrinal critique of Sufism, is in fact the religious expression of concerns and

[10]The role of the Sufi brotherhoods in Senegalese national politics has been extensively studied. See for example, Lucy C. Behrman, *Muslim Brotherhoods and Politics in Senegal* (Cambridge, Mass, 1970); Christian Coulon, *Le marabout et le prince, Islam et pouvoir au Sénégal* (Paris, 1981), and D.C. Cruise O'Brien, *The Mourides of Senegal: The Political and Economic Organization of an Islamic Brotherhood* (Oxford, 1971).

[11]See Ahmed Rufai Mohammed, "Shaikh Ahmad Rufai and Abdulmalik and the Popular Phase of Islamisation in Ebiraland," *Islam et Sociétés au Sud du Sahara*, no. 6, 1992, pp. 47-63.

preoccupations brought about by the transformations of polity, society and economy which have occurred during the past several decades. He highlights the moment in 1978 when it was decided that the effectiveness of such a movement could only be assured through the establishment of a formal organization, which came to be known as the *Jama'atu Izalat al-Bid'a wa Iqamat al-Sunna* (*Izala*). Interestingly, the stimulus which brought about the founding of *Izala* was the formal organization of the Sufis into a national interest group. Within less than ten years of its founding, *Izala* extended its organization to every corner of the country where Muslims reside, providing educational services, preaching activities and a network for the distribution of their literature and cassettes.

Muhammad Sani Umar argues that anti-Sufism, linked as it is to the social and economic transformations affecting contemporary Nigeria, represents a transition from communal to individualistic modes of religiosity. The anti-Sufis, he claims, are generally those who are benefitting from such change, and the objects of their criticism are not only the Sufis but the inherited social structures and the allegedly antiquated forms of governance represented by the emirates of the North. An echo of this argument is found in Emmanuel Grégoire's interpretation that the young merchants of Zinder, in Niger, have embraced the doctrines of *Izala* precisely because they reinforce their resistance to communal obligations, and they represent "a form of Islam which is better adapted to meeting the modern world's economic and social requirements." And Al-Karsani illustrates a similar fundamental dichotomy among Sudanese Muslims based on socio-economic differences: the popular, messianic Islam of the poor and dispossessed who await an eschatological, other-worldly solution to the resolution of their problems, versus the Islam of the Islamist intellectuals, who propose Islamically-vetted, technocratic methods to lead the country out of its misery.

### *Islamic unity and African unity*

The contributions to this book, for the most part, address events in individual countries or regions. But the processes of "rationalization" here under discussion have also provided African Muslims with access to international means of communication not easily available to them during the colonial period, and their interests are not limited to local political issues. It seems appropriate, therefore, to explore Muslim perceptions of Africa in a broader, international context.

Much has also changed in this area since the publication of *Islam in Tropical Africa*, which was quoted in our opening paragraph above.

That book was the published proceedings of the Fifth International African Seminar of the International African Institute, held at Ahmadu Bello University, Zaria, in January 1964. Exactly twenty-five years later, in 1989, Nigerian Muslims organized the first international Islam in Africa Conference in the Nigerian city of Abuja. The final communiqué of this conference stated:

> Aware that Muslims in Africa share common experiences of profound transformation of their society which has been brought about by Islam; of being the object of imperial plunder and serving as a theatre for Europeans to fight proxy wars; of being a dumping ground for cultural and ideological ideas; and yet the continent has great potential to overcome all obstacles to its progress if it reverts to its rich Islamic heritage; ...
>
> Desirous of forging a common front to unite the Ummah with a view to facing its common enemies: the imperial forces of domination and secularization; illiteracy, poverty and degradation, and to rediscover and reinstate Africa's glorious Islamic past. ...
>
> We do hereby resolve, ... etc. etc.

One of the conference resolutions was to set up an Islam in Africa Organization which would have as one of its objectives the commissioning of experts "to write the history of Islam in Africa and of Muslims and their institutions from an authentic Islamic viewpoint."

In fact, that process had already begun. Two years earlier, in 1987, the Islamic Educational, Scientific and Cultural Organization (ISESCO), which is based in Rabat, published a book entitled *Africa and Arabo-Islamic Culture*.[12] ISESCO was founded in 1982 with a grant from the Organization of the Islamic Conference. Its primary aims are to support research and education within member states. *Africa and Arabo-Islamic Culture* is a collective book to which chapters have been contributed by university-trained, academic scholars, both Muslim and non-Muslim, who are analyzing the contribution of what they call Arabo-Islamic culture to the historical development of Africa south of the Sahara. The central lines of argument in the book are, first, that Arabo-Islamic culture is a fundamental unifying factor in African culture in general and, second, that the recent resurgence of

[12]*Ifrīqiyya wa 'l-thaqāfa al-'arabiyya al-islāmiyya* (Africa and Arabo-Islamic Culture), Rabat 1987. ISESCO was founded in 1982 in order to improve cooperation among Islamic states in the fields of education, culture and scientific research; its major programmes in Africa focus on literacy training and the intensification of the teaching of Arabic. Since 1983, the organization has published *Islam Today*, a journal which appears in Arabic, English and French.

Arabo-Islamic culture has been a major force in confronting and liberating Africa from Western imperial domination.

The Islam in Africa Conference and the publication of *Africa and Arabo-Islamic Culture* mark the introduction into the Muslim discourse of a theme which has long been more characteristic of the secular African discourse: the cultural and political unity of Africa. Furthermore, the participants in this discourse employ the methods of western scholarship to demonstrate the contention that historically, the most significant contributions to this unity have been accomplished by Muslims or, to quote them directly, "by Islam."

Many non-Muslim Africans will certainly reject the idea that Islam, or Arabo-Islamic culture, has been a fundamental unifying factor in Africa. On the other hand, one contributor to *Africa and Arabo-Islamic Culture* has a point, substantiated by several of the contributions to this book, when he argues that Muslims have consistently taken the initiative in Africa in resisting what he describes as the "intellectual and cultural aggression" of the West.[13] The author of this particular article may exaggerate the degree of Muslim resistance to the West, and rather ignore the extent of Muslim collaboration, but Muslim resistance has been real and is growing among Muslim intellectuals in Africa, as this essay has already demonstrated.

These Muslim intellectuals, sometimes referred to as the "new *'ulama*", are a diverse group which includes within itself, as a group, a sound education in the Islamic religious sciences and in secular subjects as well. In addition to the challenges they are posing to secularism in all its forms, they are concerned with the Islamization of all knowledge. Thus, perhaps, their adoption of the theme of "African" unity, a concept which becomes blurred with that of the international *umma* in certain of their statements.

The dissemination of the Arabic language is an important aspect of the programme of certain of the new *'ulama*.[14] The Islam in Africa Conference resolved:

> To encourage the teaching of the Arabic language, which is the language of the Qur'an *as well as the lingua franca of the continent*, and to strive for the restoration of the use of Arabic script in

[13]See Ahmad b. 'Uthman al-Tuwaijri, "al-Tarbiyya al-islāmiyya wa 'l-athāruhā fī muwājahat al-ghazwī 'l-fikrī fī 'l-qarra al-ifrīqiyya" (Islamic Education and its Influence in Confronting Intellectual Aggression on the African Continent) in *Ifrīqiyya wa 'l-thaqāfa al-'arabiyya al-islāmiyya*, pp. 125-35.

[14]See René Otayek (ed.), *Da'wa et arabisation. Vers l'émergence d'un radicalisme islamique en Afrique noire* (Paris, forthcoming).

> vernacular [that is, in the writing of African languages such as Kiswahili and Hausa].

And of course, it is the Arabic language which is meant to constitute the "Arab" element of Arabo-Islamic culture, not the Arab nation.[15] Perhaps it is significant that, although ISESCO normally publishes in English, French *and* Arabic, it should have chosen to distribute the Arabic edition of *Africa and Arabo-Islamic Culture* first in sub-Saharan Africa, where it might appeal to a large and growing population of Muslims literate in Arabic. This potential reading public is the product of the *madrasa* schools which have developed throughout sub-Saharan Africa since the 1940s (see especially the chapters by Reichmuth and Sperling).

Arabic is the language of instruction in many of these schools, but there are many permutations of the combinations of languages taught. In Mali, most students leaving the *madrasas* will be literate only in Arabic, even if French has also been taught as a subject. In East Africa, Kiswahili often competes with Arabic as the language of instruction, especially in Tanzania. In Northern Nigeria, students become literate in Arabic, Hausa and English. But of course Arabic is given high priority in Muslim schools because knowledge of Arabic is equated with knowledge of Islam; insofar as the modernized *madrasas* are producing a new class of *'ulama*, they must provide their students with a sound foundation in Arabic. These new *'ulama* are receiving advanced training in the Islamic studies departments of African universities or in Arabic-language universities. Until recently, most higher degrees for Arabic speakers were taken in the religious sciences, but now the pattern is changing, and we find Arabic-speakers obtaining degrees in the professions and the sciences.

So what is the "Africa" which is envisaged by the authors of *Africa and Arabo-Islamic Culture* and by the organizers of the Islam in Africa Conference? It is certainly an Africa unified in Islam through the principles of the universal *umma*, an inclusivist Islam which absorbs and dissolves all differences. It is an Africa unified also by the Arabic language, the knowledge of which is inextricably linked with the knowledge of Islam. It is an Africa which has recaptured its political independence and cultural autonomy from the West, and whose destiny is linked with the future of Islam.

[15] In fact, there are differing views on this question. See, for example, Adnan Haddad, Kabemba Mufuta and Mwembo Mutunda (eds.), *De la culture négro-arabe. [Fakhr as-sudan 'ala al-Bidan] ou Titres de gloire des noirs sur les blancs* (Paris: Diffusion SEDES, 1989). The editors of this book were inspired by the same conference which produced *Africa and Arabo-Islamic Culture*, although they prefer to denote Islamic cultural unity in Africa with the term "*négro-arabe*."

But there is much which is excluded from this image of Africa by its proponents. For one thing, allusions to the reinstatement of "Africa's glorious Islamic past" mean something very different to Muslims from what they mean to non-Muslims, to whom mention of Africa's Islamic past can represent the resurgence of another form of imperial expansion: the spread of *dar al-Islam* (the land of Islam) at the expense of *dar al-kufr* (the land of unbelief). In effect, this "Africa" becomes an Islamic frontier, a political and cultural battleground on which the forces of Islam confront an opposition of their own creation. For example, in Nigeria reference to the Sokoto Caliphate as the model of a unifying Islamic state in pre-colonial Africa is seen by non-Muslims as evidence that Muslims would like to unify Nigeria through the resumption of religious conquest. Furthermore, the concept of "Arabo-Islamic" culture resonates of ambiguity on a continent which suffers from the profound tensions and persistent conflicts which exist between "Arab" and "non-Arab" Africans, whether Muslim or not. The catalog of violent conflict which plagues Sudanic Africa is tragic and depressing: Mauritania-Senegal, Mali, Chad and the Sudan.

To a certain extent, of course, the Arabic language *can* act as a unifying factor. The impetus is to equate knowledge of Arabic with knowledge of Islam, and to equate being a Muslim with the defense of a range of certain "Islamic" causes against the encroachments of Western imperial power. Muslims in Africa are virtually unanimous in their opinions on the Palestinian issue, as they seem to have been in their support of Saddam Hussein in the 1991 Gulf War. The essay of Muhammed Haron demonstrates how the Cape Town newspaper *Muslim News* focused on the Palestinian question as a means of unifying South African Muslims, especially by emphasizing the parallel nature of oppression in the two situations.

But the impact in Africa of the Islamic Revolution in Iran demonstrates the weakness of "Arabism" on the continent. The appeal of the Iranian revolution in Africa rests on two factors: its radicalism and the fact that it is *not* "Arabo-Islamic." Events in Iran demonstrated that radical Islamic political programmes could be effected by non-Arabs. The Islamic Revolution has encouraged at least two kinds of Muslim movements in Africa: the first might be described as universalist because it sees radical Islam as the solution to all of humankind's social, political and economic ills. The second might be described as particularist, because it refers to the Iranian model in order to distinguish certain local expressions of Islam from one another, as for example with the "Swahili Islam" described by Justo Lacunza Balda.

The Muslim vision of "Africa" outlined here is only slowly penetrating the consciousness of Africans and Africanists alike, but there can be little doubt that it will become increasingly competitive with the other "Africas" which are projected in the African discourse, of which three might be mentioned here for purposes of comparison.

There is the geo-political Africa of the Pan-Africanists. This is the Africa which is portrayed on a map of the globe, a politically unified Africa, liberated from the colonial and post-colonial domination of the West. It is a secular Africa in which certain Arab countries and leaders have played a significant role, not so much as Muslims but as fellow-victims of colonial oppression. One might mention as an example, President Nasser of Egypt, whose policies skillfully used the religious appeal of the University of al-Azhar to attract young students to Egypt, but who also supported Arabic-language education in sub-Saharan Africa for the purposes of constructing the foundations of a continent-wide, secular political unity. In this Africa, Islam is recognized as part of the African cultural heritage, but it moves to the political background; in the secular vision, religious preference and commitment are purely personal matters. In this Africa, the mutual commitment to the struggle for political autonomy from the West dissolves all difference.

There is also a "Black Africa," an Africa south of the Sahara, which includes the blacks of the African diaspora in Europe and the Americas and simultaneously excludes Muslim (and "white") North Africa. In contrast with the Pan-Africanists who subsume difference in a project of political unity, and the Islamists who would do so in the universal *umma*, the proponents of "Black Africa" would subsume difference in a cultural heritage which is allegedly shared by all persons of African descent. This is the Africa of *négritude*, an Africa unified by the unique essence of its culture. This is the Africa of Cheikh Anta Diop, the late Senegalese scholar who founded a school of historical research based on the hypothesis that the culture of ancient Egypt was black African. His leading disciple, Théophile Obenga, archaeologist, linguist, historian and Egyptologist, has continued Diop's scholarly work in Africa, trying to reconstruct the history of Africa's ancient culture.

Some of Diop's most devoted followers are to be found among the Africans of the diaspora, especially in the United States. Out of this milieu has emerged what is known as the Afrocentric school of history, whose proponents seek to rewrite Africa's history in order to document the cultural unity of Black Africa, a project which is implicitly, and often explicitly, critical of both Islam and the West for destroying this unity. In this Africa, therefore, Islam often joins the slave-trading and imperialist West as antagonists, as the detractors and enemies of African culture and unity. Academically, Afrocentric scholars concern themselves much less with Islam than with Western and Western-trained African scholars, about whom they are extremely critical for having distorted Africa's past. The Afrocentric school seeks to produce an African history on a grand scale, what Diop called *histoire non-événementielle*, which will demonstrate the historical unity of Africa's cultural heritage. This approach is explicitly opposed to Western scholarship's preoccupation with the micro-study which, according to the Afrocentrists, thrives on the discovery and elaboration of difference among Africans.

Afrocentricity has attracted a following which includes both a small core of research scholars and a broad popular base, especially among the Africans of the diaspora. In the United States, these ideas have developed a degree of political bite both within academia, for example in the debates about Martin Bernal's book *Black Athena*,[16] and in considerations about how Africa and Africans should be presented in school curricula as an integral part of the Western cultural heritage. For blacks of the diaspora to look to Africa for political and cultural inspiration is not a new phenomenon; one need only recall that the roots of the pan-Africanist movement are found in the Western Hemisphere among such figures as Edward Blyden, Marcus Garvey and W.E.B. DuBois, to name only a few of the leading pioneers of the movement.

There is another dimension, however, to the relationship between the African diaspora and Islam. Despite the fact that many proponents of the Afrocentric school view the spread of Islam into Africa as destructive of African culture, there is a history of Islam among the Africans of the diaspora. The traces of the early history of African Muslims in the United States are few and virtually obliterated, but the Muslim-led slave rebellions in nineteenth-century Brazil are well documented.[17] Of greater interest to the present discussion, however, is the recent history of Islam among African-Americans. Islam is growing among black Americans, albeit still only a small minority, and not only through the Nation of Islam, formerly known as the Black Muslims and founded by Elijah Muhammad. In recent years

[16]Martin Bernal, *Black Athena. The Afroasiatic Roots of Classsical Civilization. Vol I: The Fabrication of Ancient Greece 1785-1985* (London, 1987). See also the works of Molefi Kete Asante, for example, *The Afrocentric Idea* (Philadelphia, 1987.)

[17]See Allan D. Austin, *African Muslims in Antebullum America: A Sourcebook* (London:, 1984), and his paper "Islamic Identities among Africans in the New World in the days of American Slavery," presented at the conference on "Islamic Identities in Africa," SOAS, London, 18-20 April 1991.

there has been an upsurge of conversions to forms of African Islam, in particular to the Senegalese Sufi brotherhoods. The Mourides have extended their trade networks to New York City where they work as street peddlars and taxi drivers; most of them are Senegalese, but they have begun to recruit and convert black Americans.[18] More startling is the growth of the Niass Tijaniyya, which now has *zawiyas* in many major American cities, including New York, Detroit, Cincinnati, Atlanta and Washington. In Kaolack, Senegal, the seat of the brotherhood, there is a community of black Americans who have come to live and study; there is a Qur'anic school for English-speaking children, which attracts Africans as well as Americans, since this branch of the Tijaniyya is well-established in Anglophone Africa. No statistics are available which might demonstrate the demographic significance of these movements among American Muslims; no doubt they are a tiny minority. But the fact of their existence, and their present expansion, demonstrates very well the dynamic interplay of concepts of Africa and Islam in the construction of identities among persons of African descent. An analysis of the Niass brotherhood's activities in the United States would provide a valuable complement to the three essays in this book which discuss its activities in Africa, those of Ahmed Rufai Mohammed, Muhammad Sani Umar and Awad Al-Karsani.

Finally, mention should be made of one more "Africa" which appears in the discourse. This is an Africa which owes its existence solely to the fact that there is a continent of that name. There is nothing unique or essentialist about this Africa, and some members of this school of thought seem as though they might be content if the term "Africa" disappeared from our vocabularies altogether. Theirs is a universalist view in which Africa and Africans are part of larger humanity. Their Africa is politically and economically marginalized and subjugated to the West, but its future is not to be found in its own uniqueness, but in the acquisition of universal scientific and technological knowledge which can be applied independently and autonomously for the benefit of the social and economic development of the continent. Islam seems to be completely absent from this vision of Africa.

These views spring largely from a Marxist heritage, and one of their most influential spokesmen to date has been the Benin philosopher Paulin Hountondji, whose writings have contributed a provocative cutting edge to an extensive debate about the nature of

[18]See Victoria Ebin, "Mouride Traders and International Trade Networks," paper presented at the conference on "Islamic Identities in Africa," SOAS, London, 18-20 April 1991.

"African philosophy."[19] His position is vehemently opposed by those who argue that Hountondji and his cohorts are prepared completely to ignore Africa's own heritage in favour of submitting to the intellectual and cultural domination of the West. Hountondji responds that human knowledge is universal and should not be classified or graded according to national or ethnic origin; the criteria for its adoption should be based on its practical applicability in solving social and economic problems. But, he argues, if anyone is being uncritically submissive to European ideas, it is those, such as the Afrocentrists, who have adopted notions of Africa as "Other" which are the invention of the European racist and imperialist mind.[20]

Even this brief overview demonstrates that the discourse in Africa about Africa's own identity is complex and includes numerous opposing and conflicting strands. And the discourse takes on a very different shape depending on the perspective from which it is viewed. For example, if we analyze it in terms of its Muslim versus secular components, then these two sub-discourses appear to be largely conflictual and mutually exclusive. Of course, they interrelate, but usually by way of criticism and by the exaggeration of difference. So, for example, Muslims construct their own identity in part by emphasizing the alleged shortcomings of what they see as secularist values and behaviour. The secularists have often simply ignored Islam as a significant social and political factor, although this becomes increasingly difficult as Muslims continue to politicize their interpretations of Islam, as they become more Islamist.

But viewed from other perspectives, the Muslim and secular discourses are quite similar, for example in their attitudes toward the West. All Africans share the aim of liberating the continent from the political, economic and cultural domination of the West. Even the Marxist school, while embracing the intellectual and scientific heritage of the West, wants to use that knowledge to liberate Africa from Western domination. The Muslim and secular discourses are also similar in how they juxtapose notions of unity and difference in order to present and advocate their own visions of Africa and their own programmes for the liberation of the continent. Of course, each of these discourses also contructs its own particular interpretation of the "the West," but an analysis of this concept is beyond the purposes of this introductory essay. The principal conclusion to be drawn at this stage in our discussion is that the Islamist discourse about Africa is as much about "Africa" as it is about "Islam."

[19]P.J. Hountondji, *African Philosophy, Myth and Reality* (London, 1983).

[20]A recent summary of this debate is to be found in V.Y. Mudimbe, *The Invention of Africa: Gnosis, Philosophy, and the Order of Knowledge* (Bloomington, 1988).

And finally, when we shift our attention to the local level of Muslim politics in Africa, we discover an even more complex array of Muslim identities, including notions of a "South African" or a "Swahili" Islam, which seem to contradict the fundamental principles of the universal *umma*. What is at issue here, of course, is racism, and despite the insistence by the ideologues of the universalist *umma* that Islam dissolves all differences of race, black Muslims in Africa are finding unity in Islam *as blacks*. This is precisely the kind of issue which plagued socialist debates for decades: whether socialism could really confront racism, or whether blacks should unite as blacks in order successfully to confront their problems. What these examples suggest, along with many others cited in this introduction, is that when Islam becomes "rationalized" and politicized, it becomes susceptible to the same forces which mould any social and political ideology, and can in turn act in order to affect these forces. And Islam is certainly one of the most powerful ideologies functioning on the African continent today.

# ISLAMIC HEGEMONIES IN THE SUDAN

## SUFISM, MAHDISM AND ISLAMISM

*R.S. O'Fahey*

More than four decades after its publication, J.S. Trimingham's *Islam in the Sudan*[1] remains the only survey of its kind. Much research has since been done, but no scholar has attempted a synthesis to replace Trimingham, and none, I suspect, will try. Trimingham's work is not only outdated in its analyses and attitudes (many of the latter being deeply offensive to Sudanese Muslims), but the very concept of such a survey would probably have few protagonists today.

Behind such hesitancy lie doubts about the usefulness of "Islam" as an analytical concept or independent variable in the historical analysis of societal change. These doubts are, of course, part of the ongoing debate about Orientalism. Leaving to one side the confusion of Orientalism as a colonial/racist phenomenon (which may invalidate conclusions but not necessarily methodologies, especially those that are philological) with the study of religion in society, there remains the problem of whether "Islam" can be abstracted from a specific socio-political context and subsequently usefully analysed. Rather than try and answer these questions, I shall try here to examine some themes within the modern history of the northern Sudan from the perspective of successive forms of hegemonic discourse – who sets the terms of discourse, what the discourse describes, and why. It is clear at the outset that this approach has its limitations; research has been uneven, the approach here laying too great an emphasis on the written word and thus accentuating the dominance of the predominant mode of discourse in any given period. But it may be useful in not only highlighting change over time, but in exposing gaps in our understanding, thus providing an agenda for future research.

### *Sacred kings and holy lineages*

The nominal Islamization and partial Arabicization of the northern Nilotic Sudan (Sudanese Nubia) took place largely in a period aptly called the "Dark Ages," between the collapse of the northern Nubian states in the thirteenth century and the rise of the savanna-based states in the sixteenth and seventeenth centuries. The conventional picture is of the gradual undermining of the medieval Christian Nubian kingdoms by a steady inflow of Arab nomads and traders, climaxing in a change

[1](Cambridge, 1949).

in Egyptian policy from co-existence under the Fatimids to a forward aggressive policy under the Ayyubids and Mamluks.[2] Questions about how "Christian" the Christian Nubian states were, whether there really was significant Arab immigration, the reasons why Arabic replaced local languages in some areas but not in others, and why there was a shift southwards in state-forming activity in the sixteenth century have still not been satisfactorily answered. Here, there has been a significant failure in interaction between archaeological and historical research.

By the late sixteenth and early seventeenth centuries, two states dominated the northern Sudan, the Funj kingdom based on the Blue Nile with its capital at Sinnar and Darfur in the west. The origins of both states remain unclear – the question of "Funj origins" providing many innocent hours of enjoyment for British colonial officials, as the pages of *Sudan Notes and Records* testify. The origin of the last major state in Darfur, the Keira Sultanate, is marginally more clearly "known," but only by contrast to its predecessors, the Daju and Tunjur, whose history is seemingly beyond reconstruction.[3]

Both the Funj and Darfur states were in their structure and ideology sacred kingships. The political elements varied, but common to both states was a sacred king who was the physical and cosmic centre of the state (most clearly seen in the Darfur *fashir* or royal compound), an elaborate title-holding aristocracy, strict state control over trade, especially long-distance trade ("Administered trade"), and a complex social order in which everyone "knew their place."[4] However, for neither Darfur nor the Funj has it been possible to reconstruct the "pristine" pre-Islamic polity; in both cases Islam was present *ab initio,* or at least from the beginning of the state's official history.[5] Here, one is up against the problem of historiographical hegemony; perhaps Islam's most potent innovation (in the non-religious sense) was literacy. It certainly ensured that history was written, if not spoken, by Muslim clerics who until this century held a monopoly

[2]See, further, Yusuf Fadl Hasan, *The Arabs and the Sudan* (Edinburgh, 1967).

[3]My "The Tunjur: a central Sudanic mystery," *Sudan Notes and Records*, XLI, 1980, pp. 47-60, illustrates how frustrating and speculative such research is in the absence of archaeological investigation.

[4]For a survey, see R.S. O'Fahey and J.L. Spaulding, *Kingdoms of the Sudan* (London, 1974).

[5]This is well illustrated in the Keira state where on sultanic seals the earliest ruler listed is Sulayman *(fl. c.* 1650), the "founder" of the state, although kinglists make it clear that there were several generations of Keira rulers in Jabal Marra before him; see R.S. O'Fahey and M.I. Abu Salim, *Land in Dār Fūr: Charters and Related Documents from the Dār Fūr Sultanate* (Cambridge, 1983), p. 29.

over writing.[6]

In one sense this does not matter, since the Muslim clerics wrote largely about themselves, and the bias of a work such as the *Ṭabaqāt* of Wad Dayf Allah (d. 1809-10), a biographical dictionary of holy men covering the north-central Sudan, is fairly obvious.[7] The characteristic Islamic presence in both the Funj and Darfur states was the holy lineage, which usually traced its origin to an immigrant who intermarried locally.[8] The lineage gains a monopoly over education, medical and magical practice in its locality and frequently consolidates its power by receiving tax-exempt status (*jah*) or landed estates (*hakura, iqta'*) from the rulers,[9] creating what Jay Spaulding has aptly called "enclaves" encapsulated within a non-Islamic state structure.[10]

The relationship between the polity and the lineages, the nature of the latter's constituency, the modalities of Islamization in the seventeenth and eighteenth centuries are complex themes on which there is now a considerable secondary literature. I do not propose to rehearse it here, except for one aspect. In discussing the Funj state between about 1750 and its demise in 1820, Spaulding has proposed a

[6]Here there is also the complication of the "contamination" of the oral record by the written. The dominance of "The Book" in Muslim societies constantly disturbs the "integrity" of the non-Islamic oral tradition, for example in the question of "Arab" tribal genealogies. This often comes to expression in fieldwork situations. On one occasion a prominent Fur chief instead of telling me his version of his family's history had a relative read from Na'um Shuqayr's *Ta'rīkh al-Sūdān*, 3 vols (Cairo, 1903), a work indirectly the product of British Intelligence. After the quasi-ceremonial reading, elders of the *maqdum*'s entourage gave me a quite different version of the chiefly family's history (Nyala, 1969).

[7]Muhammad al-Nur b. Dayf Allah, *Kitāb al-Ṭabaqāt fī khuṣūṣ al-awliyā' wa'l-ṣāliḥīn wa'l-'ulamā' wa'l-shu'arā' fī'l-Sūdān*, ed Yusuf Fadl Hasan, 1st edn (Khartoum, 1971). For a study of "orality" versus literacy in historiographical bias, see Janet Ewald, "Speaking, writing and authority: Explorations in and from the kingdom of Taqali," *Comparative Studies in Society and History,* 30/2, 1988, pp. 199-224.

[8]There are a number of relevant studies; see, for example, P.M. Holt, "The Sons of Jabir and their Kin," in *idem, Studies in the History of the Near East* (London, 1973), pp. 88-103, and my "The Awlād 'Alī: a Fulani holy family in Dār Fūr," *Gedenkschrift Gustav Nachtigal 1874-1974: Veröffentlichungen aus dem Übersee-Museum Bremen*, C, 1, pp. 147-66. A study of two holy families of the Gezira is forthcoming, Neil McHugh, *Holymen of the Blue Nile* (Evanston, Ill., Northwestern University Press).

[9]The holy men took care to have these transactions written down. A problem here is that the overwhelming bulk of such records as have survived are from holy families so that we have no means of knowing what percentage of such grants were recorded in writing or what percentage of the totality of such grants was made to holy lineages. For texts and translations of these documents, see, for the Funj, Jay Spaulding and M.I. Abu Salim, *Public Documents from Sinnār* (East Lansing, 1989), and for Darfur, M.I. Abu Salim, *al-Fūr wa'l-arḍ: wathā'iq tamlīk* (Khartoum, 1975), and O'Fahey and Abu Salim, *Land in Dār Fūr*.

[10]*The Heroic Age in Sinnār* (East Lansing, 1985), pp. 150-98.

process in which the ideology of sacred kingship was increasingly marginalized by an Islamic quasi-bourgeois mercantile ethic. The monopoly of royal administered trade was broken down by privatization and the substitution of royal law by the *shari'a*, to the merchants' advantage; the authority and *mores* of the enclaves embraced more and more of the countryside; land and other forms of wealth became more and more commoditized, while the aristocracy committed collective suicide in a Funj "War of the Roses." Holy lineages, families such as the Ya'qubab and 'Arakiyyun of the Gezira or the Majadhib of al-Damar, successfully aggrandized themselves and even more successfully imposed their version of the Islamic *weltanschauung* both in their day and after. Spaulding sees this period of Sudanese history as decisive in the replacement of an African worldview by an Islamic vision of society.[11]

In Darfur, before the fall of the old sultanate in 1874, matters did not seemingly go so far. Why is not so easy to answer, since many of the same processes were present; for example, Darfur's external trade with Egypt in the late eighteenth century was nearly five times the volume of that of Sinnar.[12] The Darfur Sultanate undoubtedly possessed greater ethnic cohesiveness in the dominance of the Fur people – an example is the fact that Fur remained the court language up till 1916 (when Darfur was incorporated by conquest into the Condominium Sudan); whether the Funj ever had their own language remains an open question. In regard to the relationship between the state and Islam in Darfur, I have proposed a relatively stable "two-dimensionality;" in its external rhetoric and in some internal sectors (for example, judicial procedure, but not substantive law) the sultans adopted Islamic modes; in others, especially ritual and power relationships, it remained firmly a sacral state based on Fur ethnicity.[13] It is obviously a hypothetical question whether Darfur would have undergone a dissolution similar to that of Sinnar; certainly many of the same elements – the decline of the rural aristocracy, the emergence of religious and mercantile enclaves, "new men" at court, a sense of an old order passing – were present before the state was violently overthrown by al-Zubayr Pasha in 1874.

[11]*Heroic Age, passim.* Although I do not agree with Spaulding in every aspect, for example on the question of how the *shari'a* was received and administered, his total presentation is eloquent and persuasive.

[12]T. Walz, *Trade between Egypt and Bilād al-Sūdān* (Paris, 1978,) tables 1 and 2 (pp. 36 and 43-4) – these tables describe only one year's trade figures, but confirm Darfur's generally dominant share of Egypt's African trade.

[13]See my *State and Society in Dār Fūr* (London, 1980). On the Fur dimension, see now Jorg Adelberger, *Vom Sultanat zur Republik. Veränderungen in der Sozialorganisation der Fur (Sudan)* (Stuttgart, 1990).

*The new Sufis*

Conventionally, the history of the modern Sudan may be regarded as beginning with Muhammad 'Ali's decision in about 1818 to occupy the region.[14] But one might well argue that the decision by the Moroccan mystic Ahmad b. Idris (born 1749-50, died 1837) in 1815 to permit his young student, Muhammad 'Uthman al-Mirghani, to undertake a missionary journey through the Funj territories and Kordofan was an equally decisive date.[15]

The question of the neo-Sufi impact on Sudanic Africa is controversial, not least because there is no real clarity as to what is meant by neo-Sufism. In contrast to most scholars who have used the term, Fazlur Rahman, John Voll and Nehemia Levtzion among others, I do not believe it represents any form of doctrinal innovation, whether it be a less mystical mysticism, a more rigorous orthodoxy, a revival of *hadith* studies or a marrying of Wahhabism with a reformist form of Sufism.[16] What is undeniable is that in the northern Sudan from about 1780 onwards new Sufi brotherhoods appeared that were to change profoundly the religious landscape there, changes however that built upon the emerging Islamic/Arab self-consciousness apparent in the late Funj period.[17] What the new orders brought were a new educational programme, an organizational structure and a sense of belonging to a wider Muslim world.

The first new impulse came from within the Khalwatiyya tradition represented by the affiliation stemming from Muhammad b. 'Abd al-Karim al-Samman (d. 1770),[18] which was brought to the Sudan by the returned Sudanese scholar, Ahmad al-Tayyib wad al-Bashir (1742-3 to 1824). In the next generation came al-Mirghani followed by a flood of

[14]On the Turco-Egyptian period, see Richard Hill, *Egypt in the Sudan, 1820-1881* (London, 1959).

[15]See my *Enigmatic Saint: Aḥmad ibn Idrīs and the Idrīsī Tradition* (London,1990,) p. 148.

[16]*Ibid.*, pp. 1-9; these arguments are further explored in R.S. O'Fahey and Bernd Radtke, "Neo-Sufism Reconsidered," *Der Islam* (forthcoming).

[17]On this self-consciousness, see McHugh, *Holymen of the Blue Nile* .

[18]An earlier version of the Khalwatiyya may have been taken to Darfur by the Algerian, Sidi 'Abd al-Rahman b. Muhammad Abu Qabrayn (c. 1715-29 to 1793-4). He is said to have been sent to the sultanate, where he stayed for six years, as a missionary by the Egyptian Khalwati, Muhammad b. Salim al-Hifni (1689-1767). See Julia Ann Clancey-Smith, "The Saharan Raḥmāniyya: Popular protest and desert society in southeastern Algeria and the Tunisian Jarīd, c. 1759-1881," unpubl. Ph.D. thesis, University of California, 1988, pp. 38-9. There seems to be no Darfur confirmation of this episode and *tariqas* appear to be largely a twentieth-century phenomenon in the province.

largely Ibn Idris-inspired orders and teachers. The result was to cover the northern Sudan with new types of organization – Khatmiyya, Isma'iliyya, Rashidiyya, Salihiyya, Idrisiyya, Tijaniyya etc. – with many ramifications not seen there before.[19]

What was new? The holy lineages had claimed vaguely Qadiriyya or Shadhiliyya affiliations. Much of the style and content of the Islam of the holy men had owed its inspiration to Sufi Islam, but in discussing what was new one must put to one side the simplistic equation, put forward by Trimingham among others, between popular or folk Islam and Sufism. A belief in miracles (*karamat*), in hereditary charisma (*baraka*), in some form of ill-defined anti-nomianism - a dancing maraboutism somehow more acceptable to Africans - is not the totality of Sufism. Nor does a careful reading of Wad Dayf Allah's *Ṭabaqāt* sustain entirely Trimingham's picture of Islamic frontier syncretism. Ironically, if one looks at what the holy men noticed in the *Ṭabaqāt* wrote, one discovers that overwhelmingly they were concerned with the transmission, teaching and commenting upon theological (mainly the *'aqa'id* of Muhammad b. Yusuf al-Sanusi) and *shari'a* texts, in the latter case the *Mukhtaṣar* of Khalil b. Ishaq and the *Risāla* of Ibn Abi Zayd al-Qayrawani.[20] Given the role of the holy men in the sultanates as *qadis* using Islamic judicial procedure on behalf of sultanic law, such preoccupations are hardly surprising.[21]

By contrast, the new orders led an explosion of literary activity, poetry, Sufi treatises, works on grammar and rhetoric, and treatises on ritual prayer and *tajwid*; the literary production of nineteenth-century Sudan is several hundred per cent greater in volume than that of the centuries before.[22] Popular poetry in praise of the Prophet or of the saints of the brotherhoods sung at the *dhikr* or other meetings *(hawliyya, maulid*) of the orders must have played a significant role in raising the Islamic consciousness of the ordinary Sudanese. They were

[19]A detailed study is given in Ali Salih Karrar, *The Sufi Brotherhoods in the Sudan* (London, 1992). This supplements the older study on the Khatmiyya, J.O. Voll, "A history of the Khatmiyyah Tariqah in the Sudan," unpubl. Ph.D. thesis, Harvard University, 1969. A full study of the Sammaniyya is needed – there are sources in abundance, but 'Abd al-Qadir Mahmud, *al-Fikr al-ṣūfī fi'l-Sūdān* (Cairo, 1969), is a good starting point.

[20]See the analysis in my "The Eastern Sudan before 1750: biographies and bibliographies", *Bulletin of Arabic Literature in Africa*, I, 1985, pp. 60-75.

[21]On this topic, see J.L. Spaulding, "The evolution of the Islamic judiciary in Sinnār," *International Journal of African Historical Studies*, X/3, 1977, pp. 408-26, and R.S. O'Fahey, "The office of qāḍī in Dār Fūr: a preliminary enquiry," *Bulletin of the School of Oriental and African Studies*, XL/l, 1977, pp. 110-24.

[22]This is documented in detail in my forthcoming *Arabic Literature of the Sudan until 1898*. Both Ibn Idrıs and his students were concerned with the teaching of Arabic grammar.

certainly to play such a role in the Mahdist Revolution.[23]

The new orders were supra-tribal mass organizations, although over time they tended to acquire tribal monopolies. The new Sufis succeeded in linking the enclaves together in hierarchical organizations at the top of which sat the founder-saint's family, who had in most cases branches outside the Sudan; the Mirghanis retained their links with the Hijaz, the Adarisa (the descendants of Ahmad b. Idris) had their main seat in Upper Egypt, while even the purely Sudanese Rashidiyya found it more convenient to base themselves at the Haramayn. This points to another characteristic of the new orders, their internationalism. It is not that Sudanese holy men had not travelled abroad in search of knowledge and initiation before, but they appear to have done so in greater numbers in the nineteenth century and in a more networked context; one example is that a number of Sudanese students accompanied Muhammad b. ʻAli al-Sanusi (1787-1859) to Cyrenaica following the death of his spiritual master, Ibn Idris.[24] This new mobility was partly facilitated by the better communications (boats and later the telegraph) established by the Egyptian colonial regime.[25]

Although the colonial regime created a thin layer of Azhar-educated Sudanese clerics who served as *qadis, muftis* or apologists for the regime,[26] an Egyptian-style Islamic establishment did not either root itself in the Sudan or seriously compete with the brotherhoods. The colonial authorities in effect accepted the realities by giving subventions to locally-influential lineages and their schools, such as that of the Al ʻIsa of Kutranj on the Blue Nile, or in granting tax-exemptions or land to some of the brotherhoods such as the Khatmiyya or the Ismaʻiliyya of Kordofan (as the British were to do later). Nor was an Azhar education to be any guarantee of immunity from

[23]There is a considerable literature on Sudanese popular poetry; on the religious poetry the writings of Qurashi Muhammad Hasan are fundamental. I list here his main works: *Mukhtārāt min madā'iḥ Wad Saʻd,* (Khartoum, 1950); *Mahdī Allāh mulḥamat shiʻriyya* (Khartoum, 1963); *Maʻa shuʻarā' al-madā'iḥ: min al-turāth al-Shaʻbī al-Sūdānī*, 3 vols, (Khartoum, i, 1967; ii, 1968; iii, 1976; iv, forthcoming); *Shuʻarā' al-Mahdiyya* (Khartoum, 1974); *al-Madkhal ilā shiʻr al-madā'iḥ: min al-turāth al-Shaʻbī al-Sūdānī* (Khartoum, 1977) – the last is a short introduction to the subject. Sayyid Hasan has been able to recover very little poetry from before about 1800.

[24]See further, Knut S. Vikør, "Sufi and Scholar on the Desert Edge. Muḥammad b. ʻAlī al-Sanūsī (1787-1859)," unpubl. dr. philos. thesis, University of Bergen, 1991, chapter 6.

[25]The Mirghanis made use of the telegraph; Karrar, *Sufi Brotherhoods*, p. 100.

[26]These relationships were never clearcut. See, for example, my "Colonial Servant. Aḥmad al-Salāwī and the Sudan," *Der Islam* (forthcoming), and McHugh, *Holymen of the Blue Nile*.

infection by Mahdism.

By its destruction of the previous political order, through the monetization and commoditization of the economy with the consequent sharpening of socio-economic inequalities, and the imposition of a rough form of bureaucratic uniformity, the Egyptian colonial regime broke down local particularisms, introduced new fashions (literally, in terms of the *bantalun* and *tob* (cl. Ar. *thawb),* the former anathema to the Mahdi, the latter covering up earlier female "toplessness") and created an ideological void filled by the new brotherhoods.[27] Through the *tariqa* networks, which catered for all aspects of their devotees' lives, their *dhikr* and *mada' ih*, a new sense of Islamic identity emerged in the northern Sudan (but not in Darfur) sufficiently cohesive and widespread for Muhammad Ahmad, the Mahdi (1884-5), to be able to couch his call in a form of discourse enough would understand to be willing and able to respond.

### *The Mahdist idea and the Sudan*

Peter Holt in his classic study of the Mahdist state gives a somewhat hesitant introduction to the Mahdist idea in the Sudan, hesitant because there were few antecedents in Sudanese history.[28] The only previous Sudanese Mahdi was Hamad al-Nahlan (d. 1704-5), known as Wad al-Turabi, who proclaimed himself to be such while on the pilgrimage in Mecca.[29] Our increasing understanding and knowledge of the new Sufi impulses may deepen the possibilities for a better appraisal of the Mahdist idea, both intellectually and organizationally.

There appears to have been a Mahdist strain to the Idrisi tradition connected to a sense of the imminent dissolution of the world – *indiras al-Islam,* "The extinction of Islam;" the sense of living in the worst of times was a powerful factor in reinforcing Mahdist expectations.[30] The Mahdist idea pre-occupied a number of Sudanese holy men in the years

[27]On the economic consequences of Egyptian colonialism, see Anders Bjørkelo, *Prelude to the Mahdiya. Peasants and Traders in the Shendi Region, 1821-1885* (Cambridge, 1989).

[28]P.M. Holt, *The Mahdist State in the Sudan, 1881-1898,* 2nd edn (Oxford, 1970).

[29]Wad Dayf Allah, *Ṭabaqāt*, pp. 160-73.

[30]Ibn Idris uses this phrase, an old one in Sufi thought, in the lecture notes taken down from him by a Sudanese student; see *al-'Iqd al-nafīs fī naẓm jawāhir al-tadrīs l'imām ... Aḥmad Idrīs* (Cairo, 1399/1979), p. 103. Ibn Idris continues by decrying the danger to Islam from people who foolishly speculate about matters, for example *yad Allah,* "The Hand of God," in the Qur'an, that do not concern them. On one occasion Ibn Idris was allegedly asked by al-Mirghani if he was the Mahdi. This he denied but explained that, "The secret of the Mahdi is in the son of al-Sanusi" Ahmad Sidqi al-Dajjani, *al-Ḥarakat al-Sanūsiyya*, 2nd edn (Cairo 1988), p. 182.

following the Egyptian occupation; Isma'il al-Wali (1792-3 to 1863) of Kordofan, a student of Muhammad 'Uthman al-Mirghani wrote three treatises on the question,[31] while the Qadiri shaikh, Ibrahim w. al-Kabbashi (d. 1869-70), wrote a work entitled *al-Mahdī al-muntaẓar*, "The Expected Mahdi."[32] Both men had a difficult relationship with the colonial authorities, while Isma'il al-Wali's son, Muhammad al-Makki (d. 1906), was an early adherent of the Mahdi and a close advisor to his successor, the Khalifa 'Abdallahi, and a daughter of Wad al-Kabbashi was to marry 'Abd al-Rahman w. al-Nujumi, the greatest (and by his followers considered the noblest) general the Mahdi had. These works are for the moment unavailable, but another brief treatise, *Risālat al-khatm fī ba'd al-mubashshirāt*, written in 1824 by Ja'far al Sadiq b. M. 'Uthman al-Mirghani which describes various divine communications *(mubashshirāt)* to his father,[33] gives a glimpse of Muhammad 'Uthman's ideas. Thus,

> It was said to me that your intercessory station (*maqamikd al-wasila*) is together with the Prophet, Fatima, al-Hasan, al-Husayn and the Mahdi; you are the sixth..

and

> The meaning of the seal is under four aspects: the first is the Prophetic seal, the second is the Mahdist seal, the third is my seal [i.e. Muhammad 'Uthman], and the fourth seal is that of him after whom there will no other saint [*wali*].

The spiritual cosmos of Muhammad 'Uthman has yet to be fully charted, but the last remark indicates that he saw, as other Khatmiyya writings confirm, his status as being "The seal of his age," rather than as Ahmad al-Tijani saw himself, "The seal of the saints," just as the Prophet was "The seal [i.e. the last] of the prophets." That these ideas owe much to Ibn al-'Arabi is undoubted, although the complex of ideas has yet to be worked out.[34]

In 1882, a shaikh belonging to the Sammaniyya brotherhood, Muhammad Ahmad b. 'Abd Allah, revealed that he was the expected Mahdi, the one sent at the end of time to establish righteousness upon

[31]They are (1) *R. al-Bayān al-kāmil fī ma'rifat al-kawkab al-fāḍil al-imām al-mahdī wa 'l-khatim al-shāmil li-asrār al-ṭāli' wa 'l-nāzil* (1239-1823-4), (2) *K. Jāmi' ma'ānī al-kalim al-wajīz al-naẓm fī ma'rifat sayyidī al-mahdī wa 'l-khatim* (1239/1823-4, and (3) *R. al-Lam' al-bādī 'an kashf ḥaqīqat al-khatim wa 'l-imām al-hādī* (1239/1823-4). The manuscript of one of these works has recently come to light (personal communication, Dr. M.I. Abu Salim).

[32]This work is known to be extant, but is for the moment inaccessible.

[33]Published in *al-Rasā'il al-Mīrghaniyya*, 2nd edn (Cairo, 1399/1979), p. 110-12.

[34]A key work of Ibn al-'Arabi much quoted by al-Mirghani, the Mahdi and others is *'Anqā mughrib*.

the Earth before the Last Day. The Mahdist revolution (1882-5), one of the great cataclysms in modern Islamic history, swept the colonial regime of the Egyptians away and established what was the first ostensibly theocratic state in the Sudan (1885-98).

In discussing how the Mahdi both utilized and created a new Islamic hegemony or identity in the northern Sudan, one can only set forth an agenda for future research. The first and obvious *desiderata* are adequate texts of the 1,000 and more writings of the Mahdi himself, not to speak of the literary and oral poetic outpouring that accompanied the revolution. Here, a beginning has been made by Dr. Muhammad Ibrahim Abu Salim.[35] Already, some points can be made: that the Mahdi assumed a common language of discourse between himself and those to whom he addressed his proclamations, visions and warnings; that this discourse was profoundly coloured by that of Ibn al-ʻArabi as mediated by the new Sufi orders; and that the *indiras al-Islam* was now given a specific anti-colonial/proto-nationalist coloration by the Mahdi and those around him. The language of this discourse has yet to be studied, for example, how does the *hadra* or vision of Ibn al-ʻArabi relate to that of the Mahdi, in what ways does the idea of a meeting with the Prophet (*ijtimaʻ bi'l-nabi*) as an aspect of *ijtihad* relate to the idea of the Mahdi as legitimizing revolt against a corrupt Muslim government?[36] Through the Mahdi idea and the Prophetic *umma* ideal, the Mahdi totally undermined the ideological rhetoric of the Egyptian colonial regime and upstaged the brotherhoods by using their language and networks to create something new. Here, there is a parallel to what the Islamists are seeking to achieve in the Sudan today. And the latter were to build, like the Mahdi, on the twin facts of a new colonial shock, this time administered by the British, to Sudanese Muslims and a new ideological seduction, this time not a new Sufism, but an alternative rationalist political Islamism.

### *The British interlude*

A consciously institutionalized Islamic policy in the Sudan is a British

[35]The relevant works are described in R.S. O'Fahey and Anders Bjørkelo, "The Writings of Muhammad Ibrahim Salim," *Sudanic Africa*, I, 1990,. pp. 11-18. A new stage in this enterprise has been reached with the publication of *al-Athār al-kāmila li'l-imām al-Mahdī*, ed. M.I. Abu Salim, vol I, (Khartoum, 1990). This is the first of seven volumes giving adequately edited texts of all the Mahdi's writings.

[36]R. Peters, "Islam and the legitimation of power: the Mahdi-revolt in the Sudan," *Zeitschrift der Deutschen Morgenländischen Gesellschaft,* Supplement V, XI, *Deutscher Orientalistentag* (Wiesbaden, 1980), pp. 409-20, discusses this topic in *fiqh* rather than *ilham* terms.

invention. The British were obsessed by the fear of a re-run of Islamic messianism in a land whose conquest ("Reconquest" on behalf of Egypt in official parlance, to legitimize their actions) had taken them three years (1896-9) by contrast to the surgically-swift annexation of Egypt in 1882 in the face of a largely secular nationalist movement. Consequently, they watched over Sudanese Muslim leaders like hawks. Politically, the history of the British in the Sudan is a complex dance conducted by the colonial power, the revived Mahdist movement led by a son of the Mahdi, Sir Sayyid 'Abd al-Rahman al-Mahdi (d. 1959), the Khatmiyya led by Sir Sayyid 'Ali al-Mirghani (d. 1968) and various lesser Sufi figures. In the early years of colonial rule, the Mahdists were suspect and the Khatmiyya favoured; in later years, as the Khatmiyya turned to Egypt as a counterbalance to both the Mahdists and British, the latter looked with greater favour on the Mahdists. Historiographically it is important to note that most, if not all, the research done on this period has been based on the colonial archives. No one (Sudanese scholars included) has written on this period from the archives of the Mahdists or Khatmiyya, so we are dependent on British evaluations of the motives of the principal actors involved.

There are two comments that can be made in regard to the ideological position of Islam in the colonial period. First, the British brought to the Sudan policies fashioned in India. Ultimately the legal system in the Sudan as regards Muslims was derived from the Indian Penal Code of 1837 and the later Indian Civil Procedure Code.[37] To Muslims in matters of personal status (marriage, divorce, inheritance and the like), the *shari'a* was applied, but as under the Funj and Darfur Sultanates, in criminal matters secular or state law obtained. However, an important British legacy was the institutionalization of law; the creation of institutions for training *qadis*, the formalization of distinctions between state and private-status law, and a recognition of the potential for a conflict of laws.

The second point is that the political movements among the northern Sudanese as they emerged in the 1930s and '40s, be they the Umma party based on the Mahdists with its primary allegiance to the Mahdi family or the Unionists based on the Khatmiyya brotherhood owing loyalty to the Mirghani family, were thus based on supra-ethnic avowedly Islamic organizations. However, in the context of what was, by "normal" African standards, a particularly complex anti-colonial struggle (because conducted against two colonial powers, Britain and Egypt), the Sudanese parties did not put foward overtly Islamic or

[37]G. Warburg, *The Sudan under Wingate* (London, 1971), pp. 124-36. See further, Carolyn Fluehr-Lobban, *Islamic Law and Society in the Sudan* (London, 1985).

"Islamist" policies. Their strength derived from Islamic sentiments of solidarity, but these were used to articulate basically secular nationalist positions. This discontinuity between mobilization at the grassroots and the policies advocated by the leadership, who successfully co-opted the graduates of the Gordon Memorial College (later the University of Khartoum), was to provide an opening for a third group, the Muslim Brothers.

*The Return of Islam?*

The most extended and sophisticated study of the Islamist movement in the Sudan, that of Abdelwahab El-Affendi,[38] has a dual ideological purpose: to delegitimize both Sudanese Sufi-based Islam, whether it be that of the orders or the neo-Mahdists, and to marginalize the Westernized intellectuals (relatively, a powerful group in the Sudan, both north and south) by characterizing them as the transient products of a utilitarian and alien colonial educational system. By contrast, Sudanese Islamists represent a return to authenticity.

Another interpretation is to see the Islamist movement in the Sudan as a derivative of its counterpart in Egypt. The *ikhwan al-muslimun* of Egypt established in 1928 did not begin to spread in the Sudan either through missionary or *da'wa* activity or returned Sudanese students until the mid 1940s, at about the same time as the foundation of the Sudanese Communist Party (1946). An independent Sudanese movement, uniting several smaller groups, was established in 1954, but it was in its first years a propaganda rather than political movement. It only began to operate as an effective political movement when its present leader, Dr. Hasan al-Turabi, member of the other Sudanese Sufi family that had produced a Mahdi, returned from study abroad in 1962.[39]

The Islamist movement in the Sudan has, from the 1960s till the present day, been essentially a political ideological movement. As such it stands in some contrast to the "Republican Brothers" (*al-ikhwan al-jumhuriyyin*) of the late Mahmud Muhammad Taha (executed for apostasy in 1985) who are much concerned with social

[38] Abdelwahab El-Affendi, *Turabi's Revolution: Islam and Power in Sudan* (London, 1990). See also, the same author's "The ideological development of the Sudanese Ikhwan movement," *Proceedings of International Conference on Middle East Studies (BRISMES)* (Oxford, 1988), pp. 387-430, and, "Discovering the South: Sudanese dilemmas for Islam in Africa," *African Affairs,* July 1990, pp. 371-89.

[39] For an historical survey, see Susanne Wolf, "The Muslim Brotherhood in the Sudan," unpubl. Magister thesis, University of Hamburg, 1990. I am indebted to Miss Wolf for many stimulating discussions during the writing of her thesis in Bergen.

and economic issues.[40] In the democratic interlude of 1964-9 between the military regimes of 'Abbud (1958) and Numayri (1969-85), the Muslim Brothers were concerned with two issues, the struggle against the Communists, and the great issue in northern Sudanese politics, an Islamic constitution.[41] This latter issue has run like a thread through modern northern Sudanese politics since the early 1960s. Why is a complex question; John Voll suggests an answer: "As more Sudanese receive a modern style education, simple institution maintenance is not a sufficient expression of their Islamic identity. As a result it is possible to see a growing specifically Islamic content in the programs and platforms of groups in the Sudan. As this takes place, these statements take on a more explicitly fundamentalist tone."[42]

The manifest aim of the Sudanese Islamists is to create a new Sudanese Islamic identity; their means are complex and include educational initiatives, control over money from Arab oil states, banking, and the acculturation of the influx of Southerners and Westerners into the north because of war and famine.[43] A central problem is that until July 1989 and the military coup of 'Umar al-Bashir, they were only one force within the complex of northern Sudanese politics. But the truth of Voll's observation may be seen impressionistically in the changing role of ideology in the North/South conflict in the Sudan. During the first civil war, 1955-72 (the latter the year of the Addis Ababa Agreement), the conflict was scarcely ideologically articulated at all. Southern spokesmen talked vaguely of the legacy of the slave trade (rebutted by Northerners who stressed European involvement in it), the dangers of Arab Islamic

[40]For example, in combatting the crushing burden of dowry *(mahr)* on young couples, an issue that Sadiq al-Mahdi, for example, has sought to remedy. On the "Republican Brothers" see J. Rogalski, "Die Republikanischen Brüder im Sudan. Ein Beitrag zur Ideologiegeschichte des Islam in der Gegenwart," unpubl. Magister thesis, Freie Universität Berlin, 1990, and Isabel Stümpel, "Die Ideen eines sudanesischen Reformdenkers vor dem Tribunal der islamischen Religionsgelehrten – Mahmud Muhammad Taha und die Weiterenwicklung der *shari'a*," unpubl. Magister thesis, Albert Ludwigs-Universität zu Frieburg i. Br., 1990. On the killing of Mahmud Muhammad Taha, see Abdullahi A. An-Na'im, "The Islamic Law of apostacy and its modern applicability: a case from the Sudan," *Religion,* 16, 1986.

[41]See further, Abdullahi A. An-Na'im, "The elusive Islamic constitution: the Sudanese experience," *Orient,* 3, 1985, pp. 329-40.

[42]"The evolution of Islamic fundamentalism in twentieth-century Sudan," in *Islam, Nationalism and Radicalism in Egypt and the Sudan,* ed. G. Warburg and U. Kupferschmidt (New York, 1983), p. 131.

[43]Other aspects include the adoption of Western missionary and aid organization techniques by Islamist organizations, for example, the African Islamic Centre established in 1972 and the Islamic African Relief Agency established in the early 1980s.

domination (denied by Northern liberals who argued for Arabic as a neutral national language). In sum, the Southerners blamed the Northerners, the latter the British. Much of the problem in the years following Ja'far al-Numayri's take-over in 1969, when there was a will in Khartoum to try to find a settlement, was to establish the terms of reference within which the two sides could negotiate.[44] Since its outbreak in 1983, the second civil war has been characterized by an altogether more sophisticated ideological debate on both sides, wherein on the Northern side the Islamists have effectively taken over the agenda and Dr. John Garang and the Sudan Peoples Liberation Army (SPLA) have provided the first consciously articulated secularist Southern opposition.

To answer how this came about requires a deeper study of the modern urban social and economic history of the northern Sudan; surveys of the political highlights are not enough, and the former has yet to be undertaken. At a superficial level, the introduction of the "September Laws" by Numayri in September 1983 may be taken as a turning-point in that it placed the *shari'a* at the centre of the issue; the reasons that led Numayri to take this step are less important than its consequences.[45] The failure during the years following Numayri's downfall of Sudanese politicians "to devise a system that could satisfy the minority without disenfranchising the majority"[46] ended in the National Islamic Front-inspired coup of July 1989.

The regime of 'Umar al-Bashir consolidated its Islamist nature by adopting on 22 March 1991 a penal code based on an interpretation of the *shari'a*. This code, presently in force in the northern provinces including the capital, brings back the *hudud* punishments first made part of Sudanese Law in Numayri's "September Laws."[47] But the promulgation of an Islamic Law is only one aspect of a process whereby the Islamists are seeking to establish their hegemony over both the state and society. Their current means, given impetus by the 1989 *coup,* include *ad hoc* alliances with locally influential Sufi

[44]Much of the above is based on personal observation while a resident in the Sudan, 1967-71, and several subsequent visits.

[45]For a fascinating, if very personal, view of the event and its consequences, see Mansur Khalid, *al-Fajr al-khādhib. Numayrī wa-taḥrīf al-sharī'a* (Beirut, n.d.). Some of the arguments in this book have gone into the same author's *The Government They Deserve. The Role of the Elite in Sudan's Political Evolution* (London, 1990).

[46]Abdelwahab El-Affendi, , "Discovering the South," p. 380; throughout the article the author assumes that the views of Northern Sudanese Muslims are more or less coterminous with those of the Islamists.

[47]For a succinct if hostile view (i.e. because written on Western human rights premises) see "New Islamic Penal Code violates basic human rights," News from Africa Watch, 9 April 1991.

families or movements,[48] the establishment of armed militias both in the cities and countryside, purges of academics, lawyers and journalists,[49] and perhaps most important, the creation of financial institutions and trading monopolies that are increasingly independent of outside financing.

The latest phase of Islamic hegemony in the Sudan has led to a polarization of the country as it presently exists within the boundaries given by its Egyptian and British colonial masters between an Islamist Northern nationalism and a SPLA-led Southern nationalism. It may be that the Islamists of the North in their quest to fulfill the Mahdi's dream of a pure Islamic theocracy, albeit under different terms, will also follow him in effectively abandoning the South. The implications for Muslim Africa would be profound.

[48]See Awad al-Karsani's essay in this book.

[49]So far the University of Khartoum has been relatively unaffected, but the creation of new universities in Darfur, Kordofan and in the north will help to undermine its preeminence.

# ERSHIP, MUSLIM IDENTITIES AND EAST AFRICAN POLITICS

## TRADITION, BUREAUCRATIZATION AND COMMUNICATION

*François Constantin**

At first glance, it would seem that the question of religious identity is simply a problem of god(s) and belief. But identity is also related to various social processes, and believers, like everyone else, are confronted with the issues of everyday life, including family affairs and job requirements, budget and food, feelings and knowledge (which includes questions about the unknown), etc. A major feature of modernization is the development of complex and intricate systems and structures which govern more and more aspects of one's life, a process which is accompanied by the secularization of thoughts and attitudes.[1] Such changes do not result however in the disappearance of religion. Various political and social crises today reflect the real strength of religious beliefs the world over, from electoral mishaps in the United States to the fall of the Communist system in Poland.[2] These observations lead to three crucial assumptions which must be taken into account when dealing with identity problems.

One is that today religions are still effective forms of ideological mobilization, but as ideologies they also become implicated in secular conflicts. Thus religious affiliations and solidarities are challenged by other crisscrossing forms of social affiliations and solidarities.

Second is that religious identity should be considered as one specific kind of social identity, which means that religious groups involved in confrontational debates have to embrace the structures and strategies of interest groups. In the modern state system, the effectiveness of an interest group seems to require bureaucratic organization.

Third is that religiously-oriented interest groups can enter the political arena either to promote collective religious values (the *umma*, for Muslim groups, for example) or to defend the temporal interests of

* The author is deeply indebted to Dr. Louis Brenner for his kind assistance in the improvement of the English draft of this article.

[1] We refer here to the literature on political development from Karl Marx to Daniel Bell, Seymour M. Lipset or Edward Shils.

[2] See for example Robert J. Myers (ed.), "Religion and State. The struggle for legitimacy and power," *The Annals of AAPSS*, 483, January 1986, pp. 9-156; Bryan S. Turner, *Religion and Social Theory* (London/Beverly Hills, 1991); Gilles Kepel, *La revanche de Dieu* (Paris, 1991).

some of the brethren (business regulations, for instance).

Thus, as a form of social identification, religious identity is frequently mingled with other forms of identity and may exceed the limits of strictly religious claims and concerns, particularly when operating within the political system. One way to clarify this problem of identifying effective religious consciousness within interacting solidarity networks is what might be called a "top-down approach," that is, to identify religious leaders and to analyze the dialectic processes which link any one leader with, first, the group he claims to be speaking for, and, second, his social and political environment. In fact, it is easier to identify individual leaders than informal religious groups. But apart from this technical reason, the legitimacy of the "top-down approach" resides in the role of the leader as a decision-maker and a guide who is expected to transcend conflicting petty interests and to express the common interest and to identify the best choices for his followers The purpose of this paper is to apply this method to an analysis of Muslim identity in eastern Africa (Kenya, Uganda, Tanzania, Zambia and Malawi).

## *Muslim identity in the context of eastern African pluralism*

Muslims are involved in secular affairs and are thus confronted with the problems of power. They have to cope with the realities of political life which have developed according to the rules, norms, and cultural references of the post-colonial state, but they have also to take into account their own characteristics and particularly the resources and weaknesses of their own Muslim communities.

*The post-colonial state system in East Africa.* It is not our intention to develop or even to summarize the current leading theories on the post-colonial state or to enter into a debate involving such master-analysts as C. Leys, G. Hyden, R. Bates or J.-F. Bayart.[3] Their arguments draw upon examples from East African political systems, which of course share the general features of other African states. They are "new" states which have recently emerged from colonialism, which means that their governments have to cope with contrasting values,

[3]See Colin Leys, *Underdevelopment in Kenya: The Political Economy of Neo-colonialism 1964-1971* (London, 1975) and the ensuing "Kenyan debate" in the *Review of African Political Economy*; Goran Hyden, *No Shortcut to Progress: African Development Management in Perspective* (London, 1983); Robert T. Bates, *Beyond the Miracle of the Market: The Political Economy of Agrarian Development in Kenya* (Cambridge, 1989); Jean-François Bayart, *L'Etat en Afrique. La politique du ventre* (Paris, 1989).

ideals and representations inherited from both the African heritage and from European colonial legacies; they have to cope with disrupted economic systems in which subtle links connect capitalist export-oriented structures with local producers and markets within a global situation of dependence and underdevelopment. Problems of political stability, economic growth and social improvements are still severe, and various social groupings actively compete for better material and/or spiritual (ideological) conditions while foreign private and public groups intervene according to their own interests. These conditions undermine the legitimacy and efficacy of most governments.

These broad considerations are not intended as labels but as a starting-point for a more profound analysis of the current process of social and political change in Africa. But first, it is necessary to outline some of the specific characteristics of East African politics with reference to the problem of religious identity.

In comparison with the general African experience, the states of East Africa have had relatively stable governments; political changes have come about through legal processes, gradually reinforcing respect for the rule of law among the populations. Until the early 1990s, this has not meant pluralist democracy, but it has not been a very common practice that opposition might lead to exile or death. In general, various groupings were allowed to express their complaints or even criticisms provided they paid tribute to the head of state and to national unity. Of course, Uganda and Malawi have departed from this pattern on some important points, particularly with respect to human rights, but the institutions of all these states (government, parliament, courts, political parties, elections etc.) conform to the model of the modern bureaucratic state system in that they function in accordance with formal rules which regulate, more or less effectively, the expression of pluralism, including religious pluralism.

In Weberian terms, the bureaucratic state-system is necessarily secular. None of the states under discussion here has a state religion, unlike the Comoros, Mauritania or the United Kingdom. Freedom of worship is protected by law, and churches, sects and religious associations are proliferating all over the region. Such developments are usually accepted without opposition, except where they create serious unrest, such as the activities of the prophetesses A. Lenshina in Zambia and A. Lakwena in Uganda;[4] in Malawi the Watchtower has been banned. More important, the secular character of the state does

[4]See Heike Behrend, "Is Alice Lakwena a witch? The Holy Spirit Movement and its fight against evil in the north," in Holger B. Hansen, Michael Twaddle, eds, *Changing Uganda* (London, 1991), pp. 162-77; Wim M.J. Van Binsbergen, *Religious Change in Zambia: Exploratory Studies* (London, 1981), pp. 266-316.

not preclude open religious references in state rituals (oathings, festivals...) and the openly religious style of some leaders, such as Daniel arap Moi or Kenneth Kaunda, who publicly and actively participated in Christian rituals on Sundays. Such religiosity is prompted by Christian references inherited from European missionnaries, and which is invoked even when the Chief *Qadi* and the Holy Qur'an are involved in important rituals, such as the inauguration of the President of the Republic. Religion is one of the cultural references employed by political leaders to strenghten their legitimacy among people, who are thought to be more impressed by European Christian values than by any others, including Arab Islamic values.

Such statements must be modified for Tanzania, where Christian and Muslim populations are quite balanced and where a Christian (Roman Catholic) president, Julius Nyerere, was succeeded by a Muslim, A.H. Mwinyi. The religious style is still present, and the religious references in speeches are more ecumenical than ever, but of course the front pages of the Tanzanian *Daily News* now show a President visiting mosques more often than churches, although he does visit churches, just as Nyerere visited mosques. A secular state system in East Africa means a balanced attitude towards the various denominations within a global ambience of piety.[5] Such ecumenical attitudes are, however, influenced by the historical legacy of the Arab presence and the character of the Muslim communities.

*The Muslim legacy.* Until the mid-nineteenth century, Islam was closely identified with Arab domination on the East African coast, which had resulted in a kind of "cultural hegemony."[6] Islam was the ideology of the slave-owners, and the attendant legal stratification (which was not restricted to a simple two-tier system submitting African slaves to Arab masters) resulted in a contradiction: because Islam was a decisive constituent of respectability (*heshima*), access to it was limited to the social élites (i.e. the Arabs), whereas ordinary people (i.e. Africans living in the hinterland and slaves) were bound to the lower status of *washenzi* (savages) and consequently denied access

[5]Such a carefully balanced policy does not exclude conflicts, as shown by the support various religious leaders gave to political pluralism in 1990-1, particularly in Kenya.

[6]This point is developed in Frederick Cooper, "Islam and Cultural Hegemony: The Ideology of Slaveowners on the East African Coast," in Paul E. Lovejoy, ed, *The Ideology of Slavery in Africa* (Beverly Hills/London, 1981), pp. 271-307; see also Pamela W. Landberg, *Kinship and Community in a Tanzanian Coastal Village*, unpubl. Ph.D. thesis, University of California, 1977; François Constantin, "Arabie du sud-Afrique orientale. Perspectives sur une hégémonie imparfaite," *Revue canadienne d'études africaines*, 1987, 3, pp. 355-74.

to the sophisticated values of the world of Allah. Only a few *washenzi*, for various reasons, were educated in the rudiments of Islam, a process which contributed to the emergence of an intermediate group which, while attempting to separate from its African roots, was not admitted into Arab society. These frustrated "in-between people" became the Waswahili.[7]

This legacy resulted in the creation of a confused set of collective representations. For many people (particularly non-Muslims) Islam is associated with an archaic form of foreign oppression and refers to outdated values and rituals. At the same time, these Arab-Islamic values are still highly respected among traditional coastal peoples, but also among urban marginal groups who are disappointed with materialist Western and Marxist ideologies. The result is a complex array of Muslim identities, because Islamic references are not perceived in the same way by these different groups. Moreover, one group may be both fascinated by the religious call and/or by a more or less mythical Arab way of life and at the same time strongly opposed to any change or reform which might recall the former Arab domination, as shown by the 1964 revolution in Zanzibar and its aftermath, or, in a less confrontational context, by the disgruntled reactions to certain attitudes and decisions of A.H. Mwinyi, or by the opposition to economic liberalization in Zanzibar.[8]

Such conflicting representations of Islam are but one of the various lines along which Muslims divide, as clearly demonstrated by the contributions to this volume. We need only recall that the Muslims of East Africa can be either Sunni or Shi'ite, traditionalists, fundamentalists or more relaxed believers, capitalist businessmen, shopkeepers or students; they can be men or women, young or old, Digo, Hadrami or Rendille; some have obtained a Ph.D. and others no degree at all. Consequently, they are integrated into various social networks and statuses which may articulate congruent or inconsistent arguments. The degree of congruence depends not only upon the social norms which codify behaviour, but also upon individual psychology and reactions to those norms. It is not obvious that one's Islam is considered by every East African Muslim as his/her primary referent in the various aspects of his/her daily life.[9]

[7]I discussed this issue in "Condition swahili et identité politique," *Africa*, 57 (2), 1987, pp. 219-33. See Pat Caplan, Françoise Le Guennec Coppens (dir.), *Les Swahili, entre Afrique et Arabie* (Paris, 1991).

[8]Ariel Crozon, "Les Arabes à Zanzibar. Haine et fascination," in *ibid.*, pp. 179-94.

[9]See David Parkin, François Constantin, eds,"Social stratification in Swahili society," *Africa*, 59 (2), 1989, pp. 143-220; and David Parkin, "Intra- et extraversion des réseaux swahiliphones. Les Digo de Mtwapa (Kenya)," in Pat Caplan, Françoise Le Guennec-Coppens, *op.cit.*, pp. 129-43.

The sociological position of Islam adds to the constraints imposed by the plurality of social roles which everybody has to perform in East Africa. Consciousness of one's religious identity depends upon the comparative power of any religion in the social system. The demographic position of Islam is not strong, and Muslims are a minority in all the states of East Africa. Their most favourable comparative ratio is in Tanzania, where Muslims constitute about one third of the population, about equal to the number of Christians. Elsewhere, Muslims rarely exceed ten percent of the population.[10]

Such quantitative weakness is not balanced by qualitative strength. For a long time, modern education was neglected, when not completely rejected, by traditional Muslim leaders. Muslims are still generally less well-educated than Christians according to the norms of the modern Westernized state system. Higher political and government positions are strongholds of a Westernized ruling class which few people can enter with diplomas from Muslim schools, or even with degrees from an Arab university.

But if demography and the merit system in the bureaucratic state may bar the way to political power for Muslims, their capabilities can bloom in activities where practical knowledge and private networks pave the way to wealth and economic power. Some Muslims are famous as businessmen, bankers (particularly "informal" bankers) or traders. Some have obtained a *de facto* monopoly over such occupations as butchering or taxi-driving. They contribute to the working of the economic system through the distribution of goods and credit which makes them powerful actors, but people maintain a classic resentment against those who are obligatory partners, particularly when those partners are a clearly identified minority, such as the East African Asians. The periodic riots against Asian shops (not to speak of the expulsion of Asians by Idi Amin in Uganda) lead back to our problem, because Muslims are on both sides of these events, among the rioters and among the victims, as they may be when striking workers oppose their employers or when women oppose male-chauvinist laws. Muslim identity may be submerged in the conflicts emerging from these mundane issues. But even with respect to prayer, consciousness of identity is elusive because Muslims often do not all pray in the same mosques for reasons which are often far from strictly religious.

Muslim consciousness does exist, of course, among the millions

[10]Following a comparison of various demographic, ethnographic and socio-political indicators, it was concluded that Muslims represent about 8% of the population in Kenya, 35% in Tanzania, 7% in Uganda, 10% in Malawi and less than 1% in Zambia. François Constantin, *Les communautés musulmanes d'Afrique orientale* (Pau, 1983).

of believers in East Africa, even if it is not permanently active. It can emerge, at least symbolically, when praying or during religious festivals (*maulidi*); it can be activated when essential Islamic values are challenged (as in Kenya with the enforcement of the Law of Succession), and it is often invoked by political propagandists. The question then is to know how a Muslim consciousness could be propelled to the forefront without the intervention of leaders who are able to mobilize Muslims. This is the dialectical situation which links the leader with the group, where the spokesman, because he produces symbolic goods, contributes to the creation of the social reality of the group which he seeks to mobilize, as developed in P. Bourdieu's theory of representation.[11]

The leader can be considered at least as a marker of the identity of the group he is leading (or which he says he is leading). Thus we must identify those leaders who refer(red) to Islamic identity to legitimize their action. Historically, various types of leaders have emerged, which is the result of the pluralist character of the social context and of the lack of a hierarchically centralized bureaucracy in Islam. Hence the diversity which characterizes the production of Muslim leadership in East Africa. It is possible to distinguish between traditional and modern, state-oriented forms of leadership production, but we must not lose sight of a crucial problem which these leaders must manage, that is, the problem of communication, because most of these leaders seem to be unable to maintain a prevalent Muslim consciousness among their East African brethren.

### *The traditional production of leaders*

According to Max Weber, "traditional domination" rests upon the "authority of the 'eternal yesterday,' that is, of the mores sanctified through the unimaginably ancient recognition and habitual orientation to conform." His examples are the patriarch and the "patrimonial prince of yore." Indeed, "pure types are rarely found in reality," and when dealing with sociology of religion, charisma ("gift of grace") may stimulate faith in God's words in a much more emotional and communal manner than the teaching of the ordinary priest or learned man.[12] *Walis* (saints) do lead Sufi brotherhoods in East Africa ,[13] but

[11]Pierre Bourdieu, "La délégation et le fétichisme politique", *Actes de la recherche en Sciences sociales*, 52-53, 1984, pp. 49-55; and his, *Ce que parler veut dire* (Paris, 1982); Pierre Offerlé, *Les partis politiques* (Paris:, 1988).

[12]Quotations from H.H. Gerth, C. Wright Mills, eds, *From Max Weber. Essays in Sociology* (London, 1982), pp. 78-79.

[13]See August H. Nimtz, *Islam and Politics in East Africa* (Minneapolis, 1980);

brotherhoods are just one of several types of Muslim identity. Other specific religious interpretations of Islam have led to the emergence of forms of patrimonial domination in which hereditary leadership is monopolized by alleged descendants of the Prophet, as shown by important Shi'a sects, particularly the Ismailis. Likewise, East African societies have produced patrimonial "princes of yore" in the kingdoms of the Lakes region, particularly in Buganda. In this case, Muslim leadership became mixed with the aristocratic structures related to the *kabaka* (king). Thus, the essence of traditional leadership may be either religious, patrimonial or aristocratic.

*Religious origins*. Throughout the Muslim world (as in any other religion) a basic form of leadership is the authority of the teacher (here the *mwalimu*) over his pupils and former pupils, and the influence of the "priest" (here the *imam*) upon the worshippers in his mosque. Although people may identify with one another as simple participants in the same prayer sessions in the same place, such identification is often related to a sense of neighbourhood in which spatial identity prevails. Of course, Muslims might worship in a particular mosque as a sign of distinction or a way of making a statement in the context of a conflict, as with the Kibuli and Wandegeya groups in Kampala. But such situations apart, these forms of identification through the *mwalimu* or the *imam* are usually limited in their impact, and so long as these leaders do not transcend the limits of their occupational duties, they remain local elders influencing local attitudes. The international reputation of a few highly learned *shaikhs* such as Shaikh Abdallah al Farsy is a different problem. His knowledge in Islamic sciences has made him a respected theorist whose comments and activities were supposed to be far beyond mundane contingencies in which he carefully avoided becoming involved. As such, he was a symbol of the dignity of East African Islam but not a popular mobilizing leader.

Some less famous religious guides became effective popular leaders through their (alleged or proven) religious knowledge, the exemplary nature of their private lives, or their personal charisma which might be based on their wisdom, their ability to perform miracles, or the possession of *baraka*. Some of them approached sainthood, such as Shaikh Yahya bin Abdallah Ramiya, a former slave of Bagamoyo popularly known as Shaikh Ramiya, or Saleh bin Allawi Jamal al Layl, the "Habib Saleh" of Lamu, who enjoyed a more elevated status as a *sharif* coming from the Comoros. These leaders

---

François Constantin, "Charisma and the crisis of power in East Africa," in Donal C. O'Brien, C. Coulon, eds, *Charisma and Brotherhood in African Islam* (Oxford, 1988), pp. 67-90.

created a new Islamic consciousness among their followers. For various reasons, Shaikh Ramiya and Habib Saleh decided to teach Islam to the marginalized African masses, in opposition to the attitude of the local Arab élites. As a result, they achieved widespread regional fame and became the guides of such popular Muslim mass movements as the East African branch of the Qadiriyya, which expanded in the early twentieth century under the regional leadership of Shaikh Ramiya. This self-made leader was then at the centre of important networks, the influence of which was felt within the colonial political system throughout coastal Kenya and Tanganyika.[14]

The *wali* is a leader whose charisma is based on personal capabilities and gifts which are acknowledged and often exaggerated by his followers.[15] Based as it is on individual attributes, the survival and durability of any new community founded upon charismatic authority is dependent on those who will decide on the legitimacy of any successor and even of the community itself. The Riyadha mosque in Lamu remains an important educational and highly symbolic institution in East Africa, but Habib Saleh's heirs were not very successful or effective as group leaders. Shaikh Ramiya, on the other hand, unified his followers within his brotherhood with a common interpretation of Islam and through specific rituals (for example, the *maulidis*). Unity was also realized through the general acceptance that the legitimacy of succession should be based on the inheritance of knowledge and the gifts of special powers such as the ability to perform miracles. Thus, the succession of Shaikh Ramiya by his son Muhammad and his grandson Abdulrahmani was accepted by popular acclaim.[16]

Therefore, Muslim identity can be generated by an ideological system in which people accept the possibility of sainthood in a leader, in which they value Islamic knowledge (which is properly attested by chains of transmission, preferably with reference to Zanzibari *madrasas*), and in which they accept miracles and believe that such gifts can be inherited. This kind of system of thought can create strong identities (as in a brotherhood) but the contradictions of daily life expose it to the weaknesses inherent in any structure based on personal

[14]For Habib Saleh, see A.H.M. El Zein, *The Sacred Meadows: A Structural Analysis of Religious Symbolism in an East African Town (Lamu)* (Evanston, 1975); Françoise Le Guennec Coppens, "Les Masharifu Jamalilil à Lamu," in CERSOI, dir., *Islam contemporain dans l'Océan Indien* (Paris/Aix en Provence, 1981), pp. 91-102.

[15]François Constantin, "Charisma.," *op.cit.*

[16]Field research, Bagamoyo, June 1987. François Constantin, "Bagamoyó, 1987. Retour aux sources de la branche est-africaine de la Qadiriyya," *Islam et société au sud du Sahara*, 2, 1988, pp. 138-50.

leadership.

The contradictions of daily life may also contribute to a different process whereby a religious leader (e.g. an *imam*) becomes willy-nilly a political figure if not an agitator, which is certainly not the role of the *shaikh* of a *tariqa* in East Africa. During the late 1980s, harsh economic conditions and political tension led to troubles on the Kenyan coast and in Zanzibar. Some Friday sermons and other speeches by certain *imams* were interpreted by dissatisfied Muslims as an encouragement for mass demonstrations which resulted in riots. These kinds of demonstrations do not create the religious leader, who of course already exists, but they transform him, perhaps against his own will, into a popular leader who becomes exposed to police repression.[17] These kinds of events among disorganized and disgruntled people have not yet been transformed into structured movements; the group identity of the rioters is short-lived, perhaps because governments and courts wish to avoid transforming the alleged religious agitators into actual political martyrs. However these demonstrations prove that religious leadership may emerge not only from religious knowledge or supranatural gifts, but also from the effective control of the Word and of the techniques of mass manipulation by demagogic preachers.

*Patrimonial resources.* Routinization of charisma often leads to patrimonialism through which authority over the community is inherited exclusively within the lineage of the group's founder. In such conditions the followers have little or no say in the choice of the leader. In some Muslim sects, for example, supreme authority is vested in descent from the Prophet Muhammad. However, difficulties often arise after the death of a leader over the selection of the legitimate heir. These kinds of conflicts have contributed to division among Muslims, for example among the seven-*Imam* Shi'as who consider that the legitimate chain of *imams* is to be found in the direct descendants of Ismail, currently represented by Aga Khan IV. East Africa is one of the strongholds of the Ismailis, where they are represented by an important minority of Asian Muslims. They maintain their identity not only through their acceptance of the unchallenged authority of the Aga Khan, who receives a welcome worthy of a head of state when he visits, but also through a unique cultural mix which includes respect for the tenets of Islam, loyalty to Asian social structures, and assimilation of Western capitalist norms.

[17]For further information on the riots in Mombasa and Zanzibar, see the *Daily Nation* (Kenya), from 30 Oct. to 12 Nov. 1987, and *Daily News* (Tanzania), 15 June, 16 June 1988 and 31 Aug. and 1 Sept. 1988.

They further reinforce their identity by recruiting members only within the Asian community. Their only public manifestation of their participation in the international *umma* in East Africa is their heavy involvement in social activities as exemplified formerly by the influence of the East African Muslim Welfare Society (EAMWS), which was created by the Aga Khan, and today by the funding of Muslim schools and hospitals which are open to all without discrimination.

The identity of Ismailis, like other Asian Muslims in East Africa (Dawoodi Bohrans), is based less on their religious affiliation than on their ethnic and economic status. They are viewed primarily as a wealthy class of Asians who control effective means of accumulation and who are integrated into secure transnational networks which extend from Bombay to Vancouver through Cagliari. The authoritative system of regulations controlled by the Aga Khan avoids contradictions between temporal efficacy and spiritual demands. This kind of centralization does not, however, protect adherents from conflicts with governments and politicians who might succumb to demagogic xenophobia and populism, as occurred in Tanzania after the Arusha declaration and in Uganda under Idi Amin. However, such hardships help to maintain a sense of identity, and centralized patrimonial leadership has been effective in bringing about subsequent reconciliations when Ismaili know-how and investment have been sought, although Islam as such has little to do with these kinds of developments.[18]

*African aristocracy*. The historicity of African societies also influenced the installation of other forms of traditional Muslim leadership. When Islam reached the African hinterland in the nineteenth century, it was often received with great respect, and some African rulers decided to convert in order to reinforce their prestige, to improve their social status, and to increase their social distance from their ordinary subjects. Leaving aside the consequences of the subsequent arrival of Christian missionaries and European rule, the small Muslim community in Buganda reproduced the stratified power structure of the kingdom. The leader of the Muslim community was the highest-ranking Muslim in the royal aristocratic hierarchy, Prince Nuhu Mbogo, who was a relative of the *kabaka* (king). Because of the complex social and political situation in the Lakes region, Prince Mbogo did not exercize

[18]On Asian Islam in East Africa, see Cynthia Salvadori, *Through Open Doors. A View of Asian Cultures in Kenya* (Nairobi, 1983); Shirin R. Walji, "A History of the Ismaïli Community in Tanzania," unpubl. Ph.D. thesis, University of Wisconsin, 1974.

an easy authority over the Muslims, but the political domination of Buganda over the neighbouring kingdoms and chieftancies, and the alliance of the *kabaka* with the British colonial administration, enforced the supremacy of the monarchy, if not its legitimacy, even in Muslim affairs. When Prince Mbogo died (1921), he was succeeded by another Baganda prince, Badru Kakungulu, who is still at least the nominal figurehead of all Ugandan Muslim factions, although he was the actual leader of only one of them. Very few Muslims contested the selection of the Prince as their symbolic leader when they negotiated among themselves to forge the basis of a unification movement, which in the end was very short-lived.[19] But these symbolic leaders did not interfere in religious matters as such, which were the monopoly of *shaikhs*, *imams* and *muftis*.

Prince Kakungulu is now a respected elder (although he is far from neutral in factional conflicts), a status he has attained due to his aristocratic origins and his old age. He is not a particularly learned or gifted Muslim, but his leadership is based primarily on secular (i.e. non Muslim) considerations. Since the majority (and the best educated) Ugandan Muslims are Baganda, and since Baganda identity is symbolized by faithfulness to the *kabaka*, the most appropriate symbolic leader of the Ugandan Muslims would be a Muslim prince of the Baganda royal family.

The valorization of traditional hierarchies also fosters conflicting attitudes among Muslims, because a Baganda prince symbolizes both unity and conflict at the same time. Some may accept the Prince's leadership because they consider him to be a wise man (because he is old, or because he is a Baganda prince, or because he is a Muslim) or because they expect that his royal status will make him effective in negotiating Muslim interests with government. But it does not mean that everyone is content with the resultant confusion between traditional domination and religion. Politics and ethnicity invaded the religious sphere in Uganda during the last century and the "imported" religions, whatever their prestige, were never strong enough to emerge as the most important reference for identification among the interlacustrine peoples.[20]

[19]K.G. Lockard, "Religion and Political Development in Uganda, 1962-1972," unpubl. Ph.D. thesis, University of Wisconsin, 1974; François Constantin, "Minorité religieuse et luttes politiques dans l'espace ougandais," *Politique africaine*, 1 (4), Nov. 1981, pp. 71-89; Abdul B.K. Kasozi, "The UMSC: An Experiment in Muslim Administrative Centralization and Institutionalization, 1972-1982," *Journal Institute of Muslim Minority Affairs*, 6 (1) 1985, pp. 34-51.

[20]The Islamization process of the Yao (Malawi, northern Mozambique) was different. It was a response to British and Portuguese colonization where the Yao, led by their chiefs, collectively became Muslims. But the chiefs had no influence on

The post-colonial African state has had to cope with many inherited traditions, one of which is the mixing of politics, ethnicity and religion, which of course is not specific to Africa. In its efforts to improve its control over society, governments often favour the emergence of loyal and effective religious leaders, especially in situations where the religion is not hierarchically organized.

*Muslim leadership and post-colonial politics*

Religion is a political resource for politicians who are concerned with mobilization and social control. Heads of state, members of governments, MPs and party leaders are not reluctant to mix religion and politics, whatever they may say,[21] and one important part of their policy is to create and to control social organizations (if possible at the national level) which might simplify the structuration of the society.

Muslim leaders have also emerged in East Africa without any charismatic or traditional base; these have relied mainly on political support from the government or the party. This kind of leadership is often imposed from the top of the political hierarchy, and the general Muslim community has little input into the process. In fact, the issues which are at stake in these kinds of situations usually concern national and international affairs in which non-Muslim political actors and Muslim foreign institutions try to impose their own conceptions of Muslim identity through organizations or bureaucratic structures which they put in place either directly or indirectly. The ultimate aim of these interventions is not really the consolidation of national Muslim identity as such, but the integration of national Muslims into a wider world, be it the national state-system or the international *umma*.

*National politics*. The extension of political control over believers in single-party states required that religious communities should be organized along the same principles as all other communities, that is, they should be unified within a single national association which reproduced most of the principles of the state-system itself: a centralized bureaucracy capable of enforcing a sense of identity among the believers through clearly designated spokesmen. This did not immediately create problems with already centralized denominations, such as the Roman Catholic Church. But it was necessary to create national "supreme councils" for the Muslims in Kenya (Supreme

---

religious (Islamic) matters. See David Bone, "Islam in Malawi," *Journal of Religion in Africa*, XIII (2) 1982, pp. 126-38.

21"Don't mix religion and politics!" was one of Nyerere's mottos.

Council of Kenya Muslims, SUPKEM), in Tanzania (Baraza kuu Waislamu wa Tanzania, BAKWATA), in Uganda (Uganda Muslims Supreme Council, UMSC), and later in Malawi (Muslim Association in Malawi, MAM).

Since the early 1930s, Muslims (particularly Asian Muslims) had established formal associations primarily for the articulation of the economic interests of their members and for obtaining government approval or support for educational, health or other welfare activities. More specifically religious grievances might also be discussed: for example, the application of Islamic law or access to public information networks, such as broadcasting. The multiplicity of these associations often helped to maintain the divisions among Muslims based on religious (ritual), occupational, regional, ethnic or gender differences. By comparison, the supremacy of a single national body acting on behalf of all Muslims was expected to reinforce consciousness of Muslim identity and to improve the effectiveness of their activities as an interest group.

Both in Uganda and in Tanzania (in the mid-1960s) and later in Kenya (in the mid-1970s), high-level politicians (ministers, MPs, directors of public corporations) were directly involved in the negotiations and conferences which created the supreme councils.[22] Subsequently, they rarely appear as members of the boards, who are usually religious men (*shaikhs*). The politicians, however, did not participate in these negotiations as rank-and-file believers, but as a sign of the will of the party or of the government, which could also employ more authoritarian methods to enforce unity, as did Idi Amin in Uganda in 1975 when he appointed all fifteen members of the board of the UMSC, of whom five were army officers. The legitimacy within the Muslim community of such politically appointed leaders is not self-evident. Nonetheless, Muslims may accept this political subordination if the Supreme Councils demonstrate their ability to promote Islamic values and interests. People expect that dependence on the state-system will grant them access to state-controlled resources which they can share and redistribute to their brethren, whether symbolic (participation in state rituals), political (access to decision-makers) or economic (access to funds and resources).

The legitimization of leadership among Muslims in these kinds of situations supposes clientelist strategies where a leader will act as a faithful client of some politician in order to have access to state

[22]The most prominent politicians involved were A. Mayanja and A. Nekyon (members of Obote's government in Uganda in the 1960s), R. Kawawa and A. Karume (leaders of TANU and the ASP in Tanzania; and later A. Jumbe), and A. Abdallah (director of a Kenyan state-owned bank in Kenya).

resources while the grass-roots believer will respect the leader so far as he is able to "deliver the goods," either funds, permits, jobs or status. The price to pay at the successive levels of the hierarchical clientelist structure is the political conformism of the client and, as the resources become more and more limited in a context of increasing demands, possibly corruption.[23] Another dysfunction is that in such bureaucratic organizations, the oligarchical process observed by R. Michels in European political parties is working; nomination of leaders does not rely upon the members, but on self-cooptation and/or pressures from the party and the government. In the case of a serious crisis, political authorities can even stimulate old or new rival organizations, as did the Tanzanians when the then President of Zanzibar, A. Jumbe, toured the mainland to install a new national association, the Baraza wa Miskita wa Tanzania (BAMITA) which was supposed to by-pass the ineffective and corrupt BAKWATA. But the political demise of Jumbe subverted the efficacy of BAMITA, and even in Zanzibar the duties of these organizations are now performed by a governmental office, the Waqf commission.[24]

The authority of the Supreme Council is also weakened by its lack of influence in religious matters. The secular law entitles the council to organize the annual pilgrimage to Mecca (i.e. to arrange transport and accommodation, including allocation of foreign currencies) and the national celebration of the 'Id, but it has no authority in theological and intra-Islamic legal disputes, which are within the competence of the *shaikhs*, *imams*, *qadi's* courts and/or *mufti*, over whom the council has no control. The opinion is widely expressed among Muslims that the leaders of the council are more concerned with private business than with spiritual or social welfare issues, suggesting that the councils are perceived as instruments in the clientelist competition for individual prestige, power and wealth. Consequently few people identify with such official bodies, and they return to their own independent associations, and no supreme council has the power to convince its government to ban all the other competing Muslim associations.[25]

[23]A general theory on clientalism is presented in S.N. Eisenstadt, Rene Lemarchand, eds., *Political Clientelism, Patronage and Development* (Beverly Hills/London, 1981). The problem of self-esteem is at the core of Mohamed Saidi's "Islam and politics in Tanzania," paper presented at the Conference on Daawa in East Africa, Nairobi, 1989. See also P. Landberg, *op. cit.*

[24]Field research, Zanzibar, May 1989. Apart from BAKWATA and BAMITA the National Association of Koran Readers (BALUKTA) is now another important Muslim body. For the most recent attempts to "restore peace and harmony among all the faithful of Islam in Tanzania", see *Sunday News* (Tanzania), 12 Jan. 1992.

[25]In Uganda, see A.B.K. Kasozi, *op. cit.* See also François Constantin, "Muslim National Organizations and Politics in East Africa," Conference on Religion and

Government strategies in creating national councils, rather than unifying Muslims, have contributed to increasing the divisions among them, at least in East Africa where no "Muslim" political party has emerged. The absence of prominent politicians who would have promoted a programme based on Islamic ideology and on Muslim interests is very relevant to the weakness of a sense of shared Muslim identity in the region. Currently, Muslims are not considered, and do not consider themselves, as being a political force as Muslims. Muslim "big men" exist in Kenya and in Tanzania, but their power and status do not rely primarily on local Muslim connections; if it had been otherwise, they would have invested themselves in the leadership of the councils, which none of them did.[26] But this common attitude does not exclude references to Islam by politicians, particularly when the party, the government or themselves are confronted with problems of money; in these cases, Muslim politicians integrate themselves into, or activate existing, transnational Muslim networks which link East African Muslims with the wider Muslim world.

*Transnational networks*. East African Muslims are part of the *umma*, and consequently enjoy preferential links with the centre(s) of the Muslim world which is (are) interested in Muslims wherever they live throughout the world, and not only for religious reasons. This interest is motivated by the competition among Islamic centres for the leadership of the *umma*. Governments, parties, brotherhoods, international organizations, and private foundations have active international policies which are often aimed at mobilizing Muslim identity abroad, particularly on the frontier where Islam is still frail. East Africa is one of these Islamic frontiers. But again, the plurality of competing foreign organizations, instead of enhancing a shared sense of identity among East African Muslims, often results in further divisions.

Various Muslim organizations and governments have been implicated in the establishment and funding of supreme councils, which they consider to be channels for the strengthening and spread of

---

Politics in East Africa, Roskilde, 1990.

[26] Former Vice-President Jumbe of Tanzania is now considered a religious leader, although this was not the case before he left politics. In Tanganyika, before independence, some Muslims opposed to Christian domination in TANU or to independence engaged in the creation of Muslim parties (Tanganyika African Muslim Union, Central Society of Tanganyika Muslims); the most influential was the conservative All Muslim National Union of Tanganyika (AMNUT) which African Muslims such as Chief Fundikira joined when they opposed the socialist orientation of Nyerere. On AMNUT, see David Westerlund, *Ujamaa na Dini* (Stockholm, 1980).

Islam. The creation of SUPKEM in Kenya was stimulated by the Islamic World League with subsidies from the Islamic Foundation. The UMSC in Uganda was similarly funded by the governments of Saudi Arabia and Kuwait, which also assisted in the foundation of the MAM in Malawi. During his campaign for the creation of BAMITA in spring 1981, A. Jumbe explained that this new council had been proposed by the Islamic World League as a condition for further Muslim investment in education in Tanzania. Religious piety could be one motivation for this kind of commitment through financial assistance and expatriate staff, but in the context of the conflicts in the Middle East, political self-interest is also at stake. Although these interventions may strengthen Muslim consciousness of membership in the *umma*, they also have the divisive effect of constituting small pro-Saudi, pro-Libyan, pro-Iraqi or pro-Iranian factions among East African Muslims.

The dynamics of local Muslim identity are thus troubled by the activities of African or foreign preachers and/or agitators: "diplomats" or "journalists", Qur'an reciters or graduates from Arab universities, who wander through the countries of East Africa looking for contacts at the grass-roots level. They attempt to mobilize the suffering masses (even non-Muslims) and to structure the identity of disgruntled populations by developing religious and ideological arguments against Westernization and Communism and by appealing for a purification of Islam as the only solution to the general crisis of the state system. These subversive political initiatives do not seem to have been effective up to now; radical preachers have enjoyed local, shortlived successes, but exercised little sustained national or regional influence. Governments have thus far managed to control the unrest which has erupted and to punish the instigators without provoking a mass mobilization by their followers.[27] The dramatic changes in the world order and their consequences in the Third World may have reduced similar propaganda by non-accredited representatives of foreign Muslim governments, and Islamic "subversion" from abroad has thus far managed to mobilize only small fringes of particularly marginalized Muslims.[28]

[27]The most disturbing preachers in 1988-9 were the Zairo-Tanzanian "Professors," N.M. Fundi and M.A. Kawenba from Ujiji whose radicalism and attacks against Christians led Kenyan and Tanzanian governments to restrict their public meetings (*Daily News*, 9 May, 16 May, 2 Aug. 1988).

[28]It is still too early to assess the long-term influence of Khomeini and of the Iranian Islamic Republic, whose influence is clear in some of Shaikh Said Musa's writings and in the speeches of other *shaikhs*. See Justo Lacunza-Balda, "Tendances de la littérature islamique swahili," in Pat Caplan and Françoise Le Guennec-Coppens, *op. cit*, pp. 20-38.

The "true" missionnaries of Islam, that is religious men who travel through the region teaching the Qur'an in public, have not achieved much more success. For decades, the Ahmadiyya have employed various means of modern communication to attract converts to their movement. The heretical character of the Ahmadiyya does not seem to be the reason for its poor performance. Well-endowed orthodox missions, such as the Bilal mission, have also been very active, particularly in the diffusion of Islamic educational literature; the Bilal mission is probably the most important publisher of Islamic literature in East Africa. However the influence of this Pakistan-based organization is very limited. The difficulties which these missionary activities have confronted are related to the character of Islam (absence of central authority), to local history (assimilation of foreign Islam with former Arab domination) and perhaps to the attitude of the Africans towards religious beliefs. In other words, it appears to be a cultural problem, which points to the importance of communications.

### *Leadership and the technologies of identity*

The diversity of the possible sources from which Muslim leadership can be drawn raises the question of whether the efficacy of leadership in producing group consciousness is specifically related to its origins. The study of specific cases demonstrates that the sources of leadership may often overlap, and that the eventual short-term and long-term results may vary. A charismatic leader (Sh. Ramiya) can enter the bureaucracy of the colonial administration (he was appointed as a *liwali*) and remain a popular and effective contestor of the colonial Arab-British order, while a highly learned and widely respected *'alim* (as was Shaikh al-Farsy) can maintain a socially and politically conformist attitude without mobilizing the Muslims. A "leader" who has been integrated into the ruling élite of the post-colonial state may be either an insignificant puppet of the government (Supreme Council staff) or a powerful advocate for his group (the Aga Khan). The only patent relationship to be gleaned from present evidence is that hitherto no leader who has been imposed by the government through a bureaucratic structure has been perceived as a legitimate representative by the Muslim community. In Uganda, repeated autocratic appointments by Idi Amin and Milton Obote did not lead to their popular acceptance, even when the appointees possessed religious qualifications.

This apparent failure effectively to exploit the political advantages which derive from control over the bureaucracy might be explained by a lack of expertise in controlling the technologies of mass manipulation, i.e. the means of modern communication, a problem traditional leaders did not have to face. But all leaders have to adapt to the changing forms of communication which motivate people. And the most effective modern leader, the one who will be able to stimulate identity, will be the one who has the material resources to invest in the most modern methods of communications and propaganda, and who knows the themes and words to which people will respond. Lacking the expertise necessary for analyzing the mass psychology of East African Muslims, we shall limit our comments to an analysis of the political economy of leadership and of communication.

*Political economy and identity building.* The development of leadership and the mobilization of a following originate with charisma, knowledge, and hereditary and/or secular support. But leadership must be sustained by more instrumental resources, because mass mobilization requires that people be informed about the miracles, the knowledge, the "election" of the leader in order to improve his popular image as well as the status of his followers (their dignity and self-esteem) and also to maintain a social network of dependants, because the leader does not want his faithful clients to be attracted by rivals.

East African history demonstrates that successful leadership among Muslims requires economic resources. Whatever their differences of style, period and Islamic knowledge, Shaikh Ramiya, Shaikh al-Farsy or Karim Aga Khan all controlled comparatively significant economic resources which they could devote to the development and maintenance of general welfare institutions, the building of schools and health centres, the purchase of books and medicine, and the hiring of teachers and practitioners. Independent wealth also allows the leader to pay for further studies in famous Islamic institutes (and/or private European modern schools), thus enhancing his image as a learned Muslim; he also may publish religious literature and fund the building of mosques, the sophisticated architecture and design of which might reflect the superiority of the leader and of his faction, or, on the contrary, his lack of pretentiousness (although a building dedicated to Allah should necessarily be pleasant). Private wealth also allows a leader to be more generous with those followers who might be confronted with poverty, unexpected expenses or costly private rituals (marriage); he is expected to assist his brethren beyond the usual obligations of *zakat*. To be generous in this way requires a careful management of wealth. Thus, a wise Muslim leader invests for example in real estate (formerly in Bagamoyo stone town, now in London), which improves his symbolic status as well as his pocket-book or his bank account. Apart from the religious messages it encodes, such ostentatious symbolic and redistributive behaviour contributes significantly to the mobilization of followers.

Leaders who are appointed to official government bodies, like the Supreme Councils, rarely control equivalent resources. Having no important personal assets,[29] they must depend on subsidies from the government, from the party or from foreign donors. However, because the governments of East Africa are confronted with severe economic deficits, they must prioritize the various demands made upon them, and small minorities of electors or citizens are usually ignored in so far as they do not create serious disturbances. Thus, the Supreme Councils do not have access to the national resources which would enable them to compete with the activities of Muslim non-governmental associations.

To some extent, foreign donors from the Gulf, Iran or Libya do not experience these kinds of problems. The financial support which they offer to the Supreme Councils is often allocated to definite programmes or to the recruitment of expatriate teachers or staff. Thus, the ordinary Muslim considers a given programme to be the realization of a particular foreign donor (who carefully makes known that he financed the project) rather than of the Council. But when the programme is indefinitely delayed, or when scholarships are lost, the popular interpretation is that money has been diverted by members of the Council staff. Therefore, in addition to the fact that their members lack adequate religious education, social status and respectability in the eyes of the Muslim community, the Supreme Councils are further weakened by the absence of the resources necessary to develop a nation-wide mobilization policy which could supersede existing independent solidarities.

*Communication and identity.* The stability, if not stagnation, which characterizes the contemporary process of Muslim identity-building in East Africa might be explained by a failure to master the techniques of modern communications which are necessary for the mobilization of mass movements.

So far as existing leaders do not seek to increase signficantly the number of their followers, traditionalism in communications is not a serious problem, except if more aggressive rival leaders attempt to capture their constituency. In East Africa, Asian Muslims generally do not proselytize, because their religious identity is strongly related to other rigid social structures. Paradoxically, being rather affluent

[29] If they were rich and ambitious, they would have initiated a personal clientelist strategy.

Muslims, Asians pursue an active communication policy through bookshops, conferences and publications which provide general information on Islam, not only on Shi'a Islam. However, these activities are oriented more towards educated people than towards illiterate rank-and-file Muslims who cannot attend conferences in intercontinental hotels or purchase publications, and they contribute more to the integration of educated Muslims into the local or national élite than into the Muslim community. These policies are aimed more at creating social distinction than broader religious integration.

Further research is necessary in order to increase our knowledge of communication networks among Muslims in East Africa and to identify the main sources of information, comments or consultations for Muslims. These may be the mosque, a reciter of the Qur'an, a *shaikh*, the market-place, the elders, the District Commissioner or an MP, the TV or the newspapers; they could even be tape cassettes and video-tapes. One would also want to know which of these forms of communication has the broadest influence and is most effective in crystallizing some form of identity, and which form.[30] Existing information about these matters is scarce, and the only empirical observations which might be made are about the deficiencies of East African Muslims in the field of modern communications.

No national council has yet been able to produce any form of general media presentation on both the national and local levels, be it written, oral or video. Apart from the yearly *'Id* festival, councils arrange few local meetings. In Tanzania, it is unusual to find any publications by the BAKWATA or its leaders, although Islamic bookshops are comparatively well-stocked with Arab or Asian booklets, particularly the writings of the Mawlana Mawdudi, of the Bilal Mission (in English and in Kiswahili), or Iranian periodicals in pure Kiswahili (*Sauti ya Umma*). In Kenya, SUPKEM's attempt to edit a quarterly was short-lived, and the only important publisher is the international Islamic Foundation (which has its headquarters in Leicester, England); coastal Islamic movements also publish periodicals such as *The Message*.

Air time is set aside for Muslim programming on national radio and television (where this exists), but speakers often identify more with the government or the party than with any independent Muslim group, and no independent Muslim broadcasting company is operating,

[30]Nothing has been published about this since Becker's police report (in B.G. Martin, ed., "Material for the understanding of Islam in German East Africa," *Tanzanian Notes and Records*, 68, 1968, pp. 31-61). G. Nkrumah's presentation to the Islamic Identities Conference, "Muslim Associations in South Africa," provided an interesting approach for South Africa.

even supposing that any Muslim group might have asked for one. Indeed, Muslims can tune into foreign programmes, as they did in the old days when nationalists listened to Nasser's voice through the Egyptian broadcasting system. This is a way of asserting a Muslim identity which today does not seem to have a more extensive incidence than Nasser's propaganda did. East African Muslims can also buy religious cassettes which are widely sold throughout the Muslim world. But local Muslim leaders have not published tapes, even when they have recorded them.[31] Many of the cassettes which are sold in East Africa are published in Egypt, but it would be important to know how many are really sold before evaluating their possible effects on Muslim identity.

Whatever the effectiveness of the many diverse methods for mobilizing Muslims and for structuring Muslim identity, Muslims in East Africa are still reluctant to embrace the technology of modern mass communications. By such means, the fame and reputation of a local saint or *'alim* could be spread much further afield to a population whose response would not be based on literacy alone. This hesitancy might be explained by a fundamental conservatism similar to the attitude of the old establishment in opposing modernized Muslim schools. It might also be a side-effect of political control and censorship on information. But these are not convincing arguments. Some Muslims do edit periodicals and booklets and do produce radio or television reports. Shaikh al-Farsy was an active writer and editor, although he was the only East African who posed a challenge to Arab-Asian publications before the appearance of the Tanzanian Shaikh Said Musa. However, the theoretical and theological orientation of Shaikh Musa's writings and comments are more those of an intellectual than a mass mobilizer. People may, of course, respect him, as they respected Shaikh al-Farsy, even if they do not in practice identify with him or through him. The fact is that the harshness of current economic conditions makes it difficult to finance a modern communications policy. East African *shaikhs* are unable to publish their religious writings or recordings, and the prolixity of Shaikh Musa's impressive publishing programme seems to be slowing down for the same reasons.[32]

Similarly, it is now difficult to nourish traditional Muslim leadership. Shaikh Ramiya's grandson is still a respected man, but the assets which he inherited (mainly plantations) provide a much smaller return than they did half a century ago; and elaborate royal rituals no

[31] A *maulidi* led by the late Shaikh Muhammad Ramiya has been tape-recorded; one can listen to it in his son's office in Bagamoyo.

[32] See Justo Lacunza-Balda, *op. cit.*

longer distinguish Prince Badru Kakungulu. In addition to controversies about what constitutes “true” Islam (which might be described as an ideological issue), Muslim leaders are also finding it more difficult to mobilize followers on strictly religious grounds because of the economic crisis. Even the much more affluent movements emanating from foreign Arab and Islamic centres have not to date had an impressive mobilizing influence over the peoples of East Africa, who have access to a plurality of possible criteria for identification, including African-centred identities, and whose sincere allegiance to Islam does not necessarily result in a disregard for their own past, which does not include a heritage of religious militancy.

# CONSTRUCTING MUSLIM IDENTIT MALI

*Louis Brenner*[1]

For the purposes of the following discussion, identity will be considered as a process of naming: naming of self, naming of others, naming *by* others. In its most restricted sense, such naming is associated with the attaching of labels such as Muslim / non-Muslim, Wahhabi / traditional, Qadiri / Tijani / Hamallist. Although these identities can be understood to represent specific social, religious and/or political categories at a given moment in history (or at least they are often analyzed as if this were the case), such conceptualizations are inevitably reifications of more complex social and discursive processes.

Identities are constantly being constructed and reconstructed, by self and/or others, through continuing actions and discourse in a political context. Identities, both Muslim and non-Muslim, are formulated through the appropriation and reassortment of various elements or building blocks which may be religiously significant, but are also socially, politically and economically motivated. As complex clusters of attributes, they are subject to continuous reordering by self and others depending upon perceived aims, needs and constraints; they reflect political conflict and are representations of alleged social realities rather than essences in themselves.

These observations suggest that the construction of identities can be conceptualized as a system of transformations located within a broader socio-political process. This approach to the study of identity has been elaborated by J.-L. Amselle in his recent book, *Logiques métisses*,[2] and the present paper seeks further to develop his argument by examining the process of Muslim identity-building in the broader political context of contemporary Mali.

However, before we enter into this analysis, several observations about Islam as a religion are in order. Nothing which follows is intended to pass judgment on any individual's personal commitment to Islam; insofar as Islam is understood as an exploration of one's personal relationship to God, it is not for any other person to judge. Furthermore, the personal is largely inaccessible to the researcher.

[1]Research upon which this paper is based has been made possible by generous grants from several agencies: the Nuffield Foundation, the Jordan Bequest, and the Research and Publications Committee of SOAS.

[2]Jean-Loup Amselle., *Logiques métisses. Anthropologie de l'identité en Afrique et ailleurs* (Paris, 1990).

This said, however, the relationship between personal commitment and social representation is a powerful source of creative tension and contributes significantly to the internal dynamism of Muslim societies. The history of Sufism in West Africa, for example, demonstrates how a personal and private devotional practice can form the basis of a new social order and political association.[3] By contrast, the constitution of the secular state officially confines religion to the private domain; proponents of an Islamic state elevate religion to a fundamental principle of social organization. The process of identity construction includes the interplay between the personal and the social, although in the analysis which follows we will focus primarily on the latter.

*Sectarian identities*

Much recent literature about Islam in Mali has concentrated on the emergence of a religious and socio-economic grouping which is known locally as the Wahhabiyya.[4] This label was assigned to them by their opponents; they prefer to call themselves the *Ahl al-sunna* or Sunnis. In this paper, we will refer to them as Wahhabi/Sunnis, to remind the reader of the ambiguity of their identity. Both the Wahhabi/Sunnis and their opponents accept that the origins of this movement, and its ideological roots, are found outside Mali in the Middle East and more particularly in Saudi Arabia. For the Wahhabi/Sunnis themselves, this orientation symbolizes the legitimacy of their movement, associated as it is with the spiritual centre of the Muslim world and with an alleged ritual purity which rejects the many innovations of local Islamic expressions, especially Sufism. Local Malian discourse contrasts the

[3]I have written about this process elsewhere; see L. Brenner, "Muslim Thought in Eighteenth Century West Africa: The Case of Shaikh 'Uthman b. Fudi," in N. Levtzion and J. Voll (eds), *Eighteenth Century Renewal and Reform Movements in Islam* (Syracuse, 1987), pp. 39-67, and "Concepts of Tariqa in West Africa: the Case of the Qadiriyya," in D. Cruise O'Brien and C. Coulon (eds), *Charisma and Brotherhood in African Islam* (Oxford, 1988), pp. 33-52.

[4]See, for example, J.-L. Amselle, *Les négociants de la savane. Histoire et organisation sociale des Kooroko (Mali)* (Paris, 1977); L. Kaba, *The Wahhabiyya. Islamic Reform and Politics in French West Africa* (Evanston, 1974); Alliman Mahamane, "Le mouvement wahhabite à Bamako (origine et évolution)" (Bamako: ENSup, Mémoire, fin d'études,1985); J.-L. Triaud, "'Abd al-Rahman l'Africain (1908-1957), pionnier et précurseur du wahhabisme au Mali," in O. Carré et P. Dumont (eds), *Radicalismes islamiques*, vol. II, (Paris, 1986); Ronald W. Niezen, "Diverse Styles of Islamic Reform among the Songhay of Eastern Mali," unpubl. Ph.D. thesis, Cambridge University, 1987, and his article, "The 'Community of Helpers of the Sunna': Islamic Reform among the Songhay of Gao (Mali)," *Africa*, 60 (3), 1990, pp. 399-423.

Islam of the Wahhabi/Sunnis with an Islam which is described as "traditional" or "orthodox" or, more rarely, Maliki in contrast to the Hanbali preferences of the Wahhabi/Sunnis. Traditional/Orthodox Muslims criticize Wahhabi/Sunni practice precisely because it is "foreign," which often implies Arab. But the Wahhabi/Sunnis are also characterized as aggressive, self-centered and ignorant; charges of ignorance usually refer to the fact that scholars of this persuasion have not been trained by "traditional" methods in "traditional" religious institutions.

The 'international' references in this discourse are significant, because they reflect many of the tensions which the Sunni/Traditional confrontation represents, located as they are in the profound social and economic changes which Africa has experienced during the twentieth century. Much of the appeal of Wahhabi/Sunni doctrine lay in its international or universalist attributes; here was an Islam which transcended local limitations and identified with the wider Muslim world.[5] The Wahhabi/Sunnis emerged as an identifiable group in the 1940s and early 1950s within the networks of both young students and merchants who had either direct or indirect contacts with the Middle East. They were quickly recognized (as a threat) by the French, who were constantly pre-occupied with the fear that Africans might find the means to unite against their domination under the banner of Islam.[6] There was certainly an anti-French element in the movement, especially among the young scholars who became the pioneers of an educational initiative to provide Islamic schooling in competition with the French-language colonial indoctrination which they felt was transmitted in the colonial schools. But these young scholars were also critical of the pedagogical techniques of the Qur'anic schools, and they sought to develop new methods of teaching religious studies, and in particular of teaching Arabic as a living language.

Another element in the movement, not completely independent from the first, was commercial. According to Amselle, during the colonial period many people, especially former aristocrats and farmers, took to commerce in order to benefit from the economic opportunities offerred by the colonial situation. Becoming a merchant in the Malian

[5]Readers familiar with Robin Horton's analyses of the microcosm and the macrocosm in African religious concept may find echoes of his argument in the tensions described here between local and international versions of Islam in Mali. But in the present example, of course, both representations of Islam are monotheistic, albeit differing in emphasis and perception.

[6]The first systematic analysis of the Wahhabi/Sunnis in Mali was made by Marcel Cardaire, an officer in the French colonial Bureau des Affaires Musulmanes: *L'Islam et le terroir africain* (Koulouba, 1965).

context meant becoming Muslim, at a time when members of the new merchant class were taking on a Wahhabi/Sunni identity.[7]

Wahhabi/Sunni identity is therefore a combination of several elements: religious, economic, political and social. Viewed analytically, the movement represents both a historical rupture and a continuity. It is a break with the past insofar as its adherents denounced and distanced themselves from what they considered to be Traditional/Orthodox Islam in the form of the brotherhoods and local Qur'anic pedagogy. But it also demonstrates a deeper continuity as one among a lengthy series of transformations in which Muslims have reordered and reorganized themselves to respond to new demands and new conditions. This pattern of transformations can be observed in the history of Mali's Sufi brotherhoods, an examination of which demonstrates that the identity of each of them consisted of a similar array of religious, social, economic and political elements in the context of competing objectives and interests.

The central Saharan branch of the Qadiriyya, which under Sidi al-Mukhtar al-Kunti in the eighteenth century became known as the Qadiriyya-Mukhtariyya, is an excellent case in point. The initiatives instituted by Sidi al-Mukhtar represent one of the most significant social developments in West African Islamic history; under his leadership, the Qadiriyya in the region was transformed from an essentially private form of devotional mysticism into a corporate Sufism which placed great emphasis upon membership in an identifiable group. The elements which comprised this emergent identity were many and varied. They centered on a specific religious message about the spiritual power and the promised rewards of Qadiri Sufism, which were manifested in the person of Sidi al-Mukhtar himself. But beyond these particular doctrinal elements, Qadiri identity was also based upon social, economic and political interests. Sidi al-Mukhtar's organizational genius was reflected in his ability to combine within the Qadiriyya several existing networking structures and ideologies, based upon the transmission of spiritual *salasil* and scholarly *ijaza*, the lineage ideology of the Kunta (who constituted the leadership of the religious hierarchy), and the commercial interests of certain Muslim merchant communities.[8]

[7]See Amselle, *Logiques métisses*, especially ch. VIII. Amselle analyses the relevant transformation of identities in terms of a continuum between two identity poles: non-Muslim farmer and Muslim merchant.

[8]For the relationship between Muslim ideology and trading networks, see the seminal article by Abner Cohen, "Cultural Strategies in the Organization of Trading Diasporas," in C. Meillassoux (ed), *The Development of Indigenous Trade and Markets in West Africa* (Oxford, 1971).

Politically, the Qadiriyya-Mukhtariyya developed in opposition to other religious groups, particularly the *zawaya* organizations of the Kel Intasar and the Kel al-Suq; Sidi al-Mukhtar asserted that "pure" Islam was to be found only within his own community. The order also developed in explicit opposition to contemporary state or other forms of "secular" power, such as the warrior lineages of the Sahara. In his writings and in his personal behaviour, Sidi al-Mukhtar constantly drew attention to the differences between the political structures and ideologies of his own and other communities:

> [He] did not impose his authority; people submitted to him by voluntary initiation into the *tariqa*. He did not levy taxes; his followers brought him gifts, which he redistributed. He did not surround himself with pomp and panoply; he lived in simple, modest surroundings. He did not impose judgments; he mediated disputes. His followers did sometimes take up arms, but only in extreme circumstances, according to them; al-Mukhtar preferred to employ the power of his curse to discipline his enemies. The Qadiriyya-Mukhtariyya provided a model of social and political organization which contrasted starkly with existing forms of secular authority in the region.[9]

This insistence that participation in the "pure" Muslim community is founded upon voluntary participation as opposed to the exercise of violent force is a central theme in the West African Muslim discourse. And Islamic political debate in West Africa has been very much preoccupied with the question of precisely when the use of force becomes legitimate, especially against other Muslims.

This issue became the central feature of the nineteenth-century history of the Tijaniyya in West Africa. Proselytized in the region largely through the efforts of al-Hajj 'Umar Tal, this Sufi order also began its African career as a "pure" Muslim community in the sense that the Tijaniyya, under the leadership of its founder Ahmad al-Tijani, guaranteed the reward of paradise to all its adherents. But the early political import of the movement is attested in the fact that it appealed to many discontented groups, from the deposed Saifawa in Borno to the ambitious young scholars of Hamdullahi and the Futa Toro. During the years immediately following his return to West Africa, al-Hajj 'Umar attempted to construct West African Tijani identity around both its religious distinctiveness from the Qadiriyya and a political opposition to illegitimate power. In broad terms, he was repeating the pattern observed in the previous century with Sidi al-Mukhtar al-Kunti.

[9] L. Brenner, "Concepts of *tariqa* in West Africa," *op. cit.*, p. 43.

With the *jihad*, Tijani identity became significantly transformed, both from within and without. 'Umar and his associates represented the Tijaniyya as the vanguard of a rejuvenated Islam, now in holy combat against the unbelievers. But as the conflict intensified, Tijani identity became increasingly obscured in the context of a conflict which pitted Muslim against non-Muslim. When the *jihad* moved eastward and began to threaten Qadiri interests in the Niger valley, the religious confrontation between Qadiriyya and Tijaniyya became deeply politicized. Faced with such determined Muslim opposition, 'Umar's strategy was to argue that the Qadiriyya leadership, particularly in the form of Amadu Amadu of Hamdallahi, had apostasized. In other words, 'Umar sought to justify his actions by proving, through legal argumentation, that certain of these Qadiris were not Muslims at all.[10]

These developments demonstrate clearly how issues of identity reflect political conflict in Muslim societies. And it is worth remarking that, from a Muslim perspective, the more intense the political conflict, the more likely that identity distinctions will gravitate toward the issue of Muslim versus non-Muslim. This is because it is only in conflict with non-Muslims that the use of force can most successfully be legitimated. This hardening of identity through legal argumentation is a feature of highly literate scholarship, and it is characteristic of confrontational politics. Because of its legalistic nature, it is an option taken up primarily by members of the scholarly class, but it is hardly representative of the complex range of relationships between identity transformation and social conflict among Muslims in Africa.

Few Muslims seem to have accepted 'Umar's arguments about the apostasy of the Hamdullahi Muslims. Indeed, it is not clear what proportion of local Muslims ever accepted the general legitimacy of 'Umar's *jihad*, which in Mali became associated with an invading force of Tukolor (Futanke) warriors, represented in the local discourse of its opponents as an oppressive and conquering power.[11] But more illustrative of the process of transforming identities were the subsequent permutations within the Tijaniyya itself, through which persons distanced themselves from 'Umar and his *jihad*. In Mali, the most prominent of these movements was the Hamalliyya, which emerged early in the twentieth century in Nioro du Sahel (one of the

[10]The text in which this position was argued has been translated and analysed by Sidi Mohamed Mahibou and Jean-Louis Triaud in *Voilà ce qui est arrivé. Bayân mâ waqa'a d'al'Hâgg 'Umar al-Fûtî. Plaidoyer pour une guerre sainte en Afrique de l'Ouest au XIXe siècle* (Paris, 1983).

[11]See David Robinson, *The Holy War of Umar Tal: The Western Sudan in the Mid-Nineteenth Century* (Oxford, 1985).

seats of 'Umar's power) and which proclaimed itself the most "pure" form of the Tijaniyya. Under the leadership of its founder, Shaikh Hamallah, the Hamalliyya became identified with both anti-'Umarian and anti-French sentiments; here again was a reassertion of the Muslim capacity to oppose power with voluntary authority. The social appeal of the Hamalliyya was varied, but it included a strong element of political discontent; there was a significant mercantile element, but also young civil servants who were impatient with the political constraints of the colonial situation, and a strong contingent of "modernized" Musim intellectuals, as well as many Bambara who had recently converted to Islam. In other words, many Hamallists were persons caught up in the transition to the new colonial political economy.[12]

*Shifting identity referents*

Following this brief historical excursion, let us return to the process of constructing Wahhabi/Sunni and Traditional/Orthodox identities in contemporary Mali. During the twentieth century, a public discourse has evolved which submerges the complex jigsaw of Mali's Muslim heritage into a "traditional" Islam, which includes: Sufism; the bulk of religious custom associated with rites of passage such as weddings, naming ceremonies, and funerals; and particularly the practices of "*maraboutage*."

The use of the word "traditional" in this context is full of interest. First, even from the brief preceding survey of only a few selected examples, it should be evident how distortive it is to conflate the rich and complex history of West African Sufism under the reifying rubric of "traditional." All distinctions, process, and conflict, indeed all history, are obscured by such usage. But what is at issue is more than intellectual misrepresentation or simple usage; within the public discourse, "tradition" is a term whose connotations are varied and even contradictory.

In the first place, the word and its associated connotations, *as it has come to be used in Mali*, are both French. This is very significant, because it suggests the extent to which the Wahhabi/Sunni versus Traditional/Orthodox conflict has been affected by the socio-political context of the colonial period. It would seem that the French were the first to classify both the Traditionalists and the Wahhabis as

[12]See Alioune Traoré, *Cheikh Hamahoullah, homme de foi et résistant* (Paris, 1983); and L. Brenner, *West African Sufi: The Religious Heritage and Spiritual Search of Cerno Bokar Saalif Taal* (London, 1984).

such.[13] The latter refer to themselves as Sunnis, which from an internal Muslim perspective means that they are calling *themselves* Traditionalists, in that they are following the traditions of the Prophet, the *hadith* and the *sunna*, in their purest form. Similarly, from an internal Muslim perspective, one would expect that the Wahhabi/Sunnis would refer to their opponents as "innovators" (*ahl al-bid'a*), as similar groups do in Nigeria, such as the Izala. It has not been possible to trace the local origins of the term "orthodox" as it appears in this discourse, although its usage contributes to further conceptual obfuscation since Sunni is often translated from Arabic into European languages as "orthodox."

These semantic permutations suggest not only that the origins of these disputes were not independent of French interests and concerns, but also that the present debate, as it is expressed in the public domain, continues to be perceived by the general public from a French conceptual perspective. In other words, the dispute continues to be framed in public discourse by preoccupations inherited from an earlier period. The French invented "traditional" Islam (to borrow the insights of T.O. Ranger and V.Y. Mudimbe[14]), which they much preferred to "reformist" Islam (another contemporary synonym for Wahhabi inclinations), which they feared.[15] Their preference for "traditional" Islam rested upon its alleged passivity in the face of colonial domination. So committed were they to this notion of "tradition," that when Shaikh Hamallah (or Amadu Bamba or others) allegedly challenged their authority simply by refusing publicly to embrace it (a posture of distancing oneself from power, which, as we have seen, had long been a favoured Muslim strategy in West Africa), the French exiled them for being fanatics.

When we examine the evolution of this dispute into the post-colonial period, when a new discourse of nation-building emerges which highlights the themes of progress and development, we discover some interesting continuities. Members of the former Malian government of Moussa Traoré often referred to the value of the nation's

[13]This usage provides an important part of the conceptual framework of the analysis of Islam found in Marcel Cardaire's *L'Islam et le terroir africain*, *op. cit.*

[14]See, T.O. Ranger, "The Invention of Tradition in Colonial Africa," in E. Hobsbawm and T. Ranger (eds), *The Invention of Tradition* (London, 1983); and V.Y. Mudimbe, *The Invention of Africa. Gnosis, Philosophy, and the Order of Knowledge* (Bloomington, 1988).

[15]For an analysis of how the French constructed this "traditional" Islam, which they called *Islam noir*, see Christopher Harrison, *France and Islam in West Africa, 1860-1960* (Cambridge, 1988). Amselle, in *Logiques métisses*, argues that the French also invented African "traditional" religion in the region, which he calls *paganisme blanc*.

"traditions," which were broadly interpreted as obedience to authority, unity and passivity (their indebtedness to their colonial predecessors is obvious); these, they argued, were the absolute cornerstones of any possible development. Their critics dismissed these references to "tradition" as mere rhetoric designed to reinforce their domination (see two cartoons included here from Mali's independent press which illustrate this critical discourse about "tradition"). In other words, from the perspective of the Traoré régime, "tradition" continued to be equated with passivity and was therefore to be encouraged.

The Wahhabi/Sunnis find themselves in a profoundly ambiguous position. Their movement in Mali comprises two major elements: a relatively wealthy mercantile community and an expanding group of "intellectuals,"[16] mostly young men who have been educated in Muslim institutions abroad. They see themselves as true Muslim "traditionalists," and in the pre-colonial period they would have presented themselves as yet another manifestion of a "pure" Islamic community. Of course, they do that now to a certain extent, but because they are working out their destiny in a non-Islamic, post-colonial context in which they are one of the most "progressive" elements of the society (in capitalist terms), they find themselves constructing their identity in opposition to a "tradition" invented during the colonial episode.

Structurally, it might be argued that the Wahhabi/Sunnis are progressive without wanting, or being able, to admit it; after all, "progress," as it is defined in the discourse of the developing nation-state, is not a salient concept in the bulk of *hadith* or Islamic doctrinal literature. And yet the Wahhabi/Sunnis definitely represent, if not "progress," a kind of modernism in contemporary Mali. The identity which they have claimed for themselves in Mali's plural society is marked not only by doctrinal positions and commercial and educational activities, but also by a range of institutions which include mosques, modernized Muslim schools (*madrasas*), clinics, pharmacies and cultural centres. This infrastructure, mostly constructed within the past twenty years, is impressive, especially in a country where parallel public insitutions have during recent decades shown increasing signs of inefficiency and collapse. The *madrasas* account for approximately one quarter of the children in primary school; the clinics and pharmacies provide services and medicines at reduced prices.

[16]In Malian discourse, "intellectuals" can be either Muslim or secular, and the term can be used with both favourable and pejorative connotations. Thus, the Muslim "intellectual" or scholar can be a person (almost always a man) of respected and elevated status. By contrast, Western-educated "intellectuals" are sometimes denounced in Muslim circles as fallen Muslims who no longer pray.

Cartoons from *Les Echos*, Bamako

*Above*: Week of Childhood. "We must maintain traditional methods." ... But surely not this. (no. 35, 22 June 1990)

*Opposite*: 10 December, Human Rights Day.

*a*. (Poster) Every individual has the right to freedom of assembly and peaceful association. No one can be obliged to join an association.

*b*. "Papa, why isn't this article respected in our country?"

"Our tradition of wisdom demands the preservation of national unity."

*c*. "All our neighbours respect it; here, too, we are the last."

"Our tradition of wisdom demands prudence and not mimicry."

*d*. "Then why have you signed the Charter for Human Rights?"

"Our tradition of wisdom demands that we preserve our image through words without taking action."

*e*. "But why are you crying, my son?"

"Our tradition of wisdom requires me to be a coward. Sniff, sniff."

(no. 49, 7 Dec. 1990)

10 DECEMBRE :
JOURNEE DES DROITS DE L'HOMME
TOUTE PERSONNE A DROIT A LA LIBERTE DE REUNION ET D'AS-SOCIATION PACIFIQUES NUL NE PEUT ÊTRE OBLIGE DE FAIRE PARTIE D'UNE ASSOCIATION.
PAPA, POURQUOI CET ARTICLE, N'EST-IL PAS RESPECTE CHEZ NOUS ?
NOTRE TRADITION DE SAGESSE NOUS COMMANDE LA PRESERVATION DE L'UNITE NATIONALE.
TOUS NOS VOISINS LE RESPECTENT. LA AUSSI NOUS SOMMES LES DERNIERS!
NOTRE TRADITION DE SAGESSE NOUS COMMANDE LA PRUDENCE ET PAS DE MIMETISME.

*b*

*c*

MAIS ALORS. POURQU'OI AVEZ-VOUS SIGNÉ LA CHARTE DES DROITS DE L'HOMME ?
NOTRE TRADITION DE SAGESSE NOUS DEMANDE DE SOIGNER NOTRE IMAGE PAR LE VERBE SANS ACTION.
MAIS POURQUOI PLEURES-TU, MON FILS ?
NOTRE TRADITION DE SAGESSE ME COMMANDE LA LÂCHETE. SNIF! SNIF! SNIF!
KAYS.
Y.D.

*d*

*e*

These projects are examples of what the international development community would call grassroots development. They have been initiated by local communities or individuals and they are locally controlled. On some occasions the financing has also been local, based on contributions by merchants and migrant workers; but even when significant gifts or loans have come from foreign Arab/Muslim sources, a substantial amount also comes from local contributors. Despite the success of many of these initiatives, certain major actors in the development game (notably the United States and France) ignore these projects, while many Malian secularists criticize them, precisely because they are Muslim.

One reason for these attitudes is the fear which is generated among Western development officials and the secularists (almost exclusively Western-educated "intellectuals") about the political potential of Islam, particularly of "fundamentalist" Islam. Of course, in the long term, one cannot exclude the possibility that Mali will experience a significant politicization of Islamic ideology and even an experiment with an Islamic state. But present political fears are based more on ignorance and fantasy than a close understanding of the contemporary nature of Muslim groups in Mali. These fears seem to create real barriers, so that Muslim initiatives in education and health services are rarely (if ever) examined for the lessons they might offer for general development policy. Within most government ministries and among most Western foreign aid workers, Muslim insititutions are literally invisible; no one talks about them and certainly no one visits them.[17]

One of the most common criticisms of Islam in these circles has been its alleged conservatism. This charge is based in part on the pervasive moralizing discourse produced in public by Muslim spokesmen, and also by the success several years ago of Muslim interests in securing the official closing of bars and nightclubs during Ramadan. The riposte of the critics to this decree was that not all Malians were Muslim, and they should not be subject to Muslim law; this is a basic secularist principle which insists that religion is a private matter. Another factor which contributes to the conservative image of Islam is the status of women in Mali. There is no doubt that the Muslim initiatives described above are dominated by men, and that many of these men seek, through their own interpretations of Islam and its institutions, to reinforce the social dominance which Malian patriarchy has afforded them in gender relationships. But it is also

[17]This situation has changed considerably since the collapse of the Traoré régime in March 1991.

clear that women use Islam to enhance their own social position.[18] More significantly, however, sustained and substantive support for the improvement of the status of women in Mali comes primarily from Western development agencies in the form of "Women and Development" programmes, an issue about which the Malian (predominantly male) secularists are not particularly vocal!

Finally, the secularists criticize the Muslims for what has been called the materialization of Islam: the construction of visibly Muslim buildings, especially mosques. Now that Mali, and particularly Bamako, is filled to bursting with mosques, the question is regularly raised about why Muslims should spend so much money on mosques when other social needs are so pressing. The proliferation of mosques is a complex question in itself, because Muslims disagree vehemently among themselves about the social and religious implications of this phenomenon. But the criticisms of the secularists are a bit hollow, because they consistently refuse to recognize the social contributions which the Muslims have in fact made. The selectivity of their commentaries may suggest that the secularists are as much concerned about Muslim, and especially Wahhabi/Sunni, "progressivism" as about their conservatism; in other words, secularist preoccupations may be fueled by the fear that Muslim initiatives might possibly prove more effective on the ground than their own.

*Constructing a national Islamic identity*

As these observations suggest, a significant theme in contemporary Malian discourse is the confrontation between Muslim and secular identities. According to many secularists, the régime of Moussa Traoré, who held power between 1968 and 1991, increasingly adopted the trappings of a Muslim identity to the detriment of secular principles which were meant to limit religious expression to the privacy of individual conviction.[19] Mali was portrayed by Traoré and his colleagues as a Muslim country with a secular constitution, but whatever Traoré's commitment to secularism, there is no doubt that from about 1980 he had been seeking to reinforce Mali's Muslim identity.[20]

[18]See Bintou Sanankoua, "Les Associations féminines musulmanes à Bamako, " in B. Sanankoua and L. Brenner, *L'enseignement islamique au Mali* (Bamako, 1991).

[19]Moussa Traoré was removed from power in March 1991 by a *coup d'état* which was precipitated by a popular uprising.

[20]Between about 20 and 30% of Malians do not claim to be Muslim. A tiny percentage of these are Christians, but the majority are rural adherents of indigenous religious practices. The existence of this significant minority of non-Muslims means that certain rural areas have been subjected to conversion

Secular notions of governance are among the most influential of the bequests which Mali has derived from its French colonial heritage. They were embraced in principle and in fact by Mali's first independent government under Modibo Keita, and they have been firmly reinstated in the revised constitution of the Malian Third Republic, which was inaugurated in June 1992 following democratic elections. But many critics and observers alike have argued that the principles of secularism were simply given lip-service by the régime of Moussa Traoré. This is not to say that either members of government or any of the country's Islamists advocated that Mali should become an Islamic state; such a suggestion was virtually non-existent. But Traoré and various of his cabinet ministers directly involved themselves in Islamic affairs and allowed public expressions of Islam which many argued were not compatible with a secular constitution. The evidence for a deteriorating official secularism ranged from the amount of air-time granted to Muslim religious programmes in the state-owned media and the insistence by the President that his cabinet members attend Friday prayers in Bamako's central mosque, to legislation closing bars and nightclubs during Ramadan and the government's initiative in establishing Mali's national Muslim organization, the *Association malienne pour l'unité et le progrès de l'Islam* (AMUPI).

AMUPI was meant to play a central role in the construction of Mali's national Muslim identity. Internally, it was intended to define the religious arena and, through its hierarchy, to contain and control intra-Muslim conflict and to imbue the population with a sense of moral responsibility. Externally, it was to have enhanced Mali's Islamic image abroad and attracted Arab and Muslim financial assistance. The structure of AMUPI consciously reflected and reinforced existing divisions between the Wahhabi/Sunnis and the Traditional/Orthodox. The membership of all the executive committees of the association from the national to the local level were carefully selected by the government to include representatives from both factions; the presidency of most bureaux was held by an adherent of the Traditional/Orthodox school, and the secretary-generalship by a Wahhabi/Sunni. This arrangment almost completely immobilized the organization; rather than eliminate conflict, it redirected it into new channels.

With the exception of a sprinkling of Christians, the participants in the debate about secularism during the final years of Traoré's régime were all Muslims. All may not have been practising Muslims, but

---

campaigns, and in such situations representations of Muslim versus non-Muslim identities are prominent. But more generally, the public debate in Mali confronts Muslim with secular identities.

many were. And the confrontation was not really about religion as such, but about government; those who most vehemently defended secularism were by and large the same persons who led the movement for democratic pluralism.[21] For them, the Islam championed by the government was another manifestation of the state's insatiable thirst for power and control. Islam, in the guise of AMUPI, became another symbol which was intended to project an image of unity and unanimity in a country where little in fact existed. AMUPI was meant to parallel, in the religious domain, the ideological functions of Mali's single political party, the *Union Démocratique du Peuple Malien*. The UDPM defined the political arena and, through its hierarchy, exhorted a mute and passive body politic to strive for Mali's economic and social "development."

Thus, the UDPM and AMUPI played complementary roles, along with the other national associations established by the government.[22] While the UDPM expounded its policies and preached its ideology of "development," AMUPI was meant to act as the moralising arm of the united and "developing" state. Morality, it might be argued, is the rightful object of religious discourse, especially in Christianity and Islam. And Muslim spokesmen in Mali have much to say about the standards of upright behaviour and the many dangers which today allegedly threaten it. But they also propound the values and benefits of a work ethic, which is ceaselessly encouraged despite staggering levels of urban unemployment; and they defended the morality of "peaceful" resolution of conflict in a country where, under both Modibo Keita and Moussa Traoré, the reply to initiatives which challenged government policies was often summary imprisonment without trial. According to Traoré's opponents and the secularists, such harangues were empty and hollow smokescreens to hide the government's own shortcomings and misdeeds.

These political conflicts between the Traoré government and its opponents, between an allegedly "Islamizing" government and the secularists, were of concern to only a minority of Mali's population. But it was an important and influential minority, because it consisted

[21]Not exclusively, however. During one of the first major public demonstrations for multi-party democracy in Bamako in December 1990, a small group of Muslims marched shouting the slogan, "*Allahu akbar, vive la démocratie*." As the democratic movement gained momentum, an increasing number of "Muslim" endorsements of its goals were expressed – not, however, by the leadership of AMUPI.

[22]For example, the *Union Nationale des Femmes du Mali* (UNFM), the *Union Nationale de la Jeunesse du Mali* (UNJM), and the *Union Nationale des Travailleurs du Mali* (UNTM). Each of these associations was meant to unite and represent, respectively, all the country's women, youth and workers.

of those who held or who aspired to power. Nonetheless, very many Malians, primarily the poor, dismissed all these machinations as the "politics of the politicians;"[23] they had no commitment to the political contest because not only were they largely excluded from it, but they had never experienced a government which they felt had responded sincerely and effectively to their needs. In fact, it would not be an exaggeration to say that many of the poor simply wanted to avoid the attention of government and its representatives, which they saw as oppressive and exploitative.

The Muslim initiatives which have been described in this chapter are located precisely in the political space which has divided many Malians from their government. These new Muslim institutions are providing educational and medical services which the state has proven itself unable effectively to finance and to manage. Equally important, these insititutions enjoy a popular legitimacy based on local voluntarism, which is patently opposed to the intrusive and exploitative reputation of many state institutions.

The question which now poses itself is whether the democratically elected government of Mali's Third Republic can operate more effectively than its predecessors. The Islamist-secularist divide is now more sharply drawn than ever; the new constitution is firmly secularist, forbidding the formation of religiously-based political parties, but it also guarantees freedom of association and expression. A number of new Muslim organizations have come into existence, some of which have developed very active religious, educational, social and even economic programmes.

*Identity as a transformative system*

This brief analysis has concentrated on five social formations which affect the continuing construction of Muslim identities in Mali: the Wahhabi/Sunnis, the Traditional/Orthodox, the secularists, the government/administration and the international development community. Certainly, these groups are not convincingly comparable in a sociological sense; the government and its administration, as well as the development community, can act and intervene in a much more consistent and coherent manner than the other groups, whose imagined existence is often more a product of discourse than coherent action. But we are interested not only in how these groups and their members act, but also in their *representations* of themselves and of each other; and it is precisely because these actions and representations are

[23]*La politique politicienne*, see Amselle, *Logiques métisses*, p. 242.

constantly interacting that we must attempt to examine the construction of Muslim identities as a single transformative system.

As representations within discourse, the identity of *each* of these social formations is worked out with reference to *all* of the others. The complexity of such a situation means that it is difficult to envisage the overall system except through glimpses of the workings of isolated instances of naming and representation. For example, during the final decade of Traoré's régime, the "secularists" as a group were named as such because of their reactions to claims or suspicions of official government involvement in Muslim affairs. The government constantly restated its commitment to the secular state, although its critics, in this context identified as "secularists," charged that government actions belie its pronouncements. This specific debate was an integral part of a broader political opposition to Moussa Traoré; had the Muslim element been eliminated, the debate and confrontation would have continued, but without this "secularist" dimension. The democratic movement in Mali was very little concerned with issues of religion; it was profoundly secular, but found little need to present itself as such publicly.

However, in the context of confronting Muslim social initiatives, the "secularists" constantly found the need to identify themselves as such, because these initiatives were clearly presented as "Muslim," and more specifically were perceived as Wahhabi/Sunni, which in turn appear to presage Muslim political strategies. As mentioned above, the "secularists" seemed to fear the efficacy of these Muslim initiatives, while at the same time dismissing them as reactionary. One way to accomplish this was through stereotyping; the Wahhabi/Sunnis are often protrayed as "*intégristes*" or "fundamentalists."

Such stereotyping is integral to the construction of identities, and all the groups contribute to it. Because of their relative prosperity, the Wahhabi/Sunnis are often accused of having dishonestly obtained their wealth or of profligately wasting it, particularly in the construction of mosques when other social needs are so pressing. As "intellectuals," they are pilloried, usually by the Traditional/Orthodox, as being young, upstart and foreign-trained, and consequently not only alienated from the norms and needs of their own society but representing the interests of others (meaning the policies of various Arab or Muslim governments). The Wahhabi/Sunnis in turn reify "traditional" Islam into the person of the *marabout*, whom they present as an ignorant, superstitious, exploitative "charlatan." The *marabouts* are also a favoured object of abuse among secular "intellectuals," because of the role they are seen to play in providing religious and "moral" support for persons in positions of power.[24] Such practices are widespread, even endemic, and they are vehemently denounced by secular "intellectuals" as the worst kind of "tradition," which allies the secularists with the Wahhabi/Sunnis in attacking the Traditional/Orthodox, whose form of Islam has allegedly produced such "*maraboutisme*."[25]

But, as we have seen, underpinning this kind of stereotyping are real economic and political interests. My argument is that the transformative system of identity is a function of economic and political conflict; it is a public expression of such conflict. As a system, it is very open and sensitive to change and to new influences; it can give immediate expression to newly formulating interests. At the same time, the functioning of the system is subject to the dominating and hegemonic influences of the powers that be.

This essay has been examining this system primarily from a political perspective in the twentieth century. I would argue that in terms of governance there has been considerable continuity between the nineteenth and twentieth centuries in the region of present-day Mali; all successive governments have functioned as (and most have, in fact, been) exploitative conquest states. In response to the sustained tensions and conflict between the rulers and the ruled which this situation has produced, the various Muslim responses have been rather consistent; certain Muslim leaders distance themselves from power and present Islam as a refuge for the weak. This pattern can be demonstrated even if some of the most exploitative of the conquest states have been Muslim-led; it was true for Sidi al-Mukhtar al-Kunti, and it is true for contemporary Muslim initiatives in Mali.

But the twentieth century also brought some significant breaks with the past, among them the expansion of the world capitalist system into Africa and its closely associated ideology of "progress." For the French colonialists, "progress" meant making Africans more like themselves, a policy which was expressed in such notions as the *mission civilisatrice*; in post-colonial Africa, "progress" has become embedded in the ideology of "development." The theme of "progress" does not appear in any of the writings of nineteenth-century Muslims in this region; rather, these authors asserted the "purity" of their particular interpretation of Islam, a "purity" based upon a favoured link with the past and with the founders of Islam, the Prophet and his

[24]See Tidiane Diallo, "Pouvoir et marabouts en Afrique de l'Ouest," *Islam et Sociétés au Sud du Sahara*, no. 2 (1988), pp. 7-10.

[25]See Steven Feierman's astute analysis of "traditional" and "organic" intellectuals in Africa in "Health and Healing in Modern Africa," *African Studies Review*, 28 (1985), pp. 110-15.

companions. Today, Muslims still speak about such "purity," but many are also concerned about "progress," and they participate in the discourse which centres on Mali's own version of development ideology.

It is too early yet to speak about the public discourse of the Third Republic, but "development" became a dominant ideology in the Mali of Moussa Traoré. Public proclamations about "development" replaced any debate about social and economic policy. Government representatives spoke in public about little else; the content of news broadcasts and of articles in the official newspaper, *L'Essor*, were predominantly about development projects, *all of which* are initiated by foreign governments or international non-government organizations.

Mali's economic weakness, as one of the poorest countries in the world, may leave no alternative to accepting these foreign interventions, but many Malians seem to share the impression that their country is not in fact "developing." According to them, the sizeable sums of money which pour into the country each year in the name of "development" simply serve to prop up existing institutions and to provide a secure income for the fortunate few Western-educated "intellectuals" who find employment in the projects or the agencies which implement them. In other words, "development" is open to the charge that it simply reproduces the political and social *status quo*.

But most Malians also see "development" as a secular matter, and the Muslim initiatives which have been described in this paper are not perceived by secularists as development, even though most of them are locally controlled and effectively addressed to popular social needs. This situation reflects the dominance of both international and Malian secularists in determining the policy and dominating the discourse of development.

This situation is reminiscent of that which Jean Bazin analyzes with reference to religious identities and practices in pre-colonial Mali.[26] He treats the subject from a therapeutic perspective, concentrating on how religious experts responded to the requests of their clients to obtain power or wealth, or to treat their misfortunes. He describes the "magico-religious" realm as a kind of market in which two sources of expertise competed: *silamèya* and *bamanaya*. *Silamèya* is the practice of the Muslim *marabouts* who intervene primarily through the power of prayer and of the Word of the Qur'an. *Bamanaya* functions through the mediation of bloody sacrifice and powerful objects which its experts manipulate in order to activate the hidden

[26]Jean Bazin, "A chacun son Bambara," in J.-L. Amselle and E. M'Bokolo, *Au coeur de l'ethnie. Ethnies, tribalisme et Etat en Afrique* (Paris, 1985), p. 121.

forces of the cosmos. Bazin argues that *silamèya* and *bamanaya*, and the identities of their practitioners, were defined with reference to one another, in the context of competition and contrast within a given cultural milieu.

During the twentieth century, the religious experts of the past have been increasingly marginalized by "development" experts, who are the "organic intellectuals" of the late twentieth century, be they Muslim or secular. This evolution has been dominated economically and politically by the extension of world capitalism into Africa, where "development ideology" has almost completely replaced the "magico-religious" on the level of public policy. Official discourse expresses an almost total and unquestioning faith in "development" as the remedy of Mali's social and economic misfortunes. To state that this faith is as little supported by empirical evidence as is the efficacy of either *silamèya* or *bamanaya* is somewhat beside the point. Certainly, there is little indication that the ideology of development, and the economic and political conditions which produce it, will soon disappear. And the construction of identities in Mali will continue to be played out in a context of competition and contrast which is dominated by "development ideology."

# METAMORPHOSES OF THE YAO MUSLIMS

*Alan Thorold*

The Yao in southern Malawi are people for whom Islam has been taken to be a distinguishing characteristic. They are a minority in Malawi – about 10 per cent of the population are Muslims, most of whom are Yao[1] – and tend to be concentrated around the southern tip of Lake Malawi. The major Yao conversions to Islam occurred only about one hundred years ago, and since that time the Yao Muslims in Malawi have been to some extent isolated from the rest of the Muslim world. They thus represent an opportunity to trace the manner in which Islam works to transform a society from within. This is not to suggest that currents in the wider world of Islam have not affected the Yao, but that the influence which these have had upon the Yao is largely of their own choosing. The development of Islam among the Yao has, of course, occurred in conjunction with fundamental changes in the political economy of the region, but although these cannot be disregarded, it is my intention here to see if it is possible to understand part of the transformation of the Yao Muslims by way of a focus on their Islamic practice. It may be, I suggest, that there is a kind of internal logic of Islamic transformation which can be discerned.

It became clear to me while I was in Malawi[2] that the Muslims in the area were divided into three camps or factions. Most widespread and numerically strongest were adherents of the Sufi orders, known locally as *twaliki* or followers of the *tariqa*. Then there were the *sukutis* or "quietists" (the term *sukuti* is derived from the Swahili verb "to be quiet"). I had assumed from the little that has been written about the *sukuti* that they were a branch of one of the local Sufi orders, but it soon became apparent that they defined themselves in opposition to Sufi practices, and in fact were sometimes referred to as "anti-Sufi." Lastly, there was a small but very active group who will be referred to as the "new reformists" and who may be seen as the local representatives of the global Islamic revival.

To explain the emergence of these factions and describe their characteristics and differences, I shall construct a model of the development of Islam among the Yao. The elements of the model are drawn partly from Humphrey Fisher's model of Islamic conversion in

[1]David Bone estimated that 10% of the population of Malawi are Muslims in his excellent overview, "Islam in Malawi," *Journal of Religion in Africa*, 13(2), 1982, p. 130. This figure seems reasonable, although there is no recent census information on religious affiliation in Malawi.

[2]I did fieldwork in Malawi, mainly in Mangochi District, in 1986.

Africa,[3] and partly from the dichotomy which several writers have made between popular forms of Islam often associated with Sufism and the scripturalist or reformed version.[4] I suggest that there are three phases in the development of Islam in this region, each corresponding to one of the factions mentioned above. Phase 1 is that of appropriation and accommodation (Sufism). Phase 2 is that of internal reform *(sukuti)*. And Phase 3 is that of the new reformism. As I will try to indicate, each phase may be defined in terms of a characteristic relationship to the Islamic scriptures, the Book. That is to say, the role of the Book changes with the development of each phase and, in some sense, an alteration in the status of the Book inaugurates each new phase and is a part of the mechanism which introduces the new phase.

One of the consequences of the shift from one phase to the next is a transformation in the identity of the Yao Muslims. Putting it in a very schematic way, in Phase 1 such Islamic practice as is adopted is used to bolster an emerging Yao "tribal" identity. This idiosyncratic and locally controlled version of Islam makes few demands upon its adherents, yet it furnishes them with a set of cultural markers which distinguish them very clearly from their neighbours, elaborating and supplementing rather than replacing distinctive Yao rituals. The development of Phase 2 is a reaction against some of the practices associated with Phase 1, and it tends to erode the unity of the distinctively "Yao" Muslim identity. The *sukuti* movement opposes practices associated with Sufism, particularly the use of *dhikr*, but does not attempt any major social transformation of the Yao Muslims. It is with the appearance of Phase 3, the new reformist movement, that the great transformation of Yao Muslims begins. It also heralds the end of the Yao Muslims as such, since those who associate themselves with this movement see themselves primarily as Muslims, and any other identity is secondary and dispensable. The new reformists not only identify themselves as Muslim first and foremost, but they also model their behaviour and Islamic practice on that of an ideal type imported directly from the Middle East. They repudiate the earlier stages of Islam in the region and commit themselves to what they see as a global Islamic identity. The change in Islamic practice, from a pragmatic Sufism to a more and more extreme reformism is thus part

[3]H.J. Fisher, "Conversion reconsidered: Some historical aspects of religious conversion in black Africa," *Africa*, 43(1), 1973, and "The Juggernaut's Apologia: Conversion to Islam in black Africa," *Africa*, 55(2), 1985. I have used aspects of Fisher's stages ("mixing" and "reform") in my model, but more importantly, his analysis of the transforming power of Islam has influenced my own.

[4]Notably Ernest Gellner, who employs this dichotomy while indicating some of its shortcomings. See e.g. *Muslim Society* (Cambridge, 1981), p. 115.

of an ongoing metamorphosis of a local Yao Muslim identity into a supra-regional Muslim identity.

Before describing the onset of Phase 1, some preliminary historical background is required. The Yao were initially brought into contact with Islam by way of their trade with the coast, mainly at Kilwa, and, as the Yao historian Yohanna Abdallah observed, ventures to the coast soon began to have a profound influence on them: "This penetration to the coast was the reason that the Yaos began to regard the coast as their lode-star, and the arbiter of customs."[5] There is evidence that the Yao, who were settled in what is now northern Mozambique, were involved in trade with Swahili and Arabs on the coast by the beginning of the seventeenth century. In the eighteenth century the demand for ivory and the growth of slave-trading in the area drew increasing numbers of the Yao into long-distance trading. The trade in ivory and slaves also precipitated an enlargement of the Yao political process, from the village, structured around a matrilineal sorority group under the authority of the headman, to the territorial chiefdoms based on trade links and military strength. The chiefs who rose to power during this period attained their position through a combination of trading and slave-raiding, dominating by the exercise of military power reinforced by the firearms acquired from their trading partners at the coast.[6]

The nineteenth century saw a series of Yao migrations from northern Mozambique, mostly south-west toward the southern tip of Lake Malawi, though some moved north into what is now Tanzania. The cause of these migrations is not entirely clear, but would seem to have been a combination of the effects of drought and famine in northern Mozambique, conflicts with the neighbouring Makua, and conflicts between Yao chiefdoms competing for slaves.[7] The general pattern of the migrations is that as the weaker Yao chiefdoms fled from attackers and famine, they transformed themselves into invaders as they moved into what is now southern Malawi. By the time that Livingstone reached the area in the 1850s, the Yao were plundering and raiding for slaves among the Chewa and Mang'anga inhabitants, and had established themselves as the dominant political force in the region.

[5]Y.B. Abdallah, *The Yaos. Chiikala Cha WaYao*, trans. & ed. by G.M .Sanderson (Zomba, 1919), p. 27.

[6]E.A. Alpers, "Trade, State and Society among the Yao in the Nineteenth Century," *Journal of African History*, 10(3), 1969, pp. 405-7.

[7]V.L. Jhala, "The Yao in the Shire Highlands, 1861-1915: Political dominance and reaction to colonialism," *Journal of Social Sciences* [Zomba], 9(1), 1982, p. 3.

Livingstone was suitably horrified by this state of affairs and, returning to Britain in 1857, made an appeal at the Senate House in Cambridge which led to the formation of the Universities' Mission to Central Africa. The vanguard of the mission, which established itself in the Shire highlands in 1861, soon came into conflict with Yao slavers as a result of its policy of taking in and protecting runaway slaves.[8] This conflict and other difficulties forced a temporary withdrawal to Zanzibar, but in the 1870s the Church of Scotland and the Free Church of Scotland established missions in the region and the numbers of British there began to grow. In 1891 a British Protectorate was declared over the territory then known as Nyasaland, now Malawi.[9]

In the meantime the Yao chiefs became increasingly perturbed by the British presence in the region and the threat posed by it to the slave trade. A result of this was that they attempted to consolidate links with their Arab and Swahili trading partners at the coast. One of the more powerful of the slaving chiefs, Makanjila, made his allegiance clear in an exchange with a missionary, thus: "[Makanjila] in his vanity, swore what he thought an awe-inspiring oath, that if the Europeans touched the Sultan of Zanzibar, he himself would come to his rescue against the invaders. Thus showing that he regarded himself as one with the coast."[10] Makanjila, in about 1870, had been one of the first of the Yao chiefs to convert to Islam, followed soon afterwards by several other of the powerful slaving chiefs.[11]

The arrival in 1891 of Harry Johnston, the first Commissioner of the Protectorate, was quickly followed by the onset of a series of British campaigns against the Yao chiefs, and although the British forces suffered some rather severe setbacks, the "pacification" of Nyasaland and the termination of the slave trade in the region was accomplished by 1896.[12] This defeat and the end of the slave trade clearly caused a severe erosion of the chiefs' authority since a great deal of their power and wealth depended on it. Yet it was just at this time that conversion to Islam became widespread among the Yao. A missionary wrote of this as follows: "It was very noticeable how in

[8]A.E.M. Anderson-Morshead, *The History of the Universities' Mission to Central Africa* (London, 1909), pp. 21-42.

[9]C.A. Baker, "The Development of the Administration to 1897" in B. Pachai (ed), *The Early History of Malawi* (London, 1972), pp. 324-8.

[10]W.P. Johnson, "Mohammedanism and the Yaos," *Central Africa*, March 1911, p. 102.

[11]E.A. Alpers, "Towards a history of the expansion of Islam in East Africa: The matrilineal peoples of the southern interior," in T.O. Ranger and I.N. Kimambo (eds) *The Historical Study of African Religion* (London, 1972), p. 182.

[12]P.A. Cole-King, *Mangochi: the mountain, the people and the fort* (Zomba, 1982), pp. 8-12.

these years there was a recrudescence of the craze for Mohammedanism. It seemed as if the slavers, checked by the government, were determined to extend their moral force. As always, they used the native attachment to the old Yao initiation dances, encouraging these dances... in order to introduce gradually another dance which was regarded as an initiation into Mohammedanism ... its name was jandu. They used the native funeral ceremonies in the same way."[13]

Although the language is a little alarming, this description of the manner in which Islam was propagated by the chiefs and their supporters, and their reasons for doing so, seems to be accurate and convincing. In the face of British domination Islam became a means of legitimating the status of the chiefs, and the rituals which they controlled were the mechanisms by which this was accomplished. Thus by the turn of the century, many of the Yaos settled in southern Malawi were at least nominally Muslim. I have doubtless over-emphasized the political motive of these conversions, but it does seem clear that the conflict with the British was the overriding factor which precipitated a mass conversion, and to explore all the other factors which prepared the ground for this would take us too far afield here.[14] The point to be stressed is that after a long period of contact with Muslims at the coast, and the development of a political economy based largely on the slave trade, conversion occurred at a time when those links with the Swahili coast were being effectively severed, and the influence of the erstwhile trading partners was much attenuated.

These then are the conditions in which Phase 1 of our model develops – the newly-converted Yao Muslims isolated from the rest of the Muslim world and inside a British-controlled and increasingly Christian-dominated protectorate. So far the Book has not been much in evidence, and although several of the chiefs are reported to have employed Swahili scribes in the slaving era, and the association of Islam with writing and books must have been well established, there is little to suggest that literacy was a central motive for conversion.[15] Nor does it seem that the actual contents of the Qur'an were of much interest to the new converts. To the extent that the Book features in this first phase of the development of Islam, it is as part of a ritual

[13]W.P. Johnson, *My African Reminiscences* (London, 1924), p. 202.

[14]For a more extensive consideration, see A.P.H. Thorold, "Yao conversion to Islam," *Cambridge Anthropology*, 12(2), 1987.

[15]There is little evidence to support Alpers' suggestion that a desire for literacy was a significant motive for conversion among the Yao. Cf. E.A. Alpers, "Towards a history of the expansion of Islam...," p. 186, and "The Yao in Malawi: The importance of local research," in B. Pachai (ed.) *The Early History of Malawi* (London, 1972), p. 174.

system in which it operates as a sort of fetish, a source of power rather than of doctrine.

In this phase of appropriation and accommodation, the Book occupies a subordinate role, and it is certainly not the main attraction. Islamic practice revolves around a few central rituals which are often merely transformed versions of pre-Islamic Yao rituals. Most important of these was the initiation ceremony for boys. By means of the introduction of complete rather than partial circumcision, and changing the name of the ceremony to *jando* (the term used on the coast), the Yao initiation ceremony in a largely unaltered form became a method of induction into Islam. The name of the initiation for girls was likewise altered.[16]

The introduction of Sufism to the region in the early twentieth century was given an enthusiastic reception by the Yao Muslims. The Qadiriyya and Shadhiliyya had both established themselves on the coast, and were adopted by a number of Yao shaikhs who had ventured to the coastal centres and who returned to propagate elements of Sufi practice among the Yao.[17] The central ritual of the Sufis, the *dhikr* (or *sikiri* as the Yao refer to it), was swiftly incorporated by the Yao and replaced the performance of pre-Islamic dances at marriages, funerals and other ceremonies. As practised by the Yao, the performance of *sikiri* consists of a ring of dancers, usually with a core of young men, moving in unison around and around, bending and rising to expel and inhale breath. This can go on for quite a long time, certainly producing hyperventilation in the core performers, and makes for a very exhilarating spectacle.[18]

So, through the agency of the shaikhs, the Yao were able to appropriate this rather attractive aspect of Sufism, and began to refer to themselves as followers of the *tariqa* (the Sufi way). Other elements of coastal Sufism – festivals like *ziyala*, the founder's anniversary, and the use of banners and flags – joined the *sikiri* in consolidating the appeal of the *tariqa*, and the authority of the shaikhs who propagated these

[16]H.S. Stannus and J.B. Davey, "The Initiation Ceremony for Boys among the Yao of Nyasaland," *Journal of the Royal Anthropological Institute*, XLIII, 1913, p. 120. For more recent descriptions of Yao initiation ceremonies see Gerhard Kubik, "Boys' circumcision school of the Yao," *Review of Ethnology*, 6(1-7), 1978, and "Report on cultural field research in Mangochi District," *Baraza*, 2, 1984.

[17]R.C. Greenstein, "Shaykhs and tariqas: the early Muslim ulama and tariqa development in Malawi, 1885-1949," unpubl. seminar paper, Chancellor College, Zomba, 1976/7, pp. 22-3.

[18]The performances of *sikiri* which I observed in Malawi conformed in most respects to the typical *dhikr* described by J.S.Trimingham, *Islam in East Africa* (London, 1964), p. 97, and B.G. Martin, *Muslim Brotherhoods in 19th century Africa* (Cambridge, 1976), p. 2.

practices was initially unchallenged. There was a good deal of prestige attached to those Yao who made the journey to the coast, and particularly to those who had been to Zanzibar, and the title of shaikh or *mwalimu* (teacher) was given rather freely to those who returned. Few of the Yao shaikhs of this first phase were completely literate in Arabic or made any pretensions to scholarship in Islamic doctrine. But they were very active in propagating their version of Islamic practice, and persuading chiefs and headmen to build mosques and set up *madrasas* at which children were taught how to pray, to recite the *fatiha*, and other elements of this rudimentary Islamic way of life. Above all, they urged the chiefs to resist the encroachment of the Christian missions which were always eager to open schools in the region, and in this they were aided by the policy of religious neutrality which the colonial administration maintained.[19]

That, then, is an outline of Phase 1, of the appropriation and accommodation of Islam by the Yao, and until the 1930s it was entrenched more or less uniformly throughout the areas in which they were settled in southern Nyasaland. Then a series of conflicts developed among the Yao Muslims which reveal, I think, the emergence of Phase 2 of our model – that is, of an internal reform movement. The controversies seem to have initially revolved around funerals, which is significant because the ceremonies associated with the burial of Yao Muslims were a rather striking instance of the accommodation of Islamic practice to pre-Islamic Yao custom. The feasts which follow the burial of a Yao adherent of the *tariqa* are known as *sadaqa* (a term usually denoting voluntary alms), and this term is also applied by the Yao to feasts commemorating lineage ancestors.[20] A central feature of the *sadaqa* or funeral feast is the performance of *sikiri*.

The nature of the controversy can be illustrated by an interview which was conducted by Clyde Mitchell in 1948.[21] Referring to a dispute which took place in Jalasi's chiefdom in 1937, his informant says: "...long ago there was a law of Islam which says that if a burial takes place they take a flag and put it on the door where there is a death ... [and] when they have buried the body others are doing sikiri ... Ali Bisalimu [one of the antagonists] returned from a journey to the coast

[19]R.C. Greenstein, "The Nyasaland Government's policy toward African Muslims, 1900-25," in R.J. Macdonald (ed.), *From Nyasaland to Malawi* (Nairobi, 1975), p. 149.

[20]J.C. Mitchell, *The Yao Village* (Manchester, 1956), p. 140, and J.N.D. Anderson, *Islamic Law in Africa* (London, 1954), p. 169.

[21]Papers of J.C. Mitchell, 21/1 (Namwera, 25 Nov. 1948), Rhodes House Library, Oxford.

with many books ... he took a big book, named msafu [the Qur'an] which gave the old history and he found the words that putting the flag on the door and doing sikiri at the funeral is a huge sin. The Lord does not like dancing at the funeral. But to pray silently and grumble in the heart alone, until they bury the body. Then Ali Bisalimu ... started to tell all the Muslims." Not surprisingly, he met with some fierce opposition from the local adherents of the *tariqa*, and Chief Jalasi called on him to explain himself. Ali Bisalimu is said to have replied: "I am making sukutu [silence] at the funeral because at the funeral of Mohammed he did not see sikiri." But Jalasi decided thus: "We don't want sukutu in this land. Islam of the flag came long ago."

This interview is quoted at some length because it is quite revealing about the nature and origins of what became known as the *sukuti* movement in Malawi.[22] It uses the Book rather than tradition as its referent and authority, and it opposes the accretions of the Islamic practice of Phase 1, but it tends to do so negatively, by pointing to their supposed deviance, rather than by way of a positive doctrine. Nevertheless, the *sukuti* movement took root and has re-emerged in various disputes throughout the area since then. J.N.D. Anderson, who visited Nyasaland in 1950 as part of his research on Islamic law in Africa, reported that a dispute at that time became sufficiently serious for the Nyasaland administration to bring a mediator from Zanzibar to try to reconcile the parties. Once again the performance of *sikiri* at funerals was at issue, as well as the legality of eating hippopotamus meat, which the *sukutis* opposed.[23]

Shortly before I arrived in Malawi a dispute in Makanjila's chiefdom had resulted in the *sukuti* faction hiving off and building its own mosque. One of the *sukuti* leaders there informed me that again the point of contention was the conduct of funerals, and although the chief had organized a debate between the parties, a compromise could not be reached and the chief had eventually sided with the shaikhs of the *tariqa*. In the lakeside village where I stayed in another chiefdom there was a dispute about the form of the Friday prayers which reflected a more general dispute in the chief's village, where the *sukuti* faction claimed that it was wrong to perform the Friday prayer and the midday prayer together.

[22]J.M. Kiwanuka, "The Politics of Islam in Bukoba District," (unpubl. thesis, University of Dar es Salaam, 1973), p. 30, describes the emergence of a similar movement in Tanzania, although a different interpretation is given by A.H. Nimtz, *Islam and Politics in East Africa* (Minneapolis, 1980), p. 79. See also Peter Lienhardt's discussion of "A Controversy over Islamic Custom in Kilwa Kivinje, Tanzania," in I.M. Lewis (ed.), *Islam in Tropical Africa* (London, 1980), pp. 298-9.

[23]J.N.D. Anderson, *op. cit.*, p. 169.

The description of the *sukuti* movement as "anti-Sufi" seems quite accurate. It emerged in opposition to the Sufi-influenced latitude of Phase 1, but it remains dispersed and fragmented, both spatially and ideologically. Despite a tendency toward scripturalism and a more puritanical practice of Islam, there does not appear to be any unifying positive doctrine. It defines itself negatively, in opposition to the *tariqa* from which it emerges in response to a growing recognition of the significance of the Book. It also begins to undermine the Yao Muslim identity of Phase 1 in a way that the minor differences between followers of the Qadiriyya and Shadhiliyya never did.

The positive doctrine and ideological unity which the *sukuti* or internal reform movement of Phase 2 lacked, to some extent creates the opening for the arrival of the new reformists. This third phase of the development of Islam among the Yao starts to make its presence felt in Malawi in the 1970s, and although its supporters are still few in number among the Yao Muslims, its influence has grown very rapidly. It has certainly benefited from the disarray and erosion of the ranks of the *tariqa* caused by the *sukutis*, and although the new reformists tend to look more favourably upon the Islamic practice of the *sukutis* than that of the *tariqa*, they are not seeking to ally with them. One of the slogans which was popular at meetings of the reformist Muslim Students' Association underlines this: "No Qadiriyya! No Sukutiyya! Islamiyya!" But with a strong central doctrine of scripturalism and a strategy to implement it, the new reformists have set about undermining rather than directly confronting both of the other factions.

They are supported in this by relatively large material resources – funds which flowed in from donors mostly in Saudi Arabia and Kuwait. This is channelled through the Muslim Association of Malawi, an organization founded in Blantyre in the 1940s by Muslims of Asian extraction, and until recently of little consequence to the Yao Muslims. With the funds came people to administer them: a financial director from Kuwait and teachers from various parts of the Muslim world. The programme which the revived Muslim Association embarked on was directed mainly toward the provision of education for the Yao Muslim youth. Islamic centres with primary and secondary schools have been built, funds have been made available for Muslim pupils to attend these and also government schools, and scholarships have been set up to send selected students to Islamic colleges abroad. The policy of the post-Independence Malawi government to detach the mission schools from the control of the churches and to open government schools in non-Christian areas has helped the cause of the new reformists considerably, since Yao Muslims are now less resistant to the idea of sending their children to school.[24]

The Muslim Students' Association, formed in 1982 and affiliated to the Muslim Association, has been active in schools throughout the Muslim areas. The national co-ordinator in 1986, Hassan Nkata, listed some of its objectives as follows: "to create Islamic brotherhood amongst the Muslim students, to make Muslim students understand the importance of secular education and its relationship with Islam, to encourage Muslim students [to] understand Islam at an early stage (before going into the field of different jobs – this applies to those students who did not have the chance of acquiring Islamic education at a Madressa), to make authorities aware about the needs of the Muslims in the different institutions thereby creating an Islamic atmosphere everywhere."[25] In Mangochi District at the time of my visit, the activity of the Muslim Students' Association was co-ordinated by the young and energetic administrative secretary of the local branch of the Muslim Association. He arranged meetings of Muslim students in schools throughout the district, at which branches of the Students' Association were formed and committees elected. Frequent "come-together meetings" were held at the Islamic Centre then under construction outside Mangochi town. A feature of these meetings was the lectures which students were encouraged to contribute, often based on texts made available by the Muslim Association.[26] Significantly, the activities of the Muslim Students' Association were confined to schools rather than *madrasas*, limiting the possibility of conflict with local shaikhs.

The doctrine which the new reformists propagate is scripturalist in the extreme, privileging the Book as the ultimate source of authority and rejecting all Islamic practice not sanctioned by it. The strategy of enlisting the school-going youth and of using the growth of literacy in general to inculcate scripturalism seems to have been effective, and this, combined with their material resources and links with the heartlands of Islam, make the new reformists a formidable force.

It is clear that the new reformism, this third phase of Islamic transformation which threatens to eclipse the two earlier phases, is not

[24]D.S. Bone, "The Muslim Minority in Malawi and Western Education," *Journal Institute of Muslim Minority Affairs*, 6(2), 1985, p. 416.

[25]H. Nkata, "Muslim Students' Association in Malawi," *Ramadaan and Eid Annual* (Limbe, 1986), p. 127.

[26]Mostly booklets in English translations from Saudi Arabia and Kuwait, e.g. Hammudah Abdalati, *Islam in Focus* (Salimiah, 1981); Abul Ala Maududi, *Islamic Way of Life* (Riyadh, 1984); Shaykh Mohammad Ibn Abdul Wahhab, *The Three Fundamentals of Islam and their Evidences* (Riyadh, 1984). Also popular were publications and cassettes of the Durban-based A.H. Deedat.

in any simple sense an internal development. It depends upon the growing integration of Yao Muslims with the Muslim world at large, and upon factors external to Islam – in particular, changes in the education system in post-Independence Malawi, and the facility of modern travel and communications. To suggest then that this represents some sort of logical outgrowth of the earlier phases seems perhaps to strain a little against the facts, to be more Hegelian than historical. Up until the late 1970s, it seemed as though Islam among the Yao was in a state of dormancy if not atrophy. The sporadic conflicts between followers of the *tariqa* and the *sukuti* could have continued without resolution, gradually eroding the unity of the Yao Muslims. Yet it was just this divided condition of Islam in the region which gave the new reformists such a headstart, and which leads one to suggest that their success has been the logical outcome of emerging trends within the ranks of the Yao Muslims. The *sukuti* movement was able to place reform on the agenda, but operating within the horizons of the existing Islamic structures, it had neither the strategy nor the resources to effect a major transformation. The tendency towards reformism had to wait until the Yao were once again connected with the Muslim world to achieve its full effect.

From the identity which the new reformists inculcate in their followers, and particularly in the Muslim Students' Association, it would seem that one of their main objectives is to generate a sense of identity that consists of belonging to a global Muslim movement. It is an outward-looking identity, entirely opposed to the introverted identity of the Yao Muslims of Phases 1 and 2. This difference in identity is marked in many ways, but perhaps most significantly in language usage. Where Yao spiced with some Kiswahili was the language of the earlier phases, the new reformists use Chichewa (the national language of Malawi) or English at meetings, and employ Arabic greetings and formulae as much as they are able to. Above all, it is the aim of those committed to the reformist movement to go abroad, study in an Islamic institution and learn Arabic. Literacy in Arabic is rare in Malawi but it is now the aspiration of many ambitious young Muslims, and is especially desirable if acquired somewhere close to the Middle East. Within the limits of their situation as part of a Muslim minority in a state where they are viewed with some suspicion, the new reformists are trying to forge an identity based on a model of Islamic practice very different from that of their Muslim predecessors in the region.

Looking at the emergence of the phases of Islam outlined above in terms of their relationship with the Book, there is a shift from a situation in which the Book is largely effaced to one in which it is central. It was adopted in the first phase as part of a ritual system in which it was useful and docile. In the second phase it began to assert itself, exerting an influence which is corrosive of the accretions of the first phase, without yet being able to impose itself convincingly. And in the third phase, taking advantage both of the ground prepared for it by the action of the first two phases and of conditions generally conducive to scripturalism, the Book begins to assume a position of centrality and authority. The increasing prominence of the Book is accompanied by a changing identity, from a situation where Islamic practice is used to bolster a tribal identity to one where it provides access to an international movement. The Yao Muslims have been changed. The Islamic practice which they adopted and made their own has been transformed, and their identity has been transformed with it. The growth of scripturalism has been followed by the demise of a tribal identity and the emergence of a new wholly Muslim identity. Islam, which once assisted the Yao to sustain a tribal identity, has now furnished them with an entirely new identity. The Yao who appropriated Islam are ultimately being appropriated by it.

# GROWING ISLAMISM IN KANO CITY SINCE 1970

## CAUSES, FORM AND IMPLICATIONS

*Bawuro M. Barkindo**

Since 1970, Nigeria, like almost all Third World countries, has witnessed a monstrous urbanization process which has transformed urban centres from assets into huge liabilities for the nation's development. Cities are the locus of a widening gap between the rich and the poor, inadequate living conditions, transportation problems, increasing urban crimes and moral decadence.

For the majority of Muslims there is the added dilemma that the Islamic norms which had hitherto guided the religious life of Muslim urban dwellers and formed the basis of their cultural identity is fast disintegrating under the onslaught of Westernization. In many cases, even the measures adopted for dealing with urban problems are seen by Muslims as yet additional openings for the penetration and consolidation of Euro-Christian cultural values. The fact that most of the measures so far attempted to control urban problems have failed, further strengthens the conviction of Muslims that the best option is to adopt "Islamic solutions to the problems of the country."[1]

The aim of this paper is to examine the causes of this growing Islamism in Kano city since 1970 and outline its most salient features. Initially, however, a brief outline will be presented of the main features of Islamic urbanism in Kano city up to the inception of colonialism.

### *The emergence and development of an urban Islamic culture in Kano city to 1970*

Although Islam was adopted in Kano in about 1300, it was the reforms of Sarki (King) Muhammadu Rumfa (*c.* 1463-99) that laid the foundations of institutions which eventually turned Kano into an Islamic city of international repute. Thus by the mid-sixteenth century, Giovanni Anania noted that Kano was one of the three leading

*I am extremely grateful to Mallam Haruna Wakili, my colleague in the History Department, Bayero University, Kano, for his invaluable assistance in interviewing various *'ulama* for this article.

[1]Alhaji Ado Bayero, the Emir of Kano, at the meeting of the Kano State Zakkat Committee, *New Nigerian,* 21 Dec. 1990.

towns in Africa – the others being Fez and Cairo.[2] This prominent position, once attained by Kano, was maintained up to the time when it was conquered by Britain in 1903.

The physical and social characteristics of Kano city were, up to the time of British conquest, similar to those which prevailed in most urban centres in North Africa and the Middle East.[3]

In order to protect the people and their properties, the city has what Amini would call a hierarchy of veils, the most direct veil being the woman's veil.[4] Since the reforms of Sarki Rumfa in the fifteenth century, adult women were kept in purda (*kulle*). When necessity forced them to go out of the home, they were chaperoned and wore *lullubi* (cloth covering the whole body). The other veils were a series of protective walls: the courtyard wall which veiled the different apartments of the house, the outer walls of the house which veiled and protected the family and its property, and finally the formidable city walls which were further strengthened by a moat and punctuated by strong gatehouses.[5]

In addition to the wall defence systems, there was of course the state army whose main base was located in the city and its environs. It was composed of mounted troops, foot soldiers and, by the eighteenth century, the *yan bindiga* or musketeers. Within the city, the *dogarai* (policemen) apprehended offenders who were judged by the *alkali* and if convicted would be handed over to the *yari* or jailer for internment. Each ward had its own *yan tauri*, or "the invincibles," who acted as the vigilante squad of that ward. The *sarki* himself presided over his own court which heard appeals from the lower courts.

Other important characteristics of the city included the palace, the congregation mosque and the central market. The placement of the palace and the mosque near each other was directly derived from the fact that the Prophet's house at Madinah, the ideal Islamic city, was adjacent to the mosque. This underscores the Islamic injunction which enjoins the sovereign to protect religion and rule according to the laws of Allah. In addition to the central mosque, every ward in the city had its own mosque, a school and a small market which were also standard in the urban Islamic culture in the Middle East.[6]

[2]D. Lange and S. Berthoud, "L'Intérieur occidentale d'après Giovanni Lorenzo Anania (XVIème siècle)," in *Cahiers d'Histoire*, XIV, 2, 1972, p. 13.

[3]For a Middle Eastern example see Amini, "The Inward Dimension of an Islamic City - A Mystical "Sufi" Approach," *Research Report on Urbanism in Islam*, Monograph 14; University of Tokyo, 1989.

[4]*Ibid*., p. 8.

[5]B.M. Barkindo, "The Gates of Kano City : A Historical Survey," in B.M. Barkindo (ed.), *Studies in the History of Kano* ( Ibadan, 1983), pp. 1-30.

[6]Amini, The Inward Dimension of the Islamic City, p. 10.

Building regulations in the city were also governed by Islamic regulations which assert "Do not harm others and others should not harm you," further amplified by the saying of the Prophet Muhammad that "Anyone has the right to insert his joist in his neighbour's wall."[7] This explains the compact structure of the Islamic city with the outer wall of each house joining on that of its neighbour, and in this regard Kano is no different from other Muslim cities. Very narrow lanes wind through the city and widen as they approach the ward's square (*dandali*), the palace, the mosque or the market.

Up to the end of the sixteenth century, the leading *'ulama* in Kano city were temporary immigrants most of whom did not die there. From the seventeenth century, however, Kano was producing her own erudite scholars. In fact the period *c.*1620-1720 was, according to Murray Last, the "Age of Saints" in Kano city. Their sanctified graveyards called *waliyai* (i.e. "saints") have since become a focus for other burials and even of "local pilgrimage."[8] After the nineteenth-century *jihad*, Kano became one of the leading cities of scholarship in the Sokoto Caliphate attracting scholars and students (*almajirai*) from far and near.

The society was international in composition as well as outlook, divided into several ethnic, social and professional classes with many individuals belonging to more than one division. The majority, however, belonged to the Maliki *madhhab* and were predominantly Qadiri in Sufi affiliation. Islam, therefore, provided the framework for government and society.

The above is what the *Kanawa* (i.e. people of Kano) perceive as the classical urban character of their city, referred to in Hausa as the *birni*.. However, from 1903 onwards, Western education, Western materialism with its values and ethics increasingly permeated the society. This was accompanied by the loss of real political and economic powers by the traditional, political and business classes. Whether by design or accident the new political and economic structures which emerged with colonialism were located in the new suburbs collectively called *waje* (i.e. outside the city walls) where for a long time they were dominated by the new immigrants.

On the whole, the *Kanawa* passively resisted Westernization. Despite the expansion of the *birni*, there was still one *Jummat* mosque for the whole of metropolitan Kano (i.e. both the *birni* and *waje*) up to 1970. There was no modern restaurant, bar or even supermarket.

[7]*Ibid.*, p. 12.

[8]Murray Last, "Charisma and Medicine in Northern Nigeria," in D. Cruise O'Brien and C. Coulon (eds), *Charisma and Brotherhood in African Islam* ( Oxford, 1988), p. 193.

Pimps and prostitutes were never publicly tolerated and most married women stayed in purdah or went with *lullubi* whenever they ventured out of their matrimonial homes. Up to the early 1970s, the School of Arabic Studies and the Judicial School were the only Western post-primary institutions within the city. There was, however, an increase in the Islamiyya schools which attempted to combine Western education and Islamic studies in their curriculum. In short, there was an attempt to maintain the Islamic character of the city.

In the *waje* on the other hand, life was permissive. The southerners, who were predominantly Christians, had built churches and Western schools there. There were beer parlours and brothels full of prostitutes and their pimps. There were also shops full of imported European goods. It was there that artisans in the newly-imported trades and professions were located, as we have already noted. To the majority of the *Kanawa*, *birni* was home, and one only ventured to *waje* out of necessity. Its life was an evil which was tolerated because one had no choice. This view was radically changed from about 1970 onwards.

*Some of the causes of rising Islamism in Kano City since c. 1970*

Islamism did not originate among the *Kanawa* only in 1970; radicalism based on Islamic principles had long been an important feature of Kano culture. In fact, the debate among the political and educated élite about appropriate systems of government and social policies had been going on in Kano even before the *jihad* of Shehu Usman Dan Fodio in the nineteenth century and had continued after the inception of colonial rule. However, by 1970 the majority of the *Kanawa*, of whatever shade of opinion, seemed to agree that some sort of Islamic revivalism or reform was required to respond to contemporary problems.

The military coup of 1966 was a contributory factor to the developments in Kano during this period. The temporary flight of the Igbos and other southerners from Kano brought home to the *Kanawa*, for the first time, their almost total dependence on the southerners for the supply of certain goods and services which they had come to take for granted and did not feel they could do without. This was a very disturbing realization, because Western materialism had penetrated into their lives more deeply than they had imagined. Many *Kanawa* took advantage of this situation and moved to *Sabon gari* to assume the management of hotels, shops and other services. But many others were alarmed at this development, especially when, for example, a key figure like Alhaji Muhammadu Maunde, a member of the royal house, took over the management of Kings Garden and Niger hotels – then the leading establishments in Kano.

The creation of Kano State in 1967 by the government of General Yakubu Gowon saw the elevation of many of Kano's educated élite to prestigious positions as commissioners, permanent secretaries, directors etc. And many of these now left the *birni* to take up residence in the old European preserve at Nassarawa. The types of buildings there, the landscaping and even the general atmosphere were based on Western models. As time went on, there was a steady expansion of European-style bungalows, which had become a new status symbol, in Bompai and other settlements neighbouring Nassarawa.

By the early 1970s, Nigeria was wallowing in money due to the sharp rise in the price of crude oil. This was the beginning of the so-called "oil boom," which ushered in a period of reckless spending and senseless planning. Kano experienced a rapid and uncontrolled growth, as mentioned above. Hundreds of industrial estates were established in Bompai and Sharada, mostly owned by Europeans, Lebanese, Syrians and Egyptians, although a few Kano businessmen owned several factories and estates in parts of the *waje*.[9]

Both residential settlements and business enterprises were expanding in the *waje*; it was experiencing what in the Third World is generally perceived as modern development with the appearance of factories, modern hotels and restaurants, music-clubs and gambling houses, banks, shops and other business centres, petrol stations etc. Well-planned tarred roads and round-abouts with fountains were built. By contrast, the *birni* remained more or less as we described it above. However, by now the sharp division between the *birni* and *waje* which had existed until about 1969 was becoming blurred. A large number of *yan birni* (lit. "sons of the city") had already moved to the *waje* to settle, while an increasing proportion of those who still resided in the *birni* were now earning their living in the *waje*. It was during this period that certain of the *'ulama* and other Kano leaders began to be intolerant of conditions in the *waje*, which they considered to be irreligious.[10]

By the early 1970s, Kano had produced its own Westernized intellectual élite, a majority of whom were men, although there was also a large number of women. Ibrahim Yaro Muhammed, a Kano city poet, described the young members of this élite thus:

[9]I.L. Bashir, "The Growth and Development of the Manufacturing Sector of Kano's Economy, 1950-1980," Barkindo (ed.), *Kano and Some of Her Neighbours* (Zaria, 1989).

[10]Mallam Muzammil Sani Hanga, a leader of the *Umma* Intellectual Organisation in Kano, interviewed, Kano City 16 Dec. 1990.

> Young people have taken up evil ways
> They have abandoned all our respected traditions
> All our customs have been abandoned
> They have adopted European customs and they speak English
> To indicate their liberation and their worldly wisdom ...
> They no longer wear our traditional clothes
> Preferring jackets and trousers.[11]

More disturbing for some, however, has been the increasing number of Western-educated girls since the 1980s who have remained unmarried. In one of his Ramadan sermons in 1989, Shaikh Isa Waziri, one of the leading *'ulama* of Kano, called attention to this development and advised well-to-do men in the society to take extra wives as a partial solution to this "calamity," as he referred to it.

The "oil boom" led to corruption and reckless spending by the government. Many people became extremely rich and displayed their wealth by building fashionable mansions, purchasing flashy cars and the latest electronic gadgets for their homes, and taking frequent trips abroad. During the Second Republic several Kano businessmen set a new fashion by buying their own private jets.

This new-found wealth and the construction fever which gripped both the government and the private sector was the main cause for the unprecedented rural-urban migration not only in Kano State but also in all other parts of Nigeria. Many farmers and artisans simply abandoned their occupations and migrated to the cities in search of jobs or petty contracts.

Many of those who came to look for jobs in the cities were unable to find them and joined the city's unemployed. In addition, the lesser *'ulama* and their *almajirai* or students were becoming increasingly marginalized, a process which had been going on for years and which by the 1970s, had become a serious issue, as noted by Murray Last:

> No longer now are there the eventual posts as respected village scholars, now that the primary schools have their own religious instructors. No longer is there the ready hospitality (particularly in towns) and the same respect (or casual work) for the migrant students. Worst of all, perhaps, the class of austerely pious, very learned yet public scholars, who once were the models for a particular way of life, has all but disappeared.[12]

Paul Lubeck has shown that from the 1970s onwards, there had been a high representation (18.2%) of *almajirai* and sons of Islamic scholars

[11]Quoted in G. Furniss, "Social Problems in Kano in the 1970s: a Poet ' s Eye View," paper presented to the "Panel on Social History" during the African Studies Association Conference at Madison, USA, 29 October - 2nd November, 1986.

[12]Murray Last, "Religion and the State in Northern Nigeria," unpubl. paper.

among the rural migrant labourers who came into Kano city. The reason for this high percentage, he suggests, was because "Sons of *Mallams* are unable to make a secure living in traditional occupations such as tailoring or commerce which allows them to continue Islamic scholarship."[13] In short, the "oil boom" coupled with increasing Westernization had not only widened the gap between the rich and the poor but had also further marginalized some groups, among whom were the lesser Islamic scholars and their students.

Immigration into the city coupled with unemployment had led to appalling living conditions with many sleeping on the streets, in market places or in over-crowded rooms, which in turn led to an increase in crime, including rape, theft, burglary, drug addiction, drunkenness, pick-pocketing, prostitution and even murder. Young men joined together in gangs – referred to as *yan daukar amarya* (lit. "those who abduct the bride") – which abducted, raped and robbed women.

During the Second Republic the *yan tauri*, partly encouraged by rival political parties in the city and partly due to their increasing marginalization, unleashed a reign of terror. Rival groups fought among themselves, causing many casualties, some of them fatal. They also attacked innocent people, sometimes following them right into their homes.[14]

The police were made impotent, not so much because of the enormity of the crimes, but because the city dwellers were uncooperative. There were several reasons for this. First, the *Kanawa* did not trust the police, who were still considered the agents of the colonial government or of the post-Independence Northern People's Congress who had terrorized its opponents. In addition, the police were considered to be corrupt. And finally, many of the young involved in these crimes were not strangers to the city but from *Kanawa* families whom local people were reluctant to expose to the police.[15]

It was in this atmosphere that Muhammadu Marwa, nicknamed *Maitatsine* (i.e. "the one who damns") began his inflammatory sermons in the city and later mobilized his followers to defy the law. He unleashed a reign of terror on the city in which thousands lost their lives and which the army was required to quell. This crisis has been a

[13] P.M. Lubeck, "Industrial Labour in Kano: Historical Origins, Social Characteristics and Sources of Differentiation" in Barkindo, (ed.) *Studies in the History of Kano*, p.164.

[14] Alhaji Nasiru Inuwa, a senior driver in the History Department, Bayero University, Kano, in several interviews during the last few years.

[15] *Ibid.*

subject of several interpretations.[16] The *Maitatsine* phenomenon, it appears to me, is the continuation of a debate which started among the *'ulama* and members of the ruling élite on the eve of the British conquest. There were those who opted for the total rejection of European rule; they called for *jihad* and, in case of defeat, a *hijra* or mass migration to a land where they could practise their Islam without hindrance. Those who held this view included the Caliph of Sokoto himself, Attahiru Ahmadu[17] and the Emir of Kano, Alu b. Abdullahi (1894-1903).[18]

However, there were others who held the view that mass resistance or total war would result in tragedy; among these were the *wazir* of the Caliphate, Bukhari b. Ahmad,[19] and Abbas b. Abdullahi, the prince who replaced Alu as the Emir in Kano. In the event, Caliph Attahiru fought the British and, when defeated, set out on the *hijra*. He and a large number of his followers were pursued by the British forces and massacred at Bormi. Emir Alu was also arrested by the British forces and exiled to Lokoja, where he died. Wazir Bukhari and Abbas b. Abdullahi submitted to the British and were confirmed as *wazir* of Sokoto and appointed Emir of Kano respectively.

*Maitatsine* appears to have resumed this debate which, according to Dr. Dahiru Yahya, had never ceased in Kano. He condemned all things European, which he called upon people to shun, and implored them to return to Islamic ways. He damned both those who collaborated with the Europeans in any way and the rich who did not share their wealth according to the dictates of Islam, and called for a *jihad* against such people. His supporters were the lesser Qur'anic teachers, *almajirai*, the unemployed and the other marginalized groups that we have mentioned above. *Maitatsine* enjoyed a limited success partly because many of the people who did not actually join him agreed with the content of his preaching; but they disagreed with his methods.

The *Maitatsine* crisis awakened the ruling group, the business and civil service élite, as well as the leading *'ulama*, to the fact that things were bad and that something had to be done urgently to prevent them

[16]See for example, P.M. Lubeck, "Islamic Protest Under Semi-Industrial Capitalism: 'Yan Tatsine explained," *Africa*, vol 55, no. 4 (1985), pp. 369-89; A. Anwar, "The Struggle for Influence and Identity among the Ulama in Kano," unpubl. M.A. thesis, University of Maiduguri, 1989.

[17]Attahiru Ahmadu, "Wakar Zuwan Annasara" in D. Abdulkadir (ed.), *Zababbun Wakokin Da da na Yanzu* (Lagos, 1979). For an analysis of the poem, see M. Hiskett, *The Development of Islam in West Africa* (London, 1984), pp. 269-72.

[18]D.J.M. Muffet, *Concerning Brave Captains* (London, 1964).

[19]R.A. Adeleye, "The Dilemma of the Wazir: The Place of the *Risālat al-Wazīr 'ilā ahl al-'ilm wa'l-tadabbur* in the History of Sokoto Caliphate," *Journal of the Historical Society of Nigeria*, IV (2), 1968, pp. 285-311.

getting worse. A repetition of the revolt in the other Islamic centres of the north reinforced their alarm.

According to Mallam Muzammil Sani Hanga, one of Kano's leading scholars, these problems should be understood as the "Signs of the Hour," which in Islamic eschatalogy is related to the idea that at the end of every century a renewer (*mujaddid*) may arise to restore order.[20] The view of Shaikh Aminu Deen, shared in part by Mallam Muzammil, is that the current upsurge of Islamism is the result of divine intervention. He bases this view on a tradition which states that when conditions within the *umma* deteriorate, Allah will intervene to restore order, peace and the purity of Islam.[21]

An additional factor is the increased militancy of Christians, especially since the *shari'a* debates of 1977/8 and 1989, and the debates about Nigeria's membership in the Organization of the Islamic Conference. These events resulted in the appearance of numerous publications by the Christian Association of Nigeria, which in turn led to a religious awakening among Muslims. All the *'ulama* interviewed agreed on this interpretation of events, although it appears that whereas Christian militancy may have caused Islamist trends to become more aggressive, it was already active before these Christian campaigns. Already from the mid-1970s, "Islam only" had become a popular slogan among those who felt that only Islamic solutions would be able to solve Nigeria's problems.

Youth organizations have also played an important role in re-awakening Muslims, in particular the Muslim Student Society (M.S.S.) which had branches at Ahmadu Bello University in Zaria and Bayero University in Kano. The M.S.S., considered by Mallam Muzammil to be a training-ground for Muslim revolutionaries in Nigeria, organized lectures, symposia and discussions on a number of subjects, and they invited a variety of scholars both within and outside the country to address them. In April 1980, the Kano branch organized an international seminar on Muslim movements, the aim of which was to examine various successful Islamic reform movements in history, for example the *jihad* of Usman Dan Fodio, the Sudanese *Mahdiyya* and Ayatollah Khomeini's Islamic revolution, with a view to recommending a suitable model for Nigeria. They studied the texts of

[20]Mallam Muzammil Sani Hanga, interviewed in Kano city on 16 Dec. 1990.

[21]Shaikh Aminu Deen b. Abubakar, Imam of Lamido Crescent *Jummat* mosque and leader of the Da'wa Society of Nigeria, interviewed in Kano, 19 Dec. 1990. For the tradition of "Sign of the Hour" in Kano see A. Dangambo, "'The Sign of the Hour' among the Muslim Hausa, with special reference to their Verse," *Kano Studies*, N.S., vol. II, no. 1 (1980).

these and other Muslim radicals, including Muhammad Qutb of Egypt in order to see how they might be adapted to the Nigerian situation.[22]

The M.S.S. not only organized the youth but also attempted to involve various leaders, like traditional rulers, businessmen and the Western-educated élite, in many of their activities. In this way it participated in the formation of many other important Muslim organizations, such as the Council of *'Ulama*, whose primary aim was to establish closer unity among the scholars of the various Muslim brotherhoods, and the Federal Muslim Women's Association of Nigeria.

During this period, other Muslim groups also were organized: the *Izala*, the *Mahdiyya*, and the *Shi'a*. The Qadiriyya and the Tijanniyya brotherhoods also established their radical political wings in order to mobilize the youth: the *Jundullahi* and the *Fitiyanul Islam*.

*Form and content of Islamism in Kano city since 1970*

Although there is no formal or official policy which coordinates or informs these trends towards Islamism in Kano, it appears that the majority of the *Kanawa*, either as individuals or as members of groups, tend to feel that there is an urgent need to employ Islamic solutions to the urban problems which face the society. There is some indication in recent decisions by the Kano State government that its thinking is being influenced by these attitudes among the population. Let us now outline some of the salient features of Kano's recent urban Islamism.

*Establishment of more mosques*. Until 1970, there was only one *Jummat* mosque for both the *birni* and *waje*. In that year, in response to the rapid expansion of metropolitan Kano, the present Emir, Alhaji Ado Bayero, consulted a group of prominent *'ulama* on the Islamic legal implications of constructing a second *Jummat* mosque. After exhaustive deliberations, a *fatwa* was issued approving the building of a new mosque in the Fagge ward in the *waje*.[23] Since then, the Emir has sanctioned the establishment of more *Jummat* mosques, especially in the *waje*, which is expanding very rapidly.[24] Between 1980 and 1990, about ten *Jummat* mosques were built in metropolitan Kano. Some were constructed through the initiative of individuals, such as

[22]Mallam Muzammil Sani Hanga. Among the invited guests were Sadiq al-Mahdi, future Prime Minister of Sudan, who attended, and Ayatollah Khomeini, who sent his Director of Youth Organisations, Enayat Ettehad.

[23]M.S. Zahraddeen, "The Place of Mosques in the History of Kano," in Barkindo (ed.), *Studies in the History of Kano* , p. 62.

[24]*Ibid.*

that of Kurnan Asabe (built in 1972 by Alhaji Sani Marshal), and the one north of Goron Dutse in the *birni* (built in 1987 by Alhaji Isyaku Rabiu); others were built through communal efforts, such as the one at Bayero University, built in 1979.

Many other mosques were also built by wealthy individuals, Islamic organizations and brotherhoods, and educational institutions, as well as by other private and government establishments, such as the army, the police and the airport. Neither time nor money have been spared in beautifying some of these mosques, especially those owned by rich individuals, such as Alhaji Bashiru Tofa at Gandun Albasa ward in the *birni*. But some *'ulama* frown upon this rush to build more mosques; Ustaz Tijjani Bala Kalarawi, for example, maintains that rather than build more mosques, which become filled with ignorant worshippers, wealthy individuals should rather build more Islamiyya schools.[25]

*Increased activities in the mosques.* The primary activity of any mosque is the performance of the five daily Muslim prayers. But the mosque also serves as a kind of Muslim community centre where both religious and other social activities are conducted. In the period before 1970, Sufi litanies were recited in a few Qadiriyya and Tijaniyya mosques. Professor Sani Zahraddeen has noted that now

> Even in the *hijra* mosques, Sufi litanies of the Tijjaniya brotherhood are recited. One interesting development is that although the jihadists were solidly Qadiri, these mosques are now solidly Tijjani. We now find the Tijjaniya litanies in the Indabawa Mosque (introduced recently), the Jalli Mosque (introduced some years ago by Imam Tafidu), the Galadanchi Mosque (where Shaikh Maihula used to deliver his *tafsir* in Ramadan) and the Yolawa Mosque. In the Alfindiki and "Arab" mosques, the Qadiriyya litanies are recited with the accompaniment of Bandir drums.[26]

Within the last two decades there has been an increased incidence of group religious activities such as the recitation of Sufi litanies in the mosques as well as public gatherings for *tafsir* sessions during the month of Ramadan.

Another new development is the appointment as *imams* of persons who are the products of both the Western and Islamic educational systems. Shaikh Isa Waziri, the Imam of Murtala Muhammed *Jummat* mosque, is vice-principal of a post-primary school in the *birni*. Shaikh Aminu Deen b. Abubakar, the Imam of Lamido

[25]Ustaz Bala Karawi, interviewed in Kano city, 16 Dec. 1990.
[26]M.S. Zahraddeen, "The Place of Mosques in the History of Kano," pp. 62-3.

Crescent *Jummat* mosque, is a graduate, and Alhaji Imam Abbas, the Imam of Bayero University *Jummat* mosque, holds an academic diploma from that institution. These *imams* are therefore able to deliver sermons which can appeal to modern educated men and women, and consequently more people are being attracted to their sermons and *tafsir* sessions.

In recent years, the reading of the Qur'an has been introduced in some of the mosques. For example, it is recited daily between the *Maghrib* and *Ishai* prayers at the Bayero University mosque, while at the Shaikh Rabiu mosque, it is recited every Friday. This activity attracts sizeable audiences and may spread to other mosques.

Mosques which are owned or controlled by the youth organizations, such as the M.S.S., or by the *Da'wa* society and other similar groups, host various other activities like discussions, lectures and debates. In addition, marriages and naming ceremonies are now conducted in some of the mosques, especially those (like the Bayero University mosque) which are influenced by the *Izala*, who advocate the elimination of non-Islamic innovations and a return to the basic tenets of the Qur'an and the *sunna*. Also, many mosques now house libraries which include basic books on Islam which are available for consultation by the public.

*Establishment of Islamic schools.* During the reign of Emir Abdullahi Bayero (1926-52), attempts were made to integrate Western and Islamic education, in the form of the Islamiyya schools which teach Islamic religious knowledge, Arabic and Hausa language, as well as English and arithmetic. Although the first Islamiyya school was established in Zaria in the 1950s, it was in Kano that the these schools became most widely established. One reason for this is that many Kano businessmen have been willing to patronize these schools by sending their children to them and also by absorbing former pupils into their own businesses.[27]

Since the early 1970s, a considerable number of Islamiyya schools have been established in metropolitan Kano by businessmen, *'ulama*, Islamic organizations and the government. Worthy of special mention in this regard is the Kano Foundation, which has a plan to open a number of Islamiyya schools of very high standard throughout the state. A model girls' secondary school, which was established by the Foundation in Kano City in 1989, met the criticism that these new schools were destined to become élitist if they were to maintain the

[27]D.A. Maiwada, "Curriculum Development in Koranic Education," *Kano Studies*, vol. 2, no. 2 (1981), p. 150.

very high fees and strict admissions policy of the model school. All Western schools also include the teaching of Arabic and Islamic studies in their curriculum, and the quality of these courses has improved with the increased availability of well qualified teachers in these subjects. The teachers of Islamic studies in all these schools, both private and government-owned, are trained in either the prestigious School of Arabic Studies, in the Islamic teachers colleges (of which there are two new ones in municipal Kano), or in the Faculty of Arts and Islamic Studies at Bayero University.

Another significant development is the establishment of Islamic adult-education classes for married women, which are attended by both illiterate and Western-educated women; many of the latter are university graduates. In 1983, Shaikh Isa Waziri opened the first of these institutions, and since then several others have been established in metropolitan Kano, by Shaikh Aminu Deen in 1986, by Mallam Hassan Sufi in 1986/7, and by Shaikh Nasir Kabara in 1987.

*Increased religious activities.* Several years ago, the Emir expressed his disquiet about the excessive enthusiasm of young people for the game of football. His comments reflected a general concern among the public about the growing influence of Western culture, not only football but disco music, the cinema etc. Various new Islamic activities were introduced to capture the interest of the youth. Several *mallams* successfully organized their students into music groups which performed songs, usually in Arabic but sometimes in Hausa, in praise of the Prophet Muhammad, or about the basic tenets of Islam and proper Islamic moral behaviour. Some of these groups accompanied their songs with the *bandir* drums, perhaps in an effort to compete with some of the disco music groups.

Islamic quizzes were introduced in which young people were asked questions about Islamic history, the *hadith* or general Islamic knowledge. There has also been considerable enthusiasm for Qur'an recitation competitions, an activity started by Dr. Umar Bello of the Centre for Islamic Studies, Usumanu Dan Fodio University, Sokoto. Students from Kano have won several national and international competitions, which have now become very much a part of life in Kano.

*Attitude of the people.* One can also note in recent years a marked change in the public attitude of people towards Islam. Attendance has increased not only at the *Jummat* prayers, but also the other daily prayers, particularly among young people and women. There has also been a change in the way especially young men and women dress.

Men are discarding the Western fashions of suits, shirts and ties; women, especially educated ones, are wearing clothing which covers the entire body as enjoined by Islamic teachings. Shaikh Isa Waziri, however, has declared that the wearing of the *hijab* is a fashion with no religious basis,[28] a fashion which, by the way, became more popular after Hajiya Umma Bayero opened a *hijab* factory in Kano in 1987.

On the other hand, there has been an increasing incidence of intolerance of other religions, especially among the youth. Muslim students in virtually all institutions of higher learning have thus far managed to frustrate attempts by Christian students to build churches in the schools.

In October 1982, Muslim students from several post-primary institutions in the municipality destroyed a church which was under construction in Fagge ward, complaining that it was too near the *Jummat* mosque. They then went on to destroy or burn down several other churches in *Sabon gari* and Fagge areas of the *waje*. These incidents have resulted in the government hesitating to allocate land for the construction of other churches in the municipality.

*The role of Kano State government.* In addition to the State government's encouragement of Islamic education in the schools, discussed above, it has also authorized the state-owned television and radio stations to give increased air-time to Islamic activities. They broadcast sermons by the leading *'ulama*, readings from the Holy Qur'an, and *tafsir* sessions during the month of Ramadan. All the *'ulama* who were interviewed in connection with this study agree that the media have contributed significantly to the Islamic education of the public and in mobilizing them to more active participation in religious activities.

In January 1982, a national seminar on *zakkat* was organized by the Department of Islamic Studies, Bayero University in conjunction with the Islamic Foundation of Nigeria. Following the recommendations of this seminar, in 1983, the Kano State Islamic Council for Zakkat was set up at the School of Arabic Studies, the aim of which was to revive the institution of *zakkat* for assisting in the resolution of some of the social problems outlined in this paper.

In June 1987, the Kano State government set up four committees to study questions surrounding the conditions of the destitute, the *almajirai*, women and social mobilization. The membership of these committees included both lecturers from Bayero University and certain of the leading *'ulama* in Kano. The establishment of these committees

[28]Shaikh Isa Waziri, interviewed at Kano City, 10 Jan. 1991.

suggests that the State government accepted the idea that previous measures adopted to control urban social problems had failed, and that the only remaining option was to employ Islamic solutions. This attitude may have influenced the current police crackdown on prostitutes and pimps who are now being driven away from their locations in the various wards of the *waje*.

## *Conclusion*

Kano developed as a classical Islamic city, comparable to those in North Africa and the Middle East, for four centuries before the British conquest in 1903. The *Kanawa* subsequently resisted the process of Westernization which accompanied the colonial occupation, which they saw as a challenge to their Islamic way of life. Throughout the period of British rule and during the First Republic (1960-6) they attempted with some success to maintain the separate urban Islamic identity of the *birni* within the ancient walled city. This was not possible in the burgeoning suburbs of the *waje*, where the newly-introduced (Western) political, social and economic institutions were centered. Westernization took root there and gradually permeated the rest of society.

From the late 1960s, although the majority of the *Kanawa* still lived in the *birni*, the *waje* became much more important economically, politically and even socially. As the *waje* began to attract many more of the *Kanawa* as settlers or "commuters," it was no longer possible to characterize the old city and the emerging suburbs in a neat dichotomy of "us" and "them." This realization coincided with the oil boom in Nigeria and the process of rapid urbanization and its attendant problems.

These changes also coincided with a growing international Islamic revivalism, and when government measures to control the new urban problems seemed to have failed to ameliorate the worsening social situation, Muslim organizations and individuals in the city (and elsewhere) intensified their calls for Islamic solutions and began to reform existing Islamic institutions to cope with the pressing demands.

There are many over-zealous Muslims in Kano city; there are even many who advocate the total rejection of the present system of government in favour of an Islamic one. However, for the majority the recourse to Islamism is the result of their frustration with the failure of "modern" measures to cope with the worsening social and economic problems. The slogan "Islam only," therefore, is a way of saying that Islamic solutions to these problems are the only remaining options, all the others having been tried and having failed.

# ISLAM AND THE IDENTITY OF MERCHANTS IN MARADI (NIGER)

*Emmanuel Grégoire**

My research among the Hausa in Maradi (Niger) and then in Kano (northern Nigeria) initially adopted a historical perspective to examine how local merchants and entrepreneurs accumulated wealth.[1] In the framework of a study on border exchanges in West Africa, I then analyzed formal and informal trade between Niger and Nigeria. Very active underground trading patterns and smuggling networks, wherein several actors (runners, transporters and customs officers) are implicated, were thus brought to light between traders in Maradi and Kano.[2]

This research on the business world did not pay sufficient attention to a factor that carries heavy weight in Hausa areas, namely Islam. Here I hope to make up for this shortcoming by showing how closely Islam and trade are interrelated in the city of Maradi, where I recently undertook fieldwork on this topic. The objective is to understand how Islam has enabled merchants to work out a sense of identity.[3]

## *Maradi: the historical background*

Maradi had its origins in a religious movement when, in the early nineteenth century, Usman Dan Fodio and his followers launched a *jihad* against the Hausa and Borno dynasties of present-day northern Nigeria. The movement succeeded in capturing control of much of Hausaland and neighbouring regions and in establishing a Muslim state, the Sokoto Caliphate. At the northern edge of the Caliphate, Maradi was a place of refuge for the *sarki* (ruler) of Katsina, who sought to reconquer the capital whence his ancestors had been chased away by the *jihad*. At his side were the Hausa rulers of Kano and

* The author would like to thank Noal Mellott, CNRS, Paris, who translated this article from the French.

[1] See E. Grégoire, *The Alhazai of Maradi: Traditional Hausa Merchants in a Changing Sahelan City* (Boulder, Colorado, 1992), and E. Grégoire, "Formation d'un capitalisme africain. Le *alhazai* de Kano," in C. Blanc-Pamard (ed.), *La dimension economique* (Paris, 1990), pp.149-61.

[2] E. Grégoire, "Les chemins de la contrebande," *Cahiers d'Etudes Africaines* (Paris) forthcoming.

[3] See also, E. Grégoire, "Accumulation marchande et propagation de l'Islam en milieu urbain. Le cas de Maradi (Niger)", *Islam et sociétés au sud du Sahara* (Paris), no. 5 (1991), pp.43-55.

Gobir, who wanted to regain control of their own city-states. Although these princes never achieved their aims, Maradi remained for much of the nineteenth century a stronghold that warred against the Fulani emirs of Katsina and Kano.

During the colonial period, this small fortified town became an administrative centre and, during the heyday of groundnut production, a trading centre. From *chef-lieu* of a *cercle* in colonial times, Maradi has now become a *préfecture*. Meanwhile, trade with neighbouring Nigeria (Kano is only 220 km. away) had stimulated growth. The city now has more than 120,000 inhabitants – and its share of urban problems (food shortfalls, delinquency, population growth, and so on). During the 1970s, an unsuccessful attempt was made at industrialization. Above all else, Maradi is a border city with an economy based on an intense circulation of money rather than the creation of wealth.

Thanks to the groundnut trade and, later, the growth of commerce with Nigeria, a group of wealthy merchants has emerged. These men are imbued with the values of merchant capitalism and of Islam, as their name *alhazai* (singular: *alhaji*) indicates: it is the Hausa title given to Muslims who have made the pilgrimage to Mecca. In the process of accumulating their wealth, these *alhazai* have also supported the diffusion of Islam in Maradi. For them, the title of *alhaji* is a way of identifying themselves as members of a local élite. Formerly, adherence to Islam was a symbol of one's élite status, and in recent years a new generation of young traders has joined the reformist religious movement, *Izala*, which might be interpreted as yet another new way for a portion of the merchant class to assert its separate identity.

## *Accumulation and the spread of Islam*

Islam has been implanted in several African societies, especially those where trade is important. For several centuries, through trans-Saharan commerce, some traders entered into contact with Arab merchants and then converted to Islam. During their travels, they helped to spread the new religion south of the Sahara.[4] For instance, merchants from Katsina and Kano, who during the pre-colonial period had constant contacts with fellow-merchants in north African cities (such as Tripoli, Benghazi and Algiers) had an active part in diffusing Islam among the Hausa.

The Maradi area was not safe for travellers until the coming of the European powers in the early twentieth century, when Hausaland was

[4]C. Meillassoux, "Introduction" in C. Meillassoux (ed.), *L'évolution du commerce en Afrique de l'Ouest* (Oxford, 1971), pp.3-48.

divided between France and Britain. With hostilities in the region ended, people could move about without fear, for business as well as religious reasons. Trade as well as Islam could flourish. Small caravans from Maradi would sell animals and skins in Kano and then return loaded with cloth and kola nuts. Traveling to improve their knowledge of the Qur'an, *marabouts* from Maradi would spend time in the British-controlled cities of northern Nigeria. Kano, Zaria, Sokoto and Maiduguri were highly regarded as centres of Qur'anic study. Maradi itself, with a population of only 4,500 inhabitants in 1911, was still a small town where animism was strong. Only the chief and his advisers, as well as a few families of clerics from the old city-state of Katsina, were Muslim.

Following World War I, France introduced an economy based on exporting local products (groundnuts) and importing merchandise. Here, as in the rest of the colonial empire, new markets were thus opened for the mother country's industries. To reach local consumers and producers (i.e. peasants), colonial trading houses used African middlemen, who both collected groundnuts and sold trade articles. From the 1950s until the Great Drought of 1973-4, the groundnut trade boomed. More and more African traders were taken up in it; and some of them became middlemen so rich they formed a small local business élite. Exposed to influences from Nigeria, these merchants gradually converted to Islam. A *marabout* spoke about this,

> "When merchants from Maradi went to Nigeria on business, they saw how their contacts there practised religion (prayer, etc.) and then participated with them. When they came back to Niger, they changed their customs and religious beliefs. They led the men who worked with them to pray to God. That's how Islam replaced traditional religions."

Authors like Meillassoux, Hopkins and Hiskett[5] have emphasized how closely Islam and trade have been linked, and how the former has so often served as a vehicle for the latter in West Africa. As trade grew and the local economy became increasingly dependent on money, Islam was probably better suited than traditional religions for regulating social and economic relations. For merchants, becoming Muslim may have been a way of standing out (like the chief) from the ordinary people.

Thanks to their wealth and subsequently to air transportation, more and more merchants in Maradi were going on pilgrimage to

[5]See C. Meillassoux, *ibid.*; A.G. Hopkins, *An Economic History of West Africa* (New York, 1980); and M. Hiskett, *The Development of Islam in West Africa* (London, 1984).

Mecca, whence they returned with the prestigious title *alhaji*. Among the Hausa, this title also signifies success in business; through it these merchants identified themselves as members of the local business élite. Impelled by the *alhazai*, Islam gained ground in Maradi, and since 1970 it seems to have outstripped traditional religions.

Meanwhile, the growth of trade with Nigeria has considerably improved business for the Maradi *alhazai*. It produced a new generation of men who are more modern and businesslike than those involved in the groundnut trade. Although their main business is still trading, in particular the import-export trade with Nigeria, these merchants are also investing in buildings, transportation, farming, livestock and even industry.

These *alhazai* devote part of their earnings to spreading Islam: they provide *marabouts* with the means of opening Qur'anic schools, they help build mosques so that the faithful will have a place of worship, and they fund pilgrimages to Mecca for family members and close friends. As one *marabout* pointed out to me, they are "following the example of Siddiq Abubakar, a well-to-do person who provided material support to the Prophet for spreading Islam."[3] Although the *alhazai* have done much to help propagate Islam in the Maradi area, Islamization is a fundamental trend in local society. As this society undergoes change, it is looking for new frames of reference and systems of thought so as to be able to cope with the changing social and economic environment.

As the city has been Islamized, these wealthy merchants are still trying to maintain a sense of separate identity. Formerly, this status was achieved by simple adherence to Islam, by being a Muslim. Then, for a long period, the performance of the pilgrimage and the acquisition of the *alhaji* title served a similar purpose, although nowadays this title is borne by so many people that it no longer functions as a sign of distinction. It would seem that now membership in the reformist religious movement called *Izala* has become a means for young, wealthy *alhazai* to develop their own unique sense of identity. Before we comment on this movement, a brief history of major Islamic groups in Maradi is in order. Attention will be focused on differences between these groups (in doctrine as well as religious practices) and on the social repercussions of these differences.

### *The Sufi brotherhoods*

There are two major brotherhoods among Hausa Muslims: the Qadiriyya and Tijaniyya. In Maradi, Islam was first present in the form of the Qadiriyya, which was introduced into the region by the

Kunta Shaikh Sidi al-Mukhtar al-Kabir (1729/30-1811).[6] Usman Dan Fodio belonged to this brotherhood, as did the Wangarawa, an important merchant group from Mali which played a significant role in the early Islamic history of Hausaland, particularly in Katsina. Nowadays, more people in Maradi belong to this brotherhood than to any other, including some of the city's most prominent *marabouts*, including Mallam Antoma (*imam* at the mosque on Place du Chef and president of the local *marabouts'* association) and Mallam Abba (*imam* of the new Friday mosque in Zaria quarter). Most of the wealthiest *alhazai* also belong to the Qadiriyya. In Maradi, members of the Qadiriyya are referred to as *sadalu*, a term which refers to the fact that they pray with their arms at their sides.

The Tijaniyya brotherhood was founded in Algeria by Shaikh Ahmad Tijani in the eighteenth century, and spread to West Africa in the mid-nineteenth century through the activities of al-Hajj 'Umar Tal, who himself led a *jihad* in the regions of present-day Senegal and Mali.[7] The Tijaniyya, whose practices tend to be mystical, did not appear in Maradi until the mid-1950s, when it was introduced by members of its Niassiyya branch from Kano, where the Emir is an adherent of the order.[8] The Niassiyya branch of the Tijaniyya is based in Senegal, and its members pray with their arms crossed on their chests, for which reason they are referred to as *kabalu*. In Maradi, Mallam Ibrahim dan Jirataoua heads this brotherhood, and a few wealthy merchants support it.

The observable differences between *kabalu* and *sadalu* all relate to ritual, in particular to praying. In addition to differing positions of the arms during prayer,[9] the *kabalu* (Niassiyya Tijanis) recite certain Tijani litanies in groups, such as the daily *wazifa* and the *hadra* on Fridays. Although serious clashes took place between these two brotherhoods in Nigeria during the 1950s and 1960s, their members are now working together, in Maradi as in Nigeria, to oppose the *Izala* fundamentalists.

[6]J.-L. Triaud, "Le thème confrérique en Afrique de l'Ouest," in A. Popovic and G. Veinstein (eds), *Les ordres mystiques dans l'Islam* (Paris, 1986), pp.271-81.

[7]*Ibid.*

[8]O. Kane, "La confrérie Tijaniyya Ibrahima de Kano et ses liens avec la Zawiya mère de Kaolack," *Islam et sociétés au sud du Sahara* (Paris), no. 3 (1989), pp. 27-40.

[9] For a doctrinal discusion of this issue, see the chapter in this book by Muhammad Sani Umar, note 27.

*The Izala movement*

The *Jama'at izalat al-bid'a wa iqamat al-sunna* (Movement for Suppressing Innovations and Restoring the Sunna) was founded in Jos, Nigeria, in 1978 by Isma'il Idris, a former career soldier, with the support of Shaikh Abubakar Gumi, who had close ties with Saudi Arabia. Despite difficulties, *Izala* has managed to establish itself in many northern Nigerian cities,[10] whence it is now spreading to Maradi.

The *Izala*'s success has riled both the Qadiriyya and Tijaniyya. Major *marabout* families in Maradi oppose these reformers, who dare to challenge their power and criticize the holiness of their religious practices. Tension between, on the one hand, *Izala* members and, on the other, the *kabalu* and *sadalu* (joined together under the circumstances) reached such a point that the prefect and mayor summoned representatives on 5 November 1990, "to promote understanding and calm tempers." After a long, "very lively" debate, participants agreed to observe a few rules, in particular: not to preach sermons in public, not to sell cassettes of sermons, not to listen to such cassettes in the mosques, and not to go preaching from village to village. The religious peace following this meeting did not last long.

The *yan izala*, as they are called in Hausa, act like new "jihadists." Advantageously combining religion with business and social affairs, their doctrine is an ideology "tailor-made to fit" young, rich *alhazai*.[11] The *Izala* preach an authentic Islam and forbid the surviving beliefs and customs of traditional religions. A *marabout* told me,

> "We must fight animism and those who interpret the Qur'an improperly and do not practise it as it was written by the Prophet. We must get rid of the additions [innovations not prescribed in the Qur'an] and of the intermediaries between God, the Prophet and mankind. By installing intermediaries, the *sadalu* and *kabalu* have acted like animists, who saw spirits (*iskoki*) as intermediaries for communicating with the gods."

As this fierce attack against the Islamic brotherhoods indicates, there are major doctrinal disagreements between them and the *Izala*.[12] But the disagreement is not just doctrinal: it also reaches out into practices (the scheduling and length of daily prayers, distinct places of worship etc.). In this respect the *Izala* movement, like Wahhabism in

[10] *Ibid.*

[11] This is how J.-L. Amselle has described similar developments in Bamako, Mali. See Amselle, "Bamako s'arabise" in the special issue "Capitales de la couleur" of *Autrement* (Paris), 9 Oct. 1984, pp. 192-7.

[12] O. Kane, "Les mouvements religieux et le champ politique au Nigeria septentrional. Le cas du réformisme musulman à Kano," *Islam et sociétés au sud du Sahara* (Paris), no. 4 (1990), pp. 7-24.

Mali, can be said to be fundamentally opposed to the religious practices of the *marabouts*. Its followers criticize *marabouts* for their power and occult practices, for their quackery and for dealing in amulets and charms (still used in Maradi for obtaining success in work, business or love and for healing purposes). They condemn the *marabouts* as parasites living on society through such heathen practices.

Young merchants who are part of the *Izala* movement no longer send their children to Qur'anic schools. Instead, they have set up *madrasas* (known locally in French as *médersas*) for modern education in Arabic. During an interview, Alhaji Dan Tchadaoua, leader of the *Izala* in Maradi (and a rich importer-exporter), insisted on the need to develop education "which must be at the base of Islam." He criticized his elders, the wealthy *alhazai* of the 1970s and 1980s, who "put the cart before the horse" by building mosques all over the city instead of opening *madrasas* and covering the costs of teachers there. Instead of offering pilgrimages to Mecca, he continued, they should have provided material assistance to help people develop their businesses so that they could later pay for pilgrimages out of their own pockets.[13] Members of *Izala* advocate limiting the often considerable sums spent on marriages (dowries) and baptisms, charging that such expenses are a waste of money.

*Izala* represents the emergence of a new expression of Islam in Maradi, which is supported by a new generation of *alhazai*, whose conceptions of society and social relations differ from those of their elders. In their eyes Hausa society is too hierarchical, and consequently they challenge the power and authority of the elders. For example, they do not kneel in the presence of their father, mother, father-in-law, mother-in-law or any other person who must be respected because of age or social status. Traditionalists castigate them for breaking customs of this sort.

As has long been the case among wealthy Hausa families, however, the wives of these fundamentalists are supposed to live in seclusion at home; they may go out only if they wear a black veil and are dressed properly.

Many of these *alhazai* are the sons or former wards (*barwai*) of very rich Maradi merchants, who have helped them make a start in business. They persuade young migrants from the countryside to join *Izala*, and may even offer them work. This movement also recruits among school-leavers in Maradi, who see its doctrine as a form of

[13]This merchant recently offered 500,000 CFA francs (the cost of a pilgrimage to Mecca) to a *marabout* from Zinder who had won a national prize for his knowledge of the Qur'an.

Islam better adapted to the modern world. Opponents maintain that young people are attracted to *Izala* with offers of money, which some allege comes from Saudi Arabia via Nigeria, and that they are then paid to spread the new doctrine. Whether this accusation is true or not, more and more people seem to be joining the movement.

Many of these *alhazai* live in the residential part of the new Zaria quarter (also called *Izalawa*). They meet during the daytime at a place called Saudia, where they can handle affairs without being disturbed by city life or beggars and where they are building a mosque. They thus seem to be setting themselves apart from the city.

This reformist movement also has a quite different conception of money. Like other merchants in Maradi, with whom they do business, the *Izala alhazai* are involved in trade, particularly with Nigeria. Belonging to different religious groups does not stand in the way of business. But whereas their elders are ostentatious and redistribute earnings widely among clients, *marabouts* and the poor, the *Izala alhazai* have a reputation of keeping their money for themselves, of being tight-fisted. This represents a significant change of mentality. In the Sudanic and Sahelian cultures of West Africa,[14] traditional values condemn the accumulation and enjoyment of wealth by oneself. Acquiring riches is justified only if one redistributes part of them; the only reason for being wealthy is to show off one's wealth through prestigious expenditure, so as to position oneself in the social hierarchy. The *Izala* ideology runs against this conception, since it preaches individualism and a rational utilization of wealth.

Although religious cleavages run through the Muslim community in Maradi, they do not extend to the business world. A *marabout* explained, "You can do business with anybody; what's important is to earn a profit." Another went even further: "Money has no smell, and you can, indeed, do business with non-Muslims, with Christians for example." Nonetheless, one is reluctant to extend credit outside one's own group. A *marabout* told me that a *sadalu* or *kabalu* merchant avoids lending money to an *Izala*, because the latter can use the loan as a way of pressuring the lender to join the movement. Although business transcends religious affiliation, the latter does come into play in client networks. For example, a *sadalu* or *kabalu alhaji* will hire men (dependent traders, cooks, drivers, laborers etc.) who share his religious views. Likewise, young *Izala* bosses will only hire persons who agree to join their movement, and in this way they obtain new recruits in exchange for jobs.

[14] J.-L. Amselle and E. Grégoire, "Etat et capitalisme en Afrique de l'Ouest," (Paris: Document de travail, l'EHESS, 1988).

*Conclusion*

Islam is still a sign of distinction for Hausa traders in Niger as well as northern Nigeria.[15] In Maradi, Islam began growing, along with trade, during the colonial period. Nowadays, the city has become a commercial and religious center with, as a result, a burgeoning economy and population. In a study of migrations, Herry[16] has written:

> This is a specific, essential aspect of migration toward Maradi: the importance of migrations related to Islam in this area. This can be considered to be one of the major factors in the city's growth and socio-economic development.

Trade, too, attracts migrants to come and take their chances in the city.

As it has spread, Islam has adapted remarkably well to Hausa norms and customs, and even reinterpreted some of them. In Maradi, Islam is now religiously, economically and socially predominant. Through it merchants have created a sense of identity that has taken various forms over the years, the most recent being membership in the *Izala* movement.

The *Izala* ideology tends to rationalize religious practices (by rejecting pagan customs, the attribution of supernatural powers to *marabouts*, and all practices that are "not written"), social relations (by challenging tradition and customary authorities) and conceptions of money. Although, until recently, ostentation as well as the redistribution and enjoyment of wealth were frequently practised by the *alhazai* (and still are by the oldest among them), the young *alhazai* favorable to *Izala* prohibit such practices. Abstaining from enjoyment, they prefer putting wealth to more rational uses. For this reason they have become unpopular. They are often called "young rich kids," "people who want to get ahead quick" and "pampered children," because many of them come from well-to-do families. Apparently, the *Izala* ideology is to the Islamic brotherhoods what Protestantism is to Catholicism.[17]

[15]See I. Tahir, "Scholars, Sufis, Saints and Capitalism in Kano, 1904-1974," unpubl. Ph.D. thesis, University of Cambridge, 1975; and A.U. Dan Asabe, "Comparative Biographies of Selected Leaders of the Kano Commercial Establishment," unpubl. MA thesis, Bayero University (Kano), 1987.

[16]C. Herry, "Croissance urbaine et santé à Maradi (Niger). Caractéristiques démographiques, phénomènes migratoires," (GRID, University of Bordeaux II, 1990).

[17]M. Weber, *L'éthique protestante et l'esprit du capitalisme* (Paris, 1967).

*Izala* provides a framework for the increasing individualism which is appearing in response to the need to adjust to new cultural, social, economic and political contexts. The *Izala* doctrine, which so advantageously combines religion and business, may constitute a new form of Islam that is better adapted to meeting the modern world's economic and social requirements. Personal senses of identity do change over time, as we have seen. But, despite current efforts, the *Izala* movement will probably have trouble spreading into rural areas, where tradition is still strong.

# THE INFLUENCE OF THE NIASS TIJANIYYA IN THE NIGER-BENUE CONFLUENCE AREA OF NIGERIA

*Ahmed Rufai Mohammed*

*Introduction*

In the nineteenth century, the Niger-Benue confluence area consisted of a number of communities, some of which were powerful kingdoms. These included Igala, Panda, Lokoja, Ebiraland and Idoma. The appearance of Islam in the region was relatively recent, compared with its northern neighbours of Hausaland and Borno. It was probably in the 1680s that the first Muslims came to Igalaland, the most powerful state in the region, but these Muslim pioneers are better remembered for their magical practices than for their devotion to religion or proselytization. The region did not come under the direct influence of the Sokoto Caliphate, so that it remained largely non-Islamic during the nineteenth century, although the various important markets of the region, such as Ejule, Panda, Gbobe and Lokoja, attracted some Muslim elements from the Caliphate and Borno. But with the profound changes which were initiated by the British presence from the turn of the century, the Muslim presence became increasingly important, and with Islam came the Tijaniyya brotherhood.

The Tijaniyya is by far the most popular Sufi order in the Niger-Benue confluence region, where it was introduced from the North by itinerant scholars. It first established a foothold in Lokoja, from where it spread to other parts of the region. Proselytization for the "reformed" Tijaniyya under the leadership of Shaikh Ibrahim Niass, known as the "Reformer of the Age" and the "Khalifah of the Order," began in the region in 1949. This paper seeks to compare the impact of the Niass Tijaniyya upon the religio-social life of the Muslim community with that of the earlier form of the brotherhood.

*The popular appeal of the Tijaniyya*

Well over 80 per cent of Muslims in the Niger-Benue region belong to the Tijaniyya brotherhood; the Qadiriyya order is virtually non-existent in the area. It is therefore appropriate to begin by examining the factors which are responsible for the popularity of the Tijaniyya order.

Although prospective members might have been attracted to the Tijaniyya because of the prospects for material benefits, other aspects of the order seem to have played a more important role in bringing in recruits. Certainly the fact that the Tijaniyya recognizes and encourages material acquisition as well as the necessity for members to render material help to one another might have been an attraction. And although none of those interviewed claimed that they had joined the order principally for material benefit, there is no doubt that membership facilitated trade and commercial transactions, especially for those who carried out their business dealings in a city like Kano. On the other hand, the majority of the rural adherents to the Tijaniyya were farmers, and for them there were other inducements to join the order. One should also note that there was no insistence upon the seclusion of women in the order, especially in the Niass branch, which may also have been an attraction for rural populations in which women generally contribute significantly to the economic activities of the household.

Most of the itinerant scholars who propagated Islam in the area were themselves Tijanis, and therefore it was only natural that those who accepted Islam through them should emulate them and join the order. The Tijaniyya also appealed to non-literate Muslims, because although its religious rules placed a considerable devotional burden on its members, requiring them to recite the *wazifa* once a day, the *lazim* twice a day, and to attend the *hailala* every Friday, the order was non-élitist in that there were no intellectual qualifications or prerequisites for membership. The litanies were not complicated and were easier for non-literate persons to master than those of the Qadiriyya.[1]

The Tijaniyya seems to have held different attractions for the literate and non-literate. The majority of ordinary members, when asked why they had joined the order, emphasized the promise of salvation in the hereafter. The founder of the order, Shaikh Ahmad al-Tijani, offered an absolute guarantee of salvation for all members of the order, a guarantee which according to him came from the Prophet himself. He also asserted that whoever "performs the *salat al-fatih* once is guaranteed the bliss of the two abodes ... and performing it once is equivalent to the prayers of all the angels."[2] In fact, a member of the order is required to perform the *salat al-fatih* 250 times a day. Many members of the order pointed to the content of these litanies, in which one asks forgiveness from Allah repeatedly, as an indication of the reality of the salvation which has been promised to them. They also claim to have been guaranteed paradise for their parents and children as well as themselves. Although these beliefs are considered heretical by orthodox Muslims, and constitute the basis for the

[1]A. Abubakar, *al-Thaqāfat al-'arabiyya fī Nījīriyā* (Beirut, 1972), pp. 209-302.
[2]J.M. Abun Nasr, *The Tijaniyya* (London, 1965), p. 52.

condemnation of the order, they have helped in no small measure in attracting members to the Tijaniyya. Indeed, this is a wise strategy for conversion, especially among people who usually nurse great concern for the fate of their parents who were not Muslim.

Scholars in the order, on the other hand, explained their adherence to it in terms of their conviction that the Tijaniyya had come to strengthen the practice of Islam. As al-Hajj Danladi of Lokoja maintains:

> Shaikh Ahmad al-Tijani was given the *tariqa* to strengthen Islam. Before an initiate is accepted into the order he is first admonished to continue to be strict in observing the five pillars of Islam.[3]

The *mallams* feel that there is no way a member of the Tijaniyya can conduct his daily litanies without first performing his obligatory prayers, since the recitation of the litanies, which must be strictly observed, follows the prayers. This conviction on the part of the scholars that a Muslim needs to be a member of the Tijaniyya to ensure strict observation of the obligatory prayers encouraged them to propagate the order with the zeal which led to its success in the area.

Another very important feature of the order is the "trans-ethnic nature of its authority structure and community membership ... [which leads to] the reinforcement of a broader identity based on religious affiliation."[4] The Ebira, for instance, whose social organization was clan based, found in the Tijaniyya an excellent mechanism for uniting the members of different clans. The *muqaddam* of the order, irrespective of his own clan, enjoyed acceptance and reverence from the members of the order who belonged to different clans. Their membership in the Tijaniyya or *ezi ani dariqa* (the people of the path), tended to supersede other affiliations. In Lokoja, the brotherhood also furthered unity and cooperation among different ethnic groups because the membership of a *zawiya* was usually multi-ethnic, including Hausa, Nupe, Yoruba, Ebira, Igala and others.

When the movement of Shaikh Ibrahim Niass reached the Niger-Benue confluence area, it superseded all other branches of the order. The majority of those who were already Tijanis simply shifted their allegiance to his chain of initiatic authority. A central factor in this changeover was the belief that he was the *ghaith al-zaman*, the "Reformer of the Age." Leading Muslim scholars interviewed

[3] Interview with Sharif Danladi, Lokoja, February 1983.
[4] J.N. Paden, *Religion and Political Culture in Kano* (Berkeley, 1973), p. 106.

expressed their view that Shaikh Ibrahim was the "Reformer of the Age" not only for the Tijanis but for all the Muslims of the world.[5]

Mervin Hiskett has stressed race as a factor in Shaikh Ibrahim's appeal. In his view, the fact that the Shaikh, an African and a black man, had been selected by God as the holiest man on earth was a crucial factor in his ability to attract African Muslims to his following.[6] The Shaikh himself gave credence to this assertion by stressing in his *Kashf al-Ilbās* that black bodies were not prevented from coming near to God if they were those upon whom God had chosen to bestow favour.[7] The elaborate reception prepared for Shaikh Ibrahim on his first visit to Okene in 1953, which included the massing of people from all over the region and their public recitation of *dhikr*, did much to reinforce his reputation for charisma and the people's belief in his qualities as a "saviour."[8] These events attracted many people to both Islam and the Tijaniyya.[9] In fact, many men whose wives gave birth to male children around the period of Shaikh Ibrahim's visit (inlcuding some non-Muslims) named them Shehu Ibrahim.[10]

### *The pre-Niass Tijaniyya in the Niger-Benue confluence area*

Lokoja town, which was founded in 1860 by the British at the meeting point of the Niger and Benue rivers, grew into an important centre of Islamic learning, and it also played a leading role in the spread of the Tijaniyya in the region. A number of factors were responsible for this development. By the 1870s, Lokoja had grown into an important commercial centre for European manufactures, and it also served as a market for the kola trade.[11] It thus attracted traders including some Muslim scholars from the Sokoto Caliphate and Borno. During the British colonial occupation of the northern part of Nigeria at the turn

[5]Interviews with Shaikh Ahmad Rufai, Okene, August 1979; al-Hajj Shuaibu Abubakar Kenchi and Yusuf Abdullahi, Lokoja, July 1981; and Abubakar Liman, Ankpa, August 1981.

[6]M. Hiskett, "The Community of Grace and its Opponents, the Rejecters: A Debate about Theology and Mysticism in Muslim West Africa with special Reference to its Hausa Expression," *African Language Studies*, vol. XVII (1980), p. 109.

[7]*Ibid.*

[8]Interviews with Sidi Rilwan, Idah, September 1981; Ahmad Rufai, Okene, August 1979, and Abubakar Liman, Ankpa, August 1981.

[9]This is the opinion of many informants in Okene.

[10]One such non-Muslim parent was Aneika who lived in Okeneba quarter. He later converted to Islam along with all his children and brothers, and he took the name of Salahu.

[11]P. Lovejoy, *Caravans of Kola. The Hausa Kola Trade 1700-1900* (Zaria, 1980), p. 119.

of the century, most of the deposed emirs, some of whom were themselves Tijanis, along with some Tijani scholars, were banished to Lokoja. The town therefore became one of the first places in the Niger-Benue region to come into contact with adherents of the Tijaniyya order. Before the appearance of the Niass movement, two other chains of initiatic authority had been present in Lokoja, the 'Umarian and a Maghribi branch of the order.

Although Mallam Jiyya, a Nupe from Bida, has been identified as introducing the Tijaniyya into Lokoja,[12] the first *zawiya* in the town was built in 1904 by Muhammad al-Bashir, son of the jihadist al-Hajj 'Umar. Ahmad Shehu, the brother of al-Bashir and successor to al-Hajj 'Umar, led a group of Tukolor Tijanis into the Sokoto Caliphate in 1895, following defeat at the hands of the French. When Ahmad Shehu died in 1898, Muhammad al-Bashir became the leader of the Tukolor Tijani community in the Caliphate.[13] Al-Bashir fought on the side of the deposed Sultan of Sokoto against the British at Bormi in 1903, and following their defeat was exiled to Lokoja.[14]

During his exile in Lokoja, Muhammad al-Bashir propagated the Tijaniyya from his *zawiya*, which still exists in the Kabawa quarter of the town.[15] Thus, the first Sufi *zawiya* which was built in Lokoja (and in the Niger-Benue confluence area) was from the 'Umarian branch of the Tijaniyya. However, Muhammad al-Bashir propagated the order by peaceful means, and not in the militant form which had characterized his father's movement. Although al-Bashir encouraged people to join the order, he does not seem to have contemplated granting the office of *muqaddam* to any *mallam* in Lokoja. Since there is no evidence to show that he granted the title of *muqaddam* to anyone while he was alive, or any evidence that anyone requested the office from him, one might assume that the number of initiates was not sufficient to require more than one *muqaddam* at the time. This failure to appoint *muqaddams* must have accounted for the limited spread of his own branch of the order.

Mallam 'Abd as-Salam,[16] a renowned scholar and early propagator of Islam in the region, had been a student of al-Bashir, although he

[12]Interview with Ibrahim Najirgi, Lokoja, August 1981.

[13]B.O. Oloruntimehin, *The Segu Tukolor Empire* (London, 1972), p. 322.

[14]*Ibid.*, p. 323, and J.N. Paden, "The Influence of Political Elites on Political and Community Integration in Kano," unpubl. Ph.D. thesis, Harvard University, 1968, p. 237.

[15]Interviews with Hajiyya Zainab, Yusuf Abdullahi, Ibrahim Najirgi and S.A. Kenchi, Lokoja, August 1981.

[16]'Abd as-Salam was the son of Mallam Abubakar, who had accompanied Mallam Ibrahim Nagwamatse, Emir of Kontagora, into exile in Lokoja in 1902. Abubakar

obtained his title of *muqaddam* from a Maghribi *shaikh* from Fez called Sayyidi Muhammad, popularly known in Lokoja as Sidi Momoh.[17] It is not clear whether 'Abd as-Salam was initiated into the Tijaniyya by al-Bashir. Hajiyya Zainab, the daughter of al-Bashir, claims that her father initiated him, while 'Abd as-Salam's son, al-Hajj Ibrahim Najirgi, says that Mallam Jiyya initiated him. What is certain is that 'Abd as-Salam did not become a *muqaddam* until the arrival of Sayyidi Muhammad in 1917. His *silsila*, or spirtual chain of authority, is as follows:[18]

Ahmad al-Tijani (1782-1815)
↓
Muhammad al-Kabir
↓
Sayyid 'Abd al-Karim b. Muhammad al-Arabiyya
↓
Sayyidi Ahmad
↓
Sayyidi Muhammad (Sidi Momoh)
↓
'Abd as-Salam b. Abubakar (1917-34)
↓
Sherif Muhammad b. Ahmad Zangina (1934-66)
↓
Ibrahim Najirgi 'Abd as-Salam (1966-88)
↓
Suleiman b. 'Abd as-Salam (1988-present)

'Abd as-Salam built his *zawiya* in 1917,[19] and in 1920 Mawlay 'Umar, who is said to have come from Timbuktu, persuaded him to convert his stalk structure into a mud one. Both Mawlay 'Umar and Sayyidi Muhammad were international itinerant Tijani *muqaddams* who were among those suspected by the British in 1924 of being agents of a controversial Tijani leader known as Muhammad Alawi, who was located in Casablanca. Although he claimed to be a descendant of 'Ali b. Abi Talib, he was thought by the British to be of Jewish origin.[20]

---

founded the first Qur'anic school in Lokoja, which was later expanded by 'Abd as-Salam.

[17]Interveiw with Ibrahim Najirgi, Lokoja, August 1981.

[18]Ibrahim Najirgi supplied this *silsila* to the writer in August 1981. The dates refer to the period during which each of them presided over the *zawiya*, which was built by 'Abd as-Salam in 1917. Ibrahim Najirgi died in 1988, and was succeeded as head of the *zawiya* by his younger brother, Suleiman.

[19]This date was given by Ibrahim Najirgi as 1338 AH.

[20]Nigerian National Archives, Kaduna (NAK), ZARPROF, c4013, Tijani.

It was believed in official circles that Alawi had established representatives or *muqaddam* in many of the towns of Nigeria, including Lokoja, to carry out anti-British propaganda. The Tijaniyya was also suspected at the time of having some connections with the Bolsheviks in a conspiracy against British imperial hegemony. The British were paranoid about all *tariqas* during this period, but especially the Tijaniyya and the Mahdiyya. In 1923, the Mahdist leader in Nigeria, Sa'id b. Hayyatu, was banished to Lokoja, thence to Makurdi, Enugu, Port Harcourt, Victoria, and finally to Buea in British Cameroon.[21]

In 1925, an official investigation into the activities of the leader of this alleged Tijani, anti-British propaganda was carried out by the Secretary of the Northern Provinces. The Secretary requested that the Resident of Zaria Province furnish the government with information about a certain Mallam Sayyidi, who was reported to be Alawi's agent, or *wakili*, in Lokoja.[22] According to the Resident's information, Mallam Sayyidi had resided in Zaria in a house given him by the emir Aliyu Dansidi, who had been deposed in 1920 and, following a brief exile in Ankpa, sent to Lokoja in 1923. Sayyidi had himself moved to Lokoja in 1917, where he was still living. The Resident added that it was not known whether Sayyidi had any connection with Muhammad Alawi, or whether he was then acting as his agent.[23] Lokoja informants confirm that Sayyidi Muhammad had come there at the invitation of the *Maigari*, Muhammad Maikarfi, who reigned between 1916 and 1921, and was an agent of the United African Company. He was also well-known for his generous hospitality, especially to itinerant scholars.[24]

Although there can be no doubt that Sayyidi Muhammad was a Tijani *shaikh* who was propagating the order from place to place, it has not been possible to establish any connection between him and the anti-British propaganda allegedly disseminated by Alawi. Sayyidi Muhammad was highly revered in Lokoja, both as a guest of the chief and because of the quality of his spiritual chain of authority. None of his contemporaries who were interviewed were aware that he was involved in any way in anti-government propaganda. When he died in 1951, he was buried beside the grave of his former host, *sarki* Muhammad Maikarfi.[25]

[21]Tomlinson and Lethem, *History of Islamic Propaganda in Nigeria* (London, 1927), p. 18; and interview with al-Hajj Garba Sa'id, Kano, November 1982.
[22]NAK, ZARPROF, c4013, Tijani.
[23]*Ibid.*
[24]Interviews with Ibrahim Najirgi and S.A. Kenchi, Lokoja, August 1981.
[25]*Ibid.*

Mallam 'Abd as-Salam's elevation to the office of *muqaddam* contributed to the popularization of the Tijaniyya in Lokoja and neighbouring areas. This was due both to his fame as a scholar and to the sanctity of his spiritual chain of authority. He founded one of the largest Qur'anic and *'ilm* schools in Lokoja, which attracted students from the towns of the Niger-Benue, and as far away as Ikare in the western part of the country, Auchi and Jattu in the present Bendel state, and Kano. The Tijaniyya was therefore spread through his many students. One of these was a Hausa scholar-trader called 'Umar Falke, whose father sent him from Kano to study under 'Abd as-Salam in Lokoja.[26] 'Umar Falke subsequently studied various Tijani and Sunni books under Sharif Muhammad b. Ahmad Zangina, who was also from Kano and who succeeded 'Abd as-Salam as *muqaddam* of the order and head of the *zawiya*. 'Umar Falke was also appointed a *muqaddam* by Sharif Zangina, whom Falke described as the "bank of the brotherhood river, and a *mujtahid* in the propagation of the order."[27] Sharif Zangina had taken the Tijaniyya to many places in the region, including Nassarawa, Keffi, Jattu and Auchi.

There was a strong link between Lokoja and the spread of the Tijaniyya in the Niger-Benue area. The first Tijani adherent in Ebiraland was the local chief, *Attah* Ibrahim, who was initiated by an itinerant scholar from Zaria who used to stop in Okene on his way through Lokoja to the Afenmai area in the present Bendel state.[28] The *Attah* later introduced his son Abdulmalik and the latter's friend Ahmad Rufai to the order. Both of them were destined later to propagate the order in Ebiraland. According to Ahmad Rufai, the *Attah* used to invite him and Abdulmalik to sit with him on Fridays when he performed the *hailala* litany alone, although they hardly understood what was going on.[29]

In 1931, Ahmad Rufai was posted as a tax scribe to Lokoja, where he seized the opportunity to further his education in the Islamic sciences, and it was in Lokoja, on 14 May 1931, that he was granted the title of *muqaddam* in the Tijaniyya by one Mallam Gali. He also managed to obtain the major Tijani book, *Jawāhir al-ma'ānī* by 'Ali Harazim b. Barada, a close companion to the founder of the order.

[26]A. Muhammad, "A Hausa Scholar-Trader and his Library Collection: the Case Study of 'Umar Farke of Kano, Nigeria," unpubl. Ph.D. thesis, Northwestern University, 1976, p. 52.

[27]*Ibid.*, pp. 86 and 305.

[28]Interviews with Ahmad Rufai and Lawal 'Abd as-Salam, Okene, August 1979.

[29]*Ibid.* For further information on Ahmad Rufai and Abdulmalik , see A.R. Muhammad, "The popular phase of Islam in Ebiraland, Nigeria: the Roles of Sheikh Ahmed Rufai and al-Hajj Abdulmalik," *Islam et Sociétés au Sud du Sahara*, no. 6 (1992).

From this book Ahmad Rufai came to understand the spiritual values and conditions of the order, which he claimed further convinced him of the truth of the brotherhood's teachings, and he subsequently became more committed to attracting people to membership.[30]

On his return to Ebiraland, Ahmad Rufai began a proselytization campaign in order to convert people to Islam as well as to initiate some of the new converts into the Tijaniyya. While in Lokoja, he had learned that the Tijanis conducted their litanies in groups twice per day, and so he now encouraged the new initiates to attend the daily *wazifa* and the Friday *hailala* sessions in a group under his leadership. However, whenever he was absent on tax-collection duties for the Native Authority, this group practice would be suspended for want of a *muqaddam* to lead it.

Upon his return from his studies in Bida in 1936, Abdulmalik actively gave his support to the order, which attracted even more new members. He subsequently suggested that the Friday evening litany sessions, the *hailala*, be conducted at the Okeneba mosque, and Shaikh Ahmad agreed to bring his followers there from his *zawiya* in Idoji quarter. Eventually, with the increasing number of Muslims and Tijani adherents, the mosque was enlarged.

As the number of Tijani adherents increased, Shaikh Ahmad also appointed *muqaddams* for a number of district mosques, including Obehira, Okengwen, Eganyi and Ogori.[31] However, the first Tijani *muqaddam* at Ihima, al-Hajj Muhammad Sani Onitira, was initiated into the order by Shaikh Abdur-Rahman in Ibadan where he was trading in Islamic books in the 1930s. When, on his return home in the early 1940s, he decided to introduce the group litany sessions at Ikuehi/Ihima, he invited both Shaikh Ahmad Rufai and al-Hajj Abdulmalik to open his *zawiya*.[32]

The Tijaniyya brotherhood was introduced into Igalaland during the first decades of the twentieth century by immigrant scholars, most of whom came from Lokoja, or had some connection with the Tijaniyya there. The first *muqaddam* to build a *zawiya* at Dekina was Mallam Muhammad Bello, a Hausa from Kano who had reportedly been appointed *muqaddam* in Lokoja. He was prominent among the Muslim scholars who settled in Dekina; he taught both Qur'anic and

[30]Interviews with Ahmad Rufai and Lawal 'Abd as-Salam, Okene, August 1979.

[31]Information confirmed by the *muqaddams* of these localities.

[32]Interviews with Muhammad Sani Onitira, Ihima, and al-Hajj 'Abd as-Salam, the Chief Imam of Obehira, July 1982.

advanced Islamic studies. He initiated many Muslims in Dekina and the surrounding villages into the Tijaniyya.[33]

The Tijaniyya was introduced into Idah and Ankpa by Abu Keffi, although not much is known about him, except that he was the first *muqaddam* at Idah and later appointed as *muqaddam* in Ankpa Mallam Muhammad Idris, a Nupe scholar who had been initiated into the Tijaniyya in Bida before he went to Igalaland. It was probably in the 1920s that he established the first Tijani *zawiya* at Ankpa, which is still the largest in the town. The activities of the *zawiya* influenced the diffusion of the brotherhood into neighbouring villages in the decades that followed. When Muhammad Idris died in 1953, he was the Chief Imam of Ankpa; shortly before his death he bequeathed his responsibilities as *muqaddam* to his eldest son, al-Hajj Abubakar Liman.[34] It was under Liman's leadership that a strong link was developed between Ankpa, Lokoja and the Niass leadership in Kaolack.

### *The difference between the 'Umarian and the Niass Tijaniyya*

The Tijaniyya first entered West Africa via Mauritania through the good offices of Muhammad al-Hafiz b. al-Mukhtar b. Habib al-Baddi. Even before the death of the founder, Ahmad al-Tijani, Muhammad al-Hafiz had brough the Idaw 'Ali ethnic group in Mauritania into affiliation with the Tijaniyya.[35] The order also extended into northern Senegal through his influence. However, it is al-Hajj 'Umar b. Sa'id al-Futi ('Umar Tal, 1794-1864) who was responsible for the extensive proselytization by the order in West Africa during the nineteenth century. 'Umar Tal, a Tukolor from the Senegal river valley, was appointed *muqaddam* of the order in 1826 by Sidi Muhammad al-Ghali, *khalifah* of Ahmad al-Tijani in the Hijaz.[36] After spending four years in Mecca and Medina under the spiritual guidance of Sidi Muhammad, 'Umar Tal was appointed the *khalifah* of Ahmad al-Tijani for the whole of the western Sudan.

On his return from Mecca, 'Umar arrived in Borno in 1833 where he entered into doctrinal dispute with Shaikh Muhammad al-Kanemi about the belief held by the Tijanis that Ahmad al-Tijani was the seal

[33]Interviews with al-Hajj Zakari Bawa, Abdulmumin Maiyaki and al-Hajj Abdulkadir Adejo, Dekina, September 1981.

[34]Interview with al-Hajj Abubakar Liman, Ankpa, August 1981.

[35]Abun-Nasr, *The Tijaniyya*, p. 108; and O. Jah, "Sufism and the nineteenth-century Jihad Movements in the Western Sudan: a Case Study of al-Hajj 'Umar al-Futi's Philosophy of Jihad and its Sufi Bases," unpubl. Ph.D. thesis, McGill University, 1973, pp. 131-2.

[36]Jah, *Sufism*, p. 136.

of the saints.[37] He left Borno and passed through Kano to Sokoto, where he remained for five years as the guest of Sultan Muhammad Bello. It is believed in some circles that 'Umar Tal converted Muhammad Bello to the Tijaniyya before the latter's death in 1837, but the evidence remains inconclusive.[38] Unlike the Tijani leadership in North Africa, which did not show any political ambition in its propagation of the order, 'Umar Tall's conception of the order involved both spiritual and temporal authority. Having seen the example of successful *jihad* in Sokoto, he left for the Senegal region to launch his own *jihad* with the intention of creating "a state based on the archetype of Islamic society and government, and to raise the practice of Islam to the level of the ideal according to the tenets of the Tijaniyya."[39] His *jihad* succeeded in bringing a large number of people into the brotherhood. All the administrative headquarters under his authority also became the spiritual centres from where the leading *muqaddams* appointed by 'Umar directed the affairs of the brotherhood.[40]

If al-Hajj 'Umar had regarded himself as the *khalifah* of the Tijaniyya in the nineteenth-century western Sudan, Shaikh Ibrahim Niass presented himself as the *khalifah* for twentieth-century West Africa. His emergence as a leader of a new branch of the Tijaniyya began in the 1920s when he decided to establish his own *zawiya* in Medina-Kaolack (Senegal), separate from that of his brother, successor to their father, Abdullahi Niass. In 1937, Ibrahim was appointed *khalifah* of the order by Shaikh Ahmad Sukairij in Fez.[41] This appointment, as well as his claim to be the "Reformer of the Age" and the Seal of the Seal of the Saints, *Khatim khatim al-awliya*,[42] explains his popularity in West Africa, including Nigeria, Ghana, the Gambia and Equatorial Guinea. He was respected by the multitude of his followers everywhere as "scholar, mystic, master of medicine and reformer of Islam."[43] His followers believed that association with him guaranteed their salvation in the world hereafter. In his teachings,

[37] *Ibid.*, p. 136.

[38] M. Last, *The Sokoto Caliphate* (London, 1967), pp. 218-9; and L.C. Behrman, *Muslim Brotherhoods and Politics in Senegal* (Cambridge, MA, 1970), p. 19.

[39] Oloruntimehim, *The Segu Tukolor Empire*, p. 316.

[40] Louis Brenner, *West African Sufi: The Religious Heritage and Spiritual Search of Cerno Bokar Saalif Taal* (London, 1984), p. 42.

[41] *Ibid.*, p. 51.

[42] Tijanis believe in the existence of various categories of saints. Shaikh Ahmad al-Tijani was the Seal of the Saints who had permission to found a *tariqa*. After him, another gate of saints opened, those with intuitive and pure knowledge of God but who did not receive permission to found a *tariqa*. Shaikh Ibrahim was the seal of this class of saints, and is therefore referred to as the Seal of the Seal of the Saints. Interview with Alhaji Usman Bashir, Kano, July 1992.

[43] Paden, "The Influence of Political Elites," p. 97.

Shaikh Ibrahim stressed Sufi doctrines and the importance of modelling one's life on that of the Prophet.

The differences between the 'Umarian and Niass Tijaniyya were not ideological, and do not justify qualifying the latter as the "Reformed Tijaniyya," as John Paden has done.[44] Both al-Hajj 'Umar and Ibrahim Niass were Tijanis, and they adhered to the same Sufi doctrine while refraining from making any basic changes in the litanies of the order. The 'Umarian branch of course expanded through the militancy of *jihad*, whereas Ibrahim Niass not only proselytized peacefully, but insisted that the spiritual teachings of the order, known as *tarbiya*, should be made available even to those who could not read or write.[45] *Tarbiya* is a special way of gaining an intuitive knowledge of God which can only be experienced by a Sufi under the spiritual guidance of his *shaikh* or *muqaddam*. Previously, the brotherhoods had limited this spiritual training to literate adherents, or even to advanced scholars. *Tarbiya* was recognized as the most characteristic feature of the Niass Tijaniyya as it spread in the Niger-Benue area (and elsewhere in Africa).

Shaikh Ibrahim also taught that *tarbiya* should replace the spiritual retreat of *khalwa*; he wrote that "what we desire from the existence of *tarbiya* in the order is to be free from the necessity of *khalwa*."[46] It should be noted that the founder, Shaikh Ahmad al-Tijani, had not regarded *khalwa* as necessary for the spiritual enhancement of his followers; he claimed that the Prophet had ordered him to remain without solitude or isolation from the world. This assertion was the basis for Tijani confidence that "without forsaking the world they were more assured of salvation than the ascetic Sufis who spent their time in prayers and spiritual exercises because of the prophet's special prayers."[47] This attitude that Tijanis could engage fully in the activities of the world and still attain salvation was also used as a justification for the acquisition of wealth. According to Abun-Nasr, the relative prosperity of many Tijanis gave rise to the belief that Ahmad al-Tijani had not only guaranteed their salvation in the life to come, but also assured their wealth in this world.[48]

Shaikh Ibrahim always perfomed the obligatory prayers with his arms folded across his chest, *qabl*. This practice became a symbol of identity for his followers throughout West Africa. Both the 'Umarians, and non-Tijanis generally, pray with their arms at their

[44]*Ibid.*, p. 236.
[45]Hiskett, "The Community of Grace," p. 120.
[46]Quoted in *ibid.*, p. 120.
[47]Abun Nasr, *The Tijaniyya*, p. 46.
[48]*Ibid.*, p. 47.

sides. This difference in posture during prayer has led to serious disputes among the Muslim communities in Nigeria, including the Niger-Benue confluence.[49]

Another teaching of Shaikh Ibrahim which distinguished his followers from other Muslims was the prohibition of smoking. Smoking is neither directly prohibited nor encouraged by either the Qur'an or the *hadith*.

Finally, Shaikh Ibrahim placed special emphasis on the annual celebration of the birthday of the Prophet, the *maulud al-Nabi*. He considered this to be the most special night of the year, and set it aside for special preaching sessions (*wa'z*), which attracted pilgrims to Kaolack from all over West Africa, including Nigeria. Similar *maulud* celebrations were introduced into the Niger-Benue area as well.

### *Shaikh Ibrahim Niass and the popular phase of the Tijaniyya in the Niger-Benue region*

Although Shaikh Ibrahim Niass's link with Nigeria could be said to have been established in 1937 when he met the Emir of Kano, al-Hajj Abdullahi Bayero, in Mecca and renewed his Tijani *silsila*, the impact of these activities did not reach the Niger-Benue until 1949.[50] On his return from Mecca, Shaikh Ibrahim called at Fez, where the title of *khalifah* of the order was conferred upon him. He subsequently dispatched some of his leading disciples on a comprehensive tour of the major towns in West Africa to present the new *khalifah* to the people as the "Saviour of the Age."[51] One of these disciples was Shaikh Hadi, a *sharif* from Mauritania, who during 1948-9 undertook a major tour of the then Northern Region of Nigeria. In Kano, he met Shaikh Ahmad Rufai, who was there studying *tafsir* with Shaikh Atiku, a prominent Tijani leader.[52] Ahmad Rufai invited Shaikh Hadi to visit Okene, which he did in 1949, a journey which also took him to Lokoja.[53] Thus, Shaikh Hadi was the first to bring the message of the appearance

[49]For a doctrinal discussion of this dispute, see the chapter in this book by Muhammad Sani Umar, note 27. Similar conflicts have occurred elsewhere in Africa, for example in Mali where the Wahhabis pray with their arms in the *qabl* position; see the chapter by Louis Brenner.

[50]Interviews with Ahmad Rufai, Okene, August 1979, and S.A. Kenchi and al-Hajj Yusu Abdullahi, Lokoja, August 1981.

[51]According to P.B. Clarke, *West Africa and Islam* (London, 1982), p. 207, Shaikh Ibrahim declared himself the Saviour of the Age in 1930. He also declared himself to be the Reformer of the Age. Both claims are firmly believed by his followers.

[52]Paden, *Religion and Political Culture in Kano*, p. 97.

[53]Interviews with Ahmad Rufai, Okene, August 1979.

of Shaikh Ibrahim Niass as the "Reformer of the Age" to the people of the Niger-Benue confluence area.

According to Shaikh Hadi, upon hearing of the emergence of a "reformer" in Senegal, his people sent him there to confirm the news. He subsequently spent two years studying with Shaikh Niass, after which the latter appointed him as *khalifah*, or regional deputy.[54] It was then that Shaikh Hadi embarked on his tours to inform people of the appearance of the "Reformer of the Age," to initiate people into the order, to give *tarbiya* and to name appropriately qualified persons as *muqaddams*.[55]

While in Okene, Shaikh Hadi renewed the *silsila* of many Tijani members in the spiritual line of authority of Shaikh Ibrahim Niass, and he initiated many new converts to the order.[56] In Okene his host was al-Hajj Abdulmalik, who also arranged for him to stay with Shaikh Shuaibu Abubakar Kenchi in Lokoja. According to Kenchi, the entourage of Shaikh Hadi numbered forty-three persons, including those who followed him from Okene. In Lokoja, more than 5,000 Tijanis reportedly came to the Shaikh in order to renew their membership in the Tijaniyya, and he personally rewrote the *silsila* of a number of them.[57] Before his departure, Shaikh Hadi named Abubakar Kenchi *muqaddam*, entrusted him with a *tambari* or official seal of Shaikh Ibrahim Niass, and empowered him to rewrite the *silsila* of others who had renewed it during his visit.

Among the other leading scholars in Lokoja who received the Shaikh were al-Hajj Audu Dan Lele and al-Hajj Yusuf Abdullahi. But the leading Tijani *muqaddam* of the town, Sharif Muhammad b. Ahmad Zengina, neither renewed his *silsila*, nor even visited Shaikh Hadi, in spite of receiving an invitation from him. On the other hand, Sharif Zengina did not discourage any of his own followers from renewing their *silsila* if they wished to do so.[58]

A Tijani might choose to renew his *silsila* if his membership had lapsed through negligence or reluctance to carry out the required litanies of the order; or one could renew one's initiation with another popular

[54]Although the term *khalifa* literally means "successor," the Tijani use it in the sense of a deputy. Shaikh Niass appointed many of his outstanding disciples as *khalifas*, to act as regional deputies in the same manner that he had been appointed *khalifa* for all of West Africa. Shaikh Ahmad Rufai of Ebira and Yusuf Abdullahi of Lokoja, for example, claim to have been appointed *khalifas* by him.

[55]This information was given to his audience in Lokoja in 1949 when he explained his mission; interviews with S.A. Kenchi and Yusuf Abdullahi, Lokoja, August 1981.

[56]Interview with Ahmad Rufai, Okene, August 1979.

[57]Interviews with S.A. Kenchi and Yusuf Abdullahi, Lokoja, August 1981.

[58]*Ibid.*

*shaikh* for the purpose of enhancing one's position or status in the brotherhood.[59] A renewal by Sharif Zengina would have fallen within the second category, but in his case such an act might have had a counter-effect on his status in the order as a major proselytizer of the 'Umarian branch; by taking the Niass initiation he would be on an equal level with emerging young *muqaddams* like Abubakar Kenchi and Yusuf Abdullahi.

Having been launched by Shaikh Hadi, the Niass Tijaniyya was popularized and consolidated through the activity of the newly-appointed *muqaddams*. They did this through campaigns of initiation into the order, by the organization of religious ceremonies which were closely identified with the Niass Tijaniyya, and by sending members of the order on occasional visits to Kaolack, the home base of Shaikh Ibrahim Niass. Both al-Hajj Yusuf Abdullahi and Shaikh Abubakar Kenchi spearheaded the spread of the order from Lokoja into many Igala towns and villages across the River Niger. They made it a tradition to undertake itinerant visits throughout the region in order to educate Muslims about Islam and the Tijaniyya, to initiate new members into the order, and to renew the *silsila* of some members within the Niass branch of the brotherhood. Shaikh Ahmad Rufai did the same in Ebiraland.

An example of how this process worked can be seen with Abubakar Liman of Ankpa. During his visit to Okene in 1953, Shaikh Ibrahim Niass appointed Abubakar Liman *muqaddam* and authorized him to initiate persons into the order, which he subsequently began to do in Ankpa and its environs. He also hosted the visits of other *muqaddams* and *shaikhs* of the order, among the most regular and popular of whom were Abubakar Kenchi and Yusuf Abdullahi. During their visits, they would bring Abubakar Liman up to date on the recent publications of the brotherhood, and they would travel together to neighbouring villages to initiate new members. At one stage, Abubakar Liman obtained permission from Yusuf Abdullahi to grant the title of *muqaddam* to deserving Tijanis in the villages; Yusuf Abdullahi claimed to have received the authority to grant such permissions from Shaikh Niass when he was studying under him in the early 1950s. In August 1981, Abubakar Liman claimed to have appointed forty-four *muqaddams* in the Ankpa area.[60]

These initiatives were reinforced by three visits to the area by Shaikh Ibrahim Niass himself between 1953 and his death in 1975, and by the frequent visits of some of his leading disciples and some of his

[59] A. Muhammad, "A Hausa Scholar-Trader," p. 86.
[60] Interview with Abubakar Liman, Ankpa, August 1981.

children, a policy which has helped to maintain close contacts between Kaolack and the local Tijani communities, and which has continued until today. These visitors usually came first to Okene, then to Lokoja, and some of them would cross the river to Idah, Dekina and Ankpa. In each village, they would be hosted by local *muqaddam* and regarded as the guests of the entire Tijani community. They preached about Islam and the Tijaniyya in the mosques, and led the *salat* prayers and Tijani litanies. They also performed *tajdid* or renewal of membership in the order, initiated new members, and appointed as *muqaddam* those who were qualified. A few days after the arrival of these distinguished visitors, the Imam of each quarter mosque would collect voluntary donations from the community of his mosque in order to defray the costs of the visit. Any surplus would be given to the visiting *shaikh* as a gift or *sadaqa*.

*The Niass influence in the Niger-Benue confluence area*

Many aspects of Muslim religious life in the area have been influenced by the practices of the Niass Tijanis, and have contributed to the particular Muslim identity of the region.

*Tarbiya* is perhaps the most important identifying feature of the Niass Tijaniyya. It has become the great aspiration of Tijanis in the Niger-Benue confluence area to pass through the initiation of *tarbiya* and overcome the various spiritual hurdles which it requires. For them, it represents the highest level of the spiritual hierarchy in the order, and many non-literate Tijanis in the villages and towns of Ebiraland, Lokoja and Igalaland have been successfully initiated into it. They regard themselves as spiritually superior to non-initiates, and are so considered by the latter. This singular fact, that intellectualism is not the basic criterion for determining one's upward mobility in the spiritual hierarchy of the order, has made the Niass Tijaniyya popular among Muslims, especially in areas like Ebiraland and Igalaland where scholarship was not deeply rooted in the culture.

The period required to pass through the *tarbiya* initiation varies from individual to individual, and may last any time from a few days to two years. It depends on "how God eases the way for each initiate."[61] The real *tarbiya* experience is kept secret from non-initiates, although it is known to involve a series of questions and answers on the relationship between God and man.[62] When the former Grand *Qadi* of

[61]Interview with al-Hajj Yakub (Idoji/Okene, August 1979), a *muqaddam* with a special interest in guiding Tijanis through the *tarbiya*.

[62]Hiskett, "'The Community of Grace,'" pp. 120-1, indicates five stages or *hadra*, each of which contains questions aimed at eliciting specific notions.

Northern Nigeria and a leading anti-Sufi scholar, Shaikh Abubakar Mahmud Gumi, publicly challenged Shaikh Niass to justify the concept of *tarbiya*, he replied that it could not be rationally explained but only experienced.[63]

The Niass ban on smoking has also affected the general attitude of Muslims in the area, where Tijanis came to regard smoking as even more reprehensible than drinking alcohol. Muslim parents considered that any of their children who took to smoking had been cursed by God, because to them smoking was the gateway to the formation of all other evil habits, including the drinking of alcohol.

The Niass practice of folding one's arms during prayer, *qabl*, has also become popular among Muslims of the area; the majority of Muslims pray with their arms folded. However, in 1957 a serious controversy developed among the Muslims of Igalaland over the question of folding the arms or leaving them at the sides, *sadl*. It all started when a group of Muslims who prayed with their arms at their sides refused to pray behind an Imam who folded his arms. This group also regarded the recitation after prayers of *hailala* or *dhikr*, the Sufi praises to God, as an innovation, especially along the streets.[64] This was the first public expression of anti-*tariqa* sentiment in the area, and according to informants the conflict had been hatched by a group of non-Tijanis with the purpose of discrediting the order. The controversy might have exploded into a sectarian conflict but for the timely intervention of the *Attah* of Igala, who had just acceded to the throne as the first Muslim to hold this office. He decided to send a delegation to the Emir of Kano, al-Hajj Muhammad Sanusi, himself a Tijani, to clarify the situation. The delegation consisted of eleven members, two each from the towns of Idah, Dekina, Galao, Ankpa, and Sakamu Gara. One of the delegates from each town represented the *sadl* group and the other represented the *qabl* group. The eleventh member was the *wakili*, a title-holder in the *Attah*'s court who led the delegation.

Upon their arrival in Kano, and before meeting with the Emir, the members of the delegation took part in congregational prayers at the Emir's palace, where they discovered that some members of the congregation released their arms while some folded them during the prayers.[65] When the Emir later received them in audience, he ruled that both postures of *qabl* and *sadl* were accepted in Islam, but that if an Imam who made *qabl* stood to lead prayers and his followers objected to it, he should release his hands. He also said that the recitation of

[63]Paden, "The Influence of Political Elites," p. 131.

[64]Interviews with al-Hajj Zakari Bawa and Mallam Faqih 'Umar, Dekina, September 1981. Mallam Faqih represented the *qabl* group.

[65]*Ibid.*, Mallam Faqih 'Umar.

*dhikr* was acceptable in Islam, but that doing so along the streets was an innovation since a Muslim was not required to demonstrate publicly the extent of his devotion.

Although this mission resolved the dispute, Tijanis continued to recite the *dhikr* along the streets in Igalaland. Indeed, the practice increased, and *dhikr*-singing groups were formed which interspersed their singing with preaching against idol worship, condemnation of nominal Muslims, and the explanation of Islamic rituals, including all aspects of prayer. The songs were sung in both the Arabic and Igala languages.[66] These *dhikr*-singing groups now feature at Islamic ceremonies like marriage, naming and the *maulud al-nabi*. The group from al-Hajj Abubakar Liman's Qur'anic school in Ankpa, for instance, performed during the marriage ceremony of a daughter of Shaikh Ibrahim Niass, Ummu Hani, who was married at Okene in 1982 to a member of Dantata family from Kano. Ummu Hani's mother is Hajiyya Bilkis, a daughter of Abdulmalik.[67]

Another significant influence of the Niass Tijani in the area was the introduction of the annual celebration of the birth and naming days of the Prophet, the *maulud al-Nabi*. This occasion was celebrated in Kaolack with an all-night vigil during which Shaikh Niass would preach about Tijani cosmology, notions concerning the origins of the world and the life-history of the Prophet.[68] From the 1940s, this occasion attracted pilgrims from various parts of West Africa, including the Niger-Benue confluence. Before 1950, the Muslims of the area used to celebrate the *maulud* in a form known as *gani gani*, which involved some ceremonies which were a mixture of Islam and the traditional religious practices of the people.[69] *Gani gani* basically involved the beating of drums, singing (not strictly of religious compositions) and dancing round the town. It also featured the appearance of *do do*, or masquerades, in some places like Idah and Ankpa. However, following the visit of several scholars from Lokoja and Okene to Kaolack in 1952, where they observed the *maulud* of Shaikh Niass, they introduced his form of celebration into their own communities.

*Maulud* became an all-night activity during which scholars preached on the life of the Prophet and the message of the Qur'an, interspersed with the singing of praises to Allah and the Prophet, as

[66]Interview with Abubakar Liman, Ankpa, August 1981.

[67]Interview with Hajiyya Bilkis, Okene, February 1983.

[68]Paden, *Religion and Political Culture in Kano*, p. 124.

[69]For a detailed discussion of *gani gani*, see A.R. Mohammed, "History of the Spread of Islam in the Niger-Benue Confluence Area: Igalaland, Ebiraland and Lokoja, c. 1900-1960," unpubl. Ph.D. thesis, Bayero University, Kano, 1986, pp. 86-7.

well as feasting. The following seven days were dominated by various religious activities mostly involving Qur'anic students, including competitions of Qur'anic recitations, the translation of Islamic texts into the local languages, *tamthiliyya* or dramatic presentations depicting the life-histories of some of the prophets, or major events in Islamic history, and *walima*, the graduating ceremony of those pupils who had completed reading trhe Qur'an. All these activities were both entertaining and educational for young and old.

In some places, children would appear gaily in new uniforms, similar to those of the Boys Brigade and Girl Guides, to march through the streets, accompanied by drumming, singing the praises of the Prophet. The children would occasionally stop at different compounds to recite portions of the Qur'an or other Islamic texts for the occupants, who were expected to give the children some token gift in appreciation, usually cash. These activities were similar to those of some of the Christian mission schools.

*Maulud* thus became one of the most popular annual festivals in the area, comparable only to the two *sallah* festivals of *'Id al-fitr* and *'Id al-adha*. In 1974, Abubakar Liman introduced in Ankpa what he called *wadai al-maulud* (farewell to *maulud*), usually held during the last night of the month of the Prophet's birth, *Rabiul awal*. It features almost the same activities as the main *maulud* except that learned women are given an opportunity that night to speak on aspects of Islam that affect them as women.

All of these practices taken together have significantly contributed to the Islamic identity of Muslims in the Niger-Benue confluence area due to the overwhelming popularity of Niass Tijaniyya there. The fact that most of the Muslims of the region have been initiated into the Niass branch of the order has also helped them to strengthen their spiritual devotion to their religion. This is because one of the important preconditions of entry is the requirement of members to adhere strictly to the observance of the five pillars of Islam, particularly the five daily prayers. All the litanies of the order usually follow immediately after one of the obligatory prayers. Such additional emphasis on precise religious practice was very much needed by a people without a long history of Islam and can be regarded as the major contribution of the Tijaniyya to the establishment of Islam in the area.

# BEYOND SUFISM: THE CASE OF MILLENNIAL ISLAM IN THE SUDAN

*Awad Al-Sid Al-Karsani*

Millennial Islam is defined as the widespread belief that the end of the world, "which is to take place in 1400 (1979 A.D.), will be preceded by the supremacy of the false prophet (*dajjal* or Anti-Christ) followed by the Second Coming of Nabi 'Isa (Jesus Christ), after which all the world will be converted to Islam."[1] Millennialism has always been present in Islam as one of "the means of expressing dissatisfaction with the state of the society,"[2] ... "when the Islamic community has felt an imminent danger to its world of value and meaning."[3]

This paper describes the various trends of millennial Islam in the Sudan, and explains the process of the rise of new patterns of individual and organized millennial and messianic Islam in urban and rural areas, especially in the western Sudan. Although these patterns are different from early messianic experiences in the country, they are actually a continuity of such trends. The paper offers a description and an analysis of the various manifestations of these patterns, their origins, doctrines and programmes; the kinds of groups and social classes that propagate and accept their doctrines; local and international relations with other similar movements; and the kind of challenges they pose to the Sufi brotherhoods, to "Establishment Islam" and to the political system in general. The discussion of previous trends provides insight into the nature of contemporary millennial movements which are gaining ground in the Darfur region and in many urban centres in the Sudan. In Darfur these trends have resulted primarily from the work of the followers of the late Ibrahim Niass, the founder of the Tijaniyya centre at Kaolack in Senegal. Urban

[1]G.J. Lethem, *History of Islamic Political Propaganda in Nigeria* (London, 1927), p. 10. This expectation is based on a controversial prophetic tradition (*hadith*) which is well known for its importance in Shi'ite propaganda. The *hadith* states that the allotted span of the world is 1,000 years from the time of the Prophet Muhammad, to which 100 years were added for each of the four rightly-guided Caliphs, although there is no clear pronouncement concerning the fourth Caliph, 'Ali. The theory holds that in the last hundred years leading to 1400 A.H. are to occur all the changes prophesied such as the coming of the anti-Christ and the Second Coming of Jesus, who will lead the world to Islam. The Last Day will come in 1400 A.H.

[2]S. H. Nasr, *Traditional Islam in the Modern World* (London, 1987), pp. 302-3.

[3]J.S. Lavers, "Popular Islam And Unpopular Dissent: Religious Disturbances in Northern Nigeria," paper presented to the conference on "Popular Islam in Twentieth Century Africa," University of Illinois, April 1984.

millennialism is the result of different forces, which will be discussed below.

The Niassiyya movement founded by Ibrahim Niass, and which is known popularly as the *Fayda* (spiritual flood) or the *Tarbiya* (instruction), claims overall leadership of the Tijaniyya order and has been gaining considerable ground in western Sudan.[4] Their claims to universality and their religious and political activities are similar to those of many of the individual, propagandizing *fakis* who infiltrated the region in the first three decades of this century and were severely suppressed by the coercive machinery of the condominium colonial administration of the Sudan.[5] Therefore, an analysis of the impact of contemporary millennial movements requires a discussion of the state of the religious institutions in the Sudan at large and in the western Sudan in particular.

### *Sudanese Sufism*

The Qadiriyya order was the first organized Sufi brotherhood to penetrate the Sudan; before the arrival of the Tijaniyya order in western Sudan in the 1830s and the Khatmiyya order in the north in 1840s, it was the only order to enjoy allegiance and influence in the Sudan. The Qadiriyya succeeded in the Sudan because it "adapted itself readily to the peculiarities and idiosyncracies of whatever society it penetrated. There was no international organization, and its associational structure varied from one region to another."[6]

Most early Sufi centres were located in areas of economic activity, along commercial trade-routes or in regions of agricultural surplus. Different groups competed with one another in using religion to voice and further their "worldly" interests. Sufi institutions reflected how religion, economics and politics were interrelated in Sudanese Islam. In general, Sufi expressions of Islam conformed to pre-Islamic beliefs, in contrast to the Islam of the *'ulama* and certain orthodox orders, like

[4]Shaikh Ibrahim Niass was responsible for establishing many pan-Islamic organizations such as the Congregation of the Tijani Spiritual Flood and the Society of the Helpers of Religion in the 1930s and 1940s. He held the belief that the Tijaniyya order would be responsible for reviving Islam at the turn of the fifteenth *hijra* century. He argued that his movement, the *fayda*, would overflow to different places through which a multitude of people would accept the Tijaniyya. Yasir Anjola Quadri, "The Tijaniyyah in Nigeria: a Case Study," unpubl. Ph.D. thesis, University of Ibadan, 1981, p. 192.

[5]See A. Al-Karsani, "The Establishment of Neo-Mahdism in the Western Sudan, 1920-1936," *African Affairs*, vol. 86, no. 387, 1987, pp. 385-404.

[6]Neil McHugh, "Holy Men of the Blue Nile: Religious Leadership and the Genesis of the Arab Islamic Society in the Nilotic Sudan, 1500-1850," unpubl. Ph.D. thesis, Northwestern University, 1986, p. 130.

the Shadhiliyya, which "were not popular among the Sudanese because of their rigid doctrines."[7] This alienation from the Islam of the *'ulama* was deepened when in 1901 the Condominium administration established a Board of 'Ulama to collaborate with them.[8]

This dichotomy between popular and orthodox Islam was complicated by another difference between Islam in the central and western Sudan. In the central Sudan religious institutions were based on the authority of the shaikh and the hierarchies of the Sufi orders, while in the western Sudan they was based on the authority of individual *fakis* (religious men), the masters of the autonomous, one-man Qur'anic school, known locally as the *khalwa*. The *khalwa* is independent of any religious authority which transcends the domain of a single village or of several adjacent villages. The *faki* in the western Sudan was linked to the sub-units and clans of nomadic or semi-nomadic segmented societies, while in the central and northern Sudan the *faki* was integrated into the structures of the Sufi hierarchies. Consequently, the *faki* institution tends to be more mobile and open in the west.[9] Both men and women can become *fakis*; in Darfur a system of women *shaikhat* (fem. of *shaikh*) has been known since the introduction of Islam into the area in the sixteenth century. Women in Darfur and West Africa "established their own *khalawi*, attained the status of *Qonni* (i.e. senior *faki*) and initiated disciples into Sufi orders."[10]

Ecological factors have been important in shaping the religious institutions of Darfur. The meagre economic surplus of the nomads and semi-nomads prevented the rise of the complex religious hierarchies found in the northern and central Sudan and favoured the *khalwa* as a one-man institution. On the other hand, "the *faki* was prevented by the old Fur traditions from engaging in any commercial activities besides education. This hindered the evolution of the *faki* institution into an economic enterprise unless the *faki* was endowed

[7]A. Al-Karsani, "The Majdhubiyya Tariqa: its Doctrine, Organization and Politics," in M.W. Daly (ed.), *Al-Majdhubiyya and Al-Mikashfiyya: Two Sufi Tariqas in the Sudan* (London, 1985), p. 5.

[8]M. Abdel Rahim, *Imperialism and Nationalism in the Sudan*, (Khartoum, 1986), 2nd edn, p. 91.

[9]For an interesting descussion of religious institutions in Darfur see: Musa Adam Abdel Galil, "Some Economic and Political Aspects of Koranic Schools in Jebel Si," unpubl. B.Sc. (Hon.) thesis, Dept. of Social Anthropology, University of Khartoum, 1974.

[10]Quoted in Ibrahim M. Dafa' Allah, "Risālat al-asānīd wa 'l-adīla," unpubl. typescript, Al-Fasher, n.d. p. 174.

with the knowledge of religious 'writing' or medical treatment."[11] By contrast, the Islam of the brotherhoods, as we shall discuss below, was an important means of ideologically appropriating economic and surplus labour, which became the basis of stratification and a source of power and influence even among the politically insignificant small orders.

The individualistic, mobile and open nature of religious institutions in the western Sudan limited their economic role and made them susceptible to the influences of the dynamic wandering West African *fakis*. Islam in Darfur, in particular, became a mirror of the various cleavages and revolts in West Africa. Messianism and Mahdism were among the oldest religious imports from West Africa into the western Sudan. The Sudanese Mahdism of the late nineteenth century was an echo of developments in West Africa, particularly in Nigeria.

### *The millennial dimension*

In the Sudan, millennial Islam appeared as a reaction to the crushing defeat of Sudanese Mahdism in 1898 and of the West African *jihad* movements during the first two decades of the twentieth century. However, the distinct and highly elastic nature of Sudanese millennialism was reflected in the varying beliefs of its proponents. Some allowed for the contingency of

> ... temporary defeat by forseeing the overthrow of the chiliastic kingdom established by the Mahdi through the agency of the *dajjal* (Anti - Christ); al-Nabi 'Isa (the Prophet Jesus) would then return, kill the *dajjal*, and fill the earth with justice before the end of the time.[12]

Others, mainly Tijanis, preached the about nearness of the appearance of the Expected Mahdi (*al-Muntazar*) as a prelude to the approach of the Last Day. However, the two groups agreed on the imminence of great changes which would lead to the Last Day. Abdalla al-Suheini, the leader of the largest individual *faki* uprising in southern Darfur in 1921, stated: "The time is nigh ... he is out to attack the 'Turk' [the government] and he is out for no wealth or earthly power, but solely for religious ends."[13]

[11]A. Al-Karsani, "The Tijaniyya Order in the Western Sudan: A Case Study of Three Centres, Al-Fasher, An-Nahud and Khursi," unpubl. Ph.D. thesis, University of Khartoum, 1985, p. 220.

[12]M. Duffield, *Mauirno: Capitalism And Rural Development in Sudan* (London, 1981), p. 18.

[13]Quoted in Al-Karsani, "The Establishment," p. 391.

Beside such sporadic militant uprisings waged by individual *fakis*, another level of protest was expressed in the form of the millennial vision of "Shaikh Ahmad's Dream."[14] This visionary dream was a protest condemning religious laxity and immorality on the part of Muslims; it offered signs and fixed dates about the nearness of the appearance of the Mahdi, the coming of the Prophet Jesus and other events which would lead to the Last Day.[15] Though these millennial movements were defeated in the early 1930s, and Darfur was subordinated to the general stream of the Sudan's political developments, the region remained susceptible to West African messianic influences and periodic crises. The spread of the Niassiyya branch of the Tijaniyya order is a good example of the present impact of such influences.

While religious institutions in the western Sudan were undergoing radical changes resulting from the rise of the Niassiyya brotherhood in the region, those in the northern and central Sudan were witnessing changes resulting from the efforts of the Sufi leadership to improve their economic and political position. These moves, as we shall see, have adversely affected relationships between Sufi leaders and their disciples and paved the way for the rise of urban millennialism.

### *The Niassiyya connection*

The religious dimension of the Niassiyya movement is very appealing to the militant Tijanis of the western Sudan, who compare and equate the teachings of Ibrahim Niass to those of ʻUmar al-Futi. They also believe that he was "the successor of Shaykh Ahmad al-Tijani and ... the intermediary between the people and the Prophet and the Shaykh,"[16] and that shortly before his death in 1975, he predicted the appearance of the Mahdi from among the ranks of the Tijanis at the beginning of the fifteenth *hijra* century (1979). This Mahdist element seems to be a principal factor in the success of the Niassiyya in the Sudan because it complements the millennial and Mahdist heritage of the region.

Niassiyya religious doctrine includes the following:

[14]Shaikh Ahmad was the keeper of the Sacred Mosque, and the tradition of his vision is associated with Sunni protest. It was extended by Shiʻites and other political sects to express their political grievances.

[15]Among the signs which would indicate the nearness of events leading to the appearance of the Mahdi was "a she camel with a black and white tail which could come from east. ... If this camel came then all must join without delay." This event was prophesied for Darfur in 1921. See Al-Karsani, "The Tijaniyya," p. 281.

[16]Quadri , *op. cit.*, p. 194.

1. The belief that the Tijaniyya voluntary offices should be given the same degree of importance as the obligatory ones. The Niassiyya believe that the reciting of some offices without a progressional limit helps the follower to achieve his spiritual aims.

2. The performance of these special offices, as well as the possession of certain religious secrets, were characteristic of the Sudanese Niassiyya, and was important for attracting new converts to the order.

3. The Niassiyya followers are conservative in their observance and performance of the rituals. Differences in the number and timing of *hailala* and reciting *jawharat al-kamal* stem from the the Niassiyya emphasis on certain voluntary prayers and offices. The daily recitation of 70,000 *hailala* is a normal practice; in addition, their *dhikr* (remembrance) involves collective, loud, rhythmic chanting for long hours. Consequently, smoking and the use of snuff are prohibited, because smokers and snuff addicts are impatient and need breaks from *dhikr* to enjoy smoking and sniffing.

4. The Niassiyya believe that the *qutbaniyya*, the highest attainment in the Sufi hierarchy, can be achieved by the ordinary member if he performs the obligatory and voluntary offices appropriately. In the Sufi literature the *qutbaniyya* is the *maqam* (station) of the Mahdi; therefore all Niassiyya followers have an equal opportunity to achieve these two stations through their own *tarbiya* and practice of the obligatory and voluntary offices.

5. The knowledge and possession of certain "secret" religious formulas, including *al-ism al-'azam* (God's most exalted names), are indispensible to members of the Niassiyya in order to achieve the station of *qutbaniyya*.

Although Niassiyya religious doctrine, with its emphasis on any individual's potential to achieve the *qutbaniyya*, introduces a degree of individualism into Sufi practice and to a certain extent liberates followers from the yoke of total submission to a shaikh, this easing of control is mitigated by the structural organization of the order which is centred on the headquarters in Kaolack. Local town or village organizations are subordinated to a regional leadership, who in turn are subordinated to an overall national leadership who act as a local representative of Kaolack. In Kordofan, the Niassiyya centre at An-Nahud town is subordinate to the neighbouring Abu Zabad town centre, which in turn is subordinate to the national leadership at Geneina town, on the Sudanese-Chadian border.[17]

[17]Ibrahim M. Al-Tijani, *al-Samm al-zu'āf (Deadly Venom)* (Al-Fasher, 1407 [1988]), p. 2.

This rigid centralization of the Niassiyya leadership is contrary to Ahmad al-Tijani's teachings which allowed his disciples total freedom in choosing and expressing their political ideas. However, centralization has been justified by the need to mobilize Tijanis for the *jihad* against the unbelievers which will purify the world and establish the rule of the Mahdi and the global Kingdom of Islam; this is the essence of Ibrahim Niass's doctrine of the *fayda*. Niassiyya followers in many of the rural areas of Darfur are organizing themselves in communal agricultural colonies in which the shaikh decides the levels of market and subsistence production and the distribution of the money returns among the members.

In Darfur, the Niassiyya is gaining ground at the expense of the old Tijani centres. In Al-Fasher, Ibrahim, the grandson of Sidi Muhammad Salma, revolted against the family *zawiya* and established a competing Niassiyya centre. Out of the town's fifteen major Tijani *zawaya*, eleven had been completely converted to the Niassiyya. In many towns in western Kordofan the Niassiyya is spreading among Sudanese of West African origin and among small groups of natives, who are using the asceticism of the Niassiyya to attack the "worldly" inclinations of the leaders of the old Tijani centres. In other towns of Kordofan, the movement is limited to the distribution of Ibrahim Niass's book. In the central Sudan, the Niassiyya has spread only among scattered groups of individuals who have no organizational links. In the eastern Sudan, especially in the regions of agricultural capitalism, the Niassiyya has started to penetrate local West African settlements to the extent that one can argue that the spread of the Niassiyya outside Darfur is mainly dependent on the presence of West African immigrants.

The millennial programmes of the Niassiyya have influenced the political behaviour of its Sudanese followers. For example, it was claimed that an attack against a remote police station near the Sudanese-Chadian border in 1982 was organized by a band of Niassiyya followers in conjunction with the religious riots in Northern Nigeria which marked the beginning of the fifteenth *hijra* century. There were widespread rumours that the Niassiyya planned a series of disturbances in many West African countries in order to mobilize people for the *jihad* which would purify the world and pave the way for the advent of the Tijanis' expected Mahdi.

The centralization of the Niassiyya has involved political guidance and direction from Kaolack. In the 1986 elections, all members of the Niassiyya were directed by Kaolack to support the candidates of the

National Islamic Front (NIF).[18] These directives could be explained by the fact that the Niassiyya and the NIF share the objective of establishing an Islamic state. Dr. Hassan Al-Turabi, the veteran leader of the NIF, advocated the building of "a loose group of all Islamic movements,"[19] and he consequently developed close personal relations with the leaders of many international Islamic movements, including the Niassiyya. However, many of the local Niassiyya deny the intervention of Kaolack and attribute their support of the NIF to the latter's ardent quest to establish an Islamic state in the Sudan. The establishment of such a state conforms to the expectations of events which will precede the advent of the Mahdi.

Recent writings of the Niassiyya scholars in the Sudan have been directed against critics of the Tijaniyya, not in this instance the Wahhabis of Saudi Arabia who constitute the main enemy of Sufism in general and of the Tijaniyya in particular, but also against the celebrated Nigerian Tijani scholar Ibrahim b. Salih. The latter attempted, in his recent book *Al-Takfīr* (Anathematization), to prove that the basic doctrinal text of the Tijaniyya, *Jawāhir al-ma'ānī* is full of heresy and innovations, and that it is the duty of all Tijanis to free their doctrine from such unorthodox ideas. He was accused by one critic of not only being a Wahhabi himself, but also a Wahhabi agent and collaborator working for the destruction of the Tijaniyya.[20] Another Niassiyya scholar refuted Salih's basic arguments but reached the conclusion that although he is a Tijani, Salih was unable to perceive the essence of the Niassiyya *fayda*, which in turn made him unable to defend the Tijaniyya from the attacks of its enemies.[21]

Educational differences between these two scholars determined the nature of their arguments. The first scholar, who aggressively attacked Salih, was an ordinary *faki*, while the second, who was more moderate in his criticism, was a graduate of Al-Azhar University. The *faki* also cautioned Salih and other critics of the Tijaniyya that the time of the Expected Mahdi was approaching, while the Azhar graduate was silent about such issues.

The prospects of the Niassiyya in the Sudan are dependent on many local, national and international factors:

[18]Interviews with various informants in Kordofan and Darfur regions, 1988.

[19]A. El-Affendi, *Turabi's Revolution: Islam and Power in Sudan* (London, 1991), p. 145.

[20]M. Al-Tijani Ibrahim, *op.cit.*, pp. 13-15.

[21]Ibrahim Abu 'l-Qasim Al-Sanusi, *al-Tiryāq [The Panacea]*, (No publisher, no date), p. 12.

1. The membership of the Niassiyya is comprised primarily of immigrants of West African origin. This ethnic factor has limited the spread of the order outside Darfur.

2. This ethnic bias and attendant parochialism have also limited any political prospects for the Niassiyya which might possibly be achieved through the mobilization of the politically ineffective and unorganized Sudanese Tijanis into a single bloc, through which the Niassiyya might capture as much as 15 per cent of the electorate and hence become an active player in the Sudan's democratic circus of coalition politics.

3. The alliance of the Niassiyya with the NIF raises questions about the contradictions between a millennial, popular brand of Islam and a legalistic, orthodox one. Both groups agree in their ambition to establish an Islamic state, although the Niassiyya see this as but one stage in the millennial progression of history toward the coming of the Last Day. The utopian and eschatological expectations of the Niassiyya contrast sharply with the programme and ideology of the NIF leaders, who have "argued that their gains, which occured mainly within urban areas and among the educated, meant that theirs was the 'party of the future'."[22] To date, this alliance has proven of primary benefit to the more politically astute and pragmatic NIF.

4. On the other hand, protest in the form of religious expression is generated by social discontent, and millennial ideas of the sort propagated by the Niassiyya are clearly a vehicle and instrument of protest by the lower classes. The continuous state of instability brought about by the socio-economic deprivation and natural disasters which have plagued all of Sudanic Africa from Darfur right across the continent to Senegal suggests that the millennial ideology of the Niassiyya might continue to win the allegiance and support of discontented peoples in the region.

5. The Niassiyya leadership have also reached a working compromise with their former arch-enemies, the wealthy Wahhabis of Saudi Arabia. Saudi financial backing is imposing a degree of conservatism on many of the Islamic movements which have been forced to "soften" their ideals in order to obtain financial support. This issue has posed a challenge to the Kaolack leadership, although the process of interaction has helped to reconcile some of the differences between this militant, eschatological brand of West African Islam and the more tolerant religious doctrines and behaviour of the majority of Muslims. This reconciliation is designed not to compromise directly with Wahhabi doctrine but to avoid a new wave of the disparaging

[22]El-Affendi, *op.cit.*, p. 142.

critique which Wahhabi-sponsored organizations have levelled in the past against the Niassiyya's doctrine of *fayda*. This involves the reinterpretation of some of Ibrahim Niass's ideas by tranforming their direct meanings into metaphorical allusions. However, this tactic has endangered the distinct international organization of the movement by splitting it into militant and moderate factions. These developments will futher weaken the Sudanese Niassiyya.

These factors suggest that any prospects for political success by the Niassiyya is illusory, and that the order is doomed to remain a marginal, ineffective power in Sudanese politics.

## *Islam and national politics*

Since Sudanese independence in 1956, there have been various attempts to define the role of Islam in the politics of the country. The two largest Sufi orders, the Khatmiyya and the neo-Mahdists, swallowed their historic differences and jointly ruled the country during the spells of parliamentary democracy. Politics consequently became centered upon "a deep sectarian rivalry based upon the mobilization of Islam as a basis for identity in national politics."[23] The two Sufi orders exploited their political dominance in order to ensure the continuity of their vast economic interests which had been accumulated under the surveillance and patronage of the Condominium. However, in the absence of a solid and cohesive indigenous agricultural or mercantile capitalism, control of the state apparatus was essential for the creation, preservation and perpetuation of economic interests. This is why the struggle to seize the state apparatus became a vital matter for the different actors in Sudan's political circus.

The minor Sufi orders, which were politically insignificant and ineffective and which had degenerated into oblivion during the Condominium days, were no exception. The politics of manipulation pursued by the Khatmiyya and the neo-Mahdists to win new allies brought some economic and political privileges to the shaikhs of these small Sufi orders, who acquired spoils and concessions in the form of land, trade licences and the appointment of relatives and supporters to bureaucratic and political offices. In addition, many of these shaikhs put forward their own candidates to the parliament in order to protect and expand their newly-acquired interests. For many of the small Sufi orders, these new sources of revenue became more important than the ideologically appropriated revenue which they received from their followers.

[23]Peter Woodward, *Sudan since Independence* (London, 1988), p. 3.

The politicization of the small Sufi orders further increased during the periods of military rule. The banning of all political parties, trade unions and other social organizations enhanced the role of religious groups and organizations which might bridge the gap between the rulers and the ruled and help to preserve vested privileges and interests. This process was evident during Numayri's regime (1969-85). As early as 1971, Numayri established a Ministry of Endowments and Religious Affairs and directed it to rally the support of the small Sufi orders around him.

This alliance between the shaikhs of the minor Sufi orders and Numayri continued until his downfall in 1985. The shaikhs of these small Sufi orders won different concessions from the state: free pilgrimage and medical treatment abroad, government grants to expand the realm of their religious and educational activities, and permissions to collect donations abroad. This policy was so successful that by 1976 all the Sufi orders except the Khatmiyya and the neo-Mahdists had rallied behind Numayri's regime. Many of the relatives and followers of the shaikhs of the small Sufi orders were appointed to ministerial posts, key bureaucracy positions and leading positions in the Sudan Socialist Union (SSU), the single party of the regime. In view of this close relationship between Numayri and the small Sufi orders, one of their shaikhs asked for the establishment of a 'secretariat' within the SSU to represent their interests.[24] Many of the shaikhs outmanoeuvred the official representatives of Numayri's regime and manipulated the regional and provincial hierarchies to serve their own interests. Thus, during the late 1970s, which was a time of severe economic crisis and scarcity of goods, "items that [were] difficult to get (e.g. gas, sugar, tea, flour and other rationed items) [were] distributed to the *maseed* [religious education centres] in sufficient quantities and without delay."[25] In fact, most of these goods found their way onto the black market. This engagement in black-marketeering activities as a means to accumulate wealth sowed discord between these shaikhs and their poor followers, because the shaikhs were creating their wealth at the distribution level in full view of their disciples. By contrast, the rich Khatmiyya and neo-Mahdists, who created their wealth and capital on the production level, succeeded in keeping their followers intact during Numayri's regime.

The changing economic and political fortunes of the shaikhs of the small Sufi orders were accompanied by a drastic qualitative change in the educational experience of many of them, who now obtained either

[24]Idris S. El Hassan, "On Ideology: The Case of Religion in Northern Sudan," unpubl. Ph.D. thesis, University of Connecticut, 1980, p. 176.
[25]*Ibid.*, p. 187.

secondary or university diplomas or degrees. The refusal to perform or to recognize certain traditional Sufi practices by some of the new generation of shaikhs who had attained these levels of educational achievement had a profound social impact on the members of the orders. On the other hand, their modern education helped these leaders to give the appearance of conforming to the puritanism of the Wahhabis, whose program endangers the very existence of the Sufi religious élite. This situation worked in favour of those shaikhs of the small Sufi orders who sought donations from the rich Arab countries to assist in spreading Islam and in establishing more Islamic educational institutions.

These changes in the behaviour and practices of the new generation of shaikhs reflected their alienation from the peasant societies from which they had sprung, and deeply affected their relations with their peasant disciples, especially during Numayri's regime. Sufism and Sufi centres were no longer sanctuaries for the persecuted, where women would pray for children and men would seek success in worldly matters.[26] The complete identification of these orders with the repression and corruption of Numayri's regime compelled many of their followers either to abandon Sufism altogether and join other existing Islamic movements, or to look for some other alternative.

Long before attaining its independence the Sudan had experienced the rise of non-sectarian Islamic groups, the most important of which, in terms of their influence among both educated and non-educated sections of the society, were the Republican Brothers, the Muslim Brothers, and the Wahhabis (*Ansar al-Sunna*).

The Wahhabis began in the Sudan in the 1930s by attacking the Sufis and denouncing their practices as *bida'* (innovations). However, in 1954 they joined forces with certain *'ulama* and with the Muslim Brothers in the "Islamic Constitution Committee," which sought to promulgate an Islamic constitution as a prelude to the establishment of an Islamic state in the Sudan. These puritan, orthodox Wahhabis never formed a political party to advance their own cause, but they acted as a pressure group to urge successive governments to promulgate an Islamic constitution, curb Christian missionary activities, and spread Islamic missionary activities in the south and in the Nuba mountains.

The Wahhabis, thanks to generous grants and donations from the Saudis and to the encouragement of the Ministry of Endowments and Religious Affairs, were able to extend their activities far afield and establish mosques, educational centres and clinics in many towns and big villages. Although the Wahhabis did win some followers from

[26]A. Schimmel, *The Mystical Dimensions of Islam* (Chapel Hill, 1975), p. 239.

among the former disciples of the small Sufi orders, their literalism and destruction of the shrines of Sufi saints in other Muslim countries limited their advance and expansion in the Sudan.

The Republican Brothers were the "rationalists" of the Sudan. They propagated a "Second Message of Islam" which upheld the ethical and moral teachings of Islam, especially those tenets which were revealed during the Meccan period. They believed that the Qur'an was to be judged in the light of historical experience, advocated equality between men and women, and proposed that gradual reform and moral reinforcement were the only means of building an Islamic society. Unlike the Wahhabis, they formed an élite political party which was opposed to sectarianism and traditionalism. Though the Republican Brothers never participated in elections, they were critical "of the apathy and the irrelevance of the élite."[27] The élitist and educationalist nature of the Republican Brothers' movement was the main factor behind its inability to gain recruits from among the Sufis and those who had abandoned Sufism. It also explains why the movement withered after the execution of its leader, M.M. Taha, for "heresy" and "apostasy" in January 1985.

The Sudanese branch of the Muslim Brotherhood Society (*al-Ikhwan al-Muslimun*) was established in 1946. It had evolved originally as an anti-Communist group of religious zealots in schools and as a pressure-group to promulgate an Islamic constitution for the Sudan. Unlike the Republican Brothers, the Muslim Brothers actively participated in day-to-day politics; pragmatism and political expediency were substituted for puritanism, and the movement gained much capital out of its new utilitarianism. Between 1964 and 1985 it developed from a closed organization into an open, mass party (the Islamic Charter Front, the Islamic Trend and the NIF).

The National Reconciliation concluded in 1977 between Numayri and some sections of the opposition marked a U-turn in the history of this movement, which exploited the reconciliation and expanded its influence into various sections of the state apparatus and consolidated its grip of control over the universities and other educational institutions. However, this relationship between Numayri and the Muslim Brothers entered a new stage when Numayri allowed the movement to establish Islamic financial institutions, banks and investment companies. The movement exploited these institutions to control the commanding heights of the Sudanese economy and extend financial facilities to the small-business sector, artisans and key-figures in Numayri's regime, as an incentive to join or support the movement.

[27]Mansour Khalid, *The Government They Deserve* (London, 1990), p. 87.

This policy of infiltrating the regime seems to have been a success to the extent that the movement from 1979 onwards not only became independent of its sectarian allies, but came into direct competition with them.

These three movements cannot be adequately assessed without a discussion of the position of Islam in national politics. One cannot deny that the promulgation of an Islamic constitution was a central issue in post-Independence politics. This situation was not the result of conflicts between forces of traditionalism and modernity, because the traditional forces, including the shaikhs of the small Ṣufi orders, had undergone a process of "urbanization, and other forms of social change which have served to weaken the older groups."[28] The conflict was mainly among the various forces of modernity, both religious and secular. In the Sudan, the secular forces were weak because of their fragile base in the society due to the repression and banning of their activities during more than two decades of military rule. By contrast, an increasing identification with Islam was encouraged by external religious influences from the Middle East. The three movements discussed above were therefore influenced by both modernist and fundamentalist trends.

Although the movement to promulgate an Islamic consititution began in 1954, democratic governments were unable to adopt such a constitution either in 1958 or 1968. The application of the Shari'a in 1983 constituted a direct intervention by the state to impose Islamization from above at a time when Numayri was looking to religion to serve as an ideology to legitimize his rule, salvage his tottering regime, mask its rampant corruption, and take "the wind out of the sails of all the Sudanese Islamic movements."[29]

In the international arena, the success of the Iranian revolution in 1979, the Sacred Mosque takeover by "Mahdist" elements in 1979, and the Northern Nigerian religious riots in 1982 were interpreted by Numayri as signs presaging either the fulfilment of millennial expectations or his own downfall. The transformation of the Sudan in 1983 into an Islamic state was both a reaction to previous local and international developments and a quirk of Numayri's personality, which "oscillates between the irrational and the superstitious."[30] However, the application of the Shari'a came at a time when social and economic problems, resulting from Numayri's pell-mell capitalism in the late 1970s, were widening the gap between rich and poor in both urban and rural areas. Furthermore, the repression and terror that accompanied the

[28]Woodward, *Sudan since Independence*, p. 3.
[29]Mansour Khalid, *Numeiri and the Revolution of Dis-May* (London, 1985), p. 259.
[30]*Ibid.*, p. 254.

application of the Shari'a made many people question and doubt the sincerity of Numayri as well as his supporters from the country's Islamic movements. The large-scale repression and terror committed by the regime on a starving people raised questions about the nature of "Numayri's Islam" and its relation to the values and heritage of the dominant popular Islam. Thus, in this atomsphere of complete identification between Numayri, the orthodox and fundamentalist Islamic movements, and the shaikhs of the small Sufi orders, who are the custodians and keepers of popular Islam, one might expect the rise of a crisis of identity among the religiously oriented sections of the oppressed and depressed urban populations.

### *Urban millennialism*

Urban millennialism, an old phenomenon in the Sudan, has been rejuvenated as a result of rising social and economic inequalities and the repressive nature of Numayri's regime. In the past, urban millennial Islam was mainly disorganized and spontaneous. The new wave of millennial Islam is organized and has borrowed many of its ideas from an old form of "Shaikh Ahmad's Dream," one version of which, circulated in 1982, holds:

> The selfish rich person is too much engrossed in his own luxury to care for his poor brother, and every kind of corruption, usury, and disregard for meticulous weights and measures and drinks has been perpetrated, all in the absence of love or charity.[31]

Another copy, which appeared in 1986, states:

> Women do not obey their husbands. They appear in front of men unveiled and they go outside their houses without the knowledge of their husbands. The rich do not pay their Zakat, or help the poor, or perform pilgrimage to Mecca, and they do not command the Good and prohibit the Evil.[32]

An important difference between the millennial visions of the 1980s and those of the 1920s is the absence of any signs connoting the nearness of the occurrence of great changes which will lead to the Last Day. There is no mention of the "Mahdi" or "*Dajjal*". They tend to caution people about the present

[31]"Shaikh Ahmad's Dream," 1982. All translations were compared with official translations from the 1920s which are held in the National Records Office, Khartoum.

[32]"Shaikh Ahmad's Dream, " 1986.

> ... abominable state of affairs which calls for God's mercy. Would you, Shaikh Ahmad, warn them before the wrath of the Lord falls upon their heads and the doors of mercy are closed?[33]

The growing social and economic rift between the different social classes is criticized and attributed to a metaphysical cause, namely that the people were suffering because they had strayed from religion and "God's Path."

> Indeed the evils of this generation have gone too far in the way of wickedness and heresy. They deny the true faith and cling to the illusion of this passing show but the time is drawing near.[34]

The only solution offered by the visions to the social and economic inequalities is that:

> The time is drawing near and the door of penitence will then be indefinitely closed. ... Men and women will begin to perish, and then Islam will fall back into its former state of decay and oblivion.[35]

All the different versions of these urban millennial leaflets stop at the level of criticizing the *status quo*. They offer no alternative programme for any kind of socio-economic or political change save the repetition of the warnings that the "time is drawing near" when "the door of penitence will be indefinitely closed."

It is of interest to note that these leaflets, which were handwritten during the 1920s, are now typed and distributed in large numbers. Some contend that they are the work of certain secret messianic groups and Islamic movements such as the Islamic Liberation Party and other Egyptian groups.

In Khartoum University and other institutions of higher education, there are two small groups which have been spearheading millennial activities: *Jama'at al-Balagh* and *Jama'at al-Mušlimin. Jama'at al-Balagh* is an extension of an Egyptian organization which preaches against moral laxity, attacks every kind of corruption, and concentrates on the issue of the individual's responsibility for achieving his own salvation before the wrath to come. The other group, *Jama'at al-Muslimin*, was founded by al-Siddig al-Hajj, the present Emir of the organization and a teaching assistant in the University of Khartoum. The group advocates the use of the sciences, mainly mathematics, as a means to discover and understand the secrets of the Qur'an.[36] Its

[33] *Ibid.*
[34] "Shaikh Ahmad's Dream," 1982.
[35] "Shaikh Ahmad's Dream," 1986.
[36] Al-Siddig al-Hajj, *Taisīr al-mu'jiza fī 'l-Qur'ān al-karīm bi'l-'addād thalāthat 'ashr* [The Number Thirteen and the Discovery of the Qur'an's Statistical Miracle], (Khartoum, 1988).

members also believe that theirs is the only "true" Islamic group whose members will be "saved," while all others have strayed and will be condemned. This extreme stand by the *Jama'at al-Muslimin* is clear in their claim that the Republican Brothers and all other educated Muslims who refuse to pray with them are infidels and should be excommunicated.[37] The Emir has been seeking to achieve, under his own leadership, the unity and ideological conformity which are needed to establish the millennial, universal kingdom of Islam under the domain of the Qur'an and the Prophetic traditions. According to him, the Mahdi's rule will come after the establishment of the universal Kingdom of Islam.[38]

These two groups have little chance of appealing to the illiterate and semi-literate rank-and-file masses. And as small élite groups, they are not posing any kind of immediate danger to other similar Islamic movements. However, they demonstrate how a highly militant, organized and dedicated individual can build an organization around apolitical and morally reinforcing activities.

A comparison between Sudanese and Nigerian patterns of millennial Islam shows that both have had recourse to some form of "Shaikh Ahmad's Dream" to express popular discontent and grievances. On the other hand, Nigerian millennialism has tended toward militant action. The distribution of millennial leaflets, which usually "appear as indices of tension, of worry, of alarm about 'the times' among the lower levels of the community,"[39] is usually accompanied by sporadic waves of violence. In the Sudan, the impact of these leaflets still remains with the limits of criticism of the *status quo*.

The distribution of these leaflets did, however, annoy the puritan orthodox Wahhabis in the Sudan. In an attempt to counter these millennial ideas, they issued a small, free pamphlet which questioned the authenticiy of "Shaikh Ahmad's Dream." In it, they argued:

> No one has the knowledge of Time ... the Prophetic traditions have explained some of the events leading to the Last Day and there is no need for such an unorthodox dream which is filled with lies.[40]

[37] Al-Siddig al-Hajj, "Letter to the students of the University of Khartoum: A call to vote for the Jama'at al-Muslimun," no date, p. 7.

[38] Interview with al-Siddig al-Hajj, Khartoum, 1991.

[39] J.S. Lavers, *op. cit.*, p. 2.

[40] A. Ben Bazz, *Tanbīh hamm 'alā kadhib al-waṣiyya* [The Fallacy of the Dream], (Riyyad, 1402 [1982]), pp. 14-15.

*Conclusion*

This essay has attempted to argue that Islam in the Sudan is used as a vehicle to express ideological, socio-economic and political cleavages. It has given birth to and nursed many different and competing identities, such as modernist/traditionalist, urban/rural, millennial, autocratic and populist. All these forces, with local or international connections, have been trying, in one way or another, to take over the apparatus of state in order to serve their own objectives and interests.

The Islamic movements which have flourished or been founded in the post-Independence period have been striving to constitute an alternative to the declining influence of popular Sufi identity. These movements are an expression not only of religious ideals, but also of distinct and diverging socio-economic interests. However, either because of their "literate" and rigid ideological overtones, or because of their economic malpractices, they have not succeeded in attracting either those of Sufi persuasion or the poor suffering sections of the urban population.

Periodic state interventions, especially under military rule, to impose a certain Islamic identity on the people brings new regroupings and alliances between the military rulers, leaders of the small Sufi orders, and some of the Islamic movements. These regroupings reflect a keen desire to preserve or further socio-economic interests. The state uses ideology to consolidate its position and further the interests of its own clients and its allies.

During the 1970s and the early 1980s, the policy of "public patronizing of minor Sufi orders by Numayri personally, as well as by the state,"[41] motivated the shaikhs of these small Sufi orders to seek enrichment in business enterprise. The old patronage relationship between them and their followers was affected by the new financial status of these shaikhs, who became independent of the financial donations of their followers. Also, the educational background of many of these Sufi shaikhs made them refrain from performing or recognizing certain traditional Sufi practices, which had an immense social impact on their followers.

The shared economic interests of the previous Sufi leaders with some of the Islamic movements (mainly the Wahhabis and the NIF) resulted in orienting the tolerant, peaceful and compromizing character of the brotherhoods, especially the urban and semi-urban ones, toward a more "fundamentalist" identity, which in this context was synonymous with wealth and economic success.

[41]Peter Woodward, *Sudan 1898-1989: The Unstable State* (Boulder, CO, 1990), p. 181.

The psychologically oppressed Sufi followers started to understand that the shaikhs of the brotherhoods were no longer either bearers of the old Sufi heritage or "mediators" who would help them achieve salvation. The individual follower was compelled to search for his own salvation beyond the confines of these "worldly-motivated" brotherhoods.

It is in light of this tragedy that the different proponents of the various fundamentalist and millennial Islamic movements are trying to replace the popular Sufi brotherhoods and absorb their former adherents. However, this clash of fundamentalist with popular Sufi identities has begun to pose certain challenges to the two dominant brotherhoods, the Khatmiyya and the neo-Mahdists, especially during the third democratic experiment (1985-89). This clash manifested itself in a severe struggle to manipulate the apparatus of state and the economy to their own benefit and resulted in the *coup d'état* of July 1989 which was strongly backed by the NIF. Given the nature of this political struggle, we can understand that the leaders of a millennial Islam, who are advancing themselves as the voices of the discontented and oppressed individual in both rural and urban areas, are likely to remain marginal, ineffective and insignificant players in the Sudan's political circus.

# CHANGING ISLAMIC IDENTITY IN NIGERIA FROM THE 1960s TO THE 1980s: FROM SUFISM TO ANTI-SUFISM

*Muhammad Sani Umar**

*Introduction*

The long history of Sufism in the area of present-day Nigeria is an important background to understanding the current change of Islamic identity from Sufism to anti-Sufism.[1] Sufi concepts such as *kashf, wilaya, baraka* and *karama* were invoked by the leaders of the Sokoto *jihad* as one basis for the legitimacy of their leadership, while individual and communal identities in the Sokoto Caliphate were sustained around the Qadiriyya. Shaikh Usman dan Fodio was regarded as a *qutb* and of most of the leaders of the Sokoto *jihad* as *awliya*, and the Qadiriyya was adopted as a kind of official Sufi order. According to some sources, Shaikh Usman had said that it was not permissible for any member of his community to leave the Qadiriyya.[2] It is therefore not surprising that there seem to have been no anti-Sufi currents in Nigeria up to the first half of the twentieth century. In addition, the supposition that there might have been a Wahhabi influence on the leaders of the Sokoto *jihad*[3] has also been contested.[4]

*I would like to register my appreciation to Professor John O. Hunwick for his sustained interest in this work; his comments on earlier drafts have been encouraging and most helpful. My gratitude is also due to Professor Muhammad Sani Zahradeen for his kind advice and instructive supervision during my student days at Bayero University, where I first presented some of the materials and ideas in this chapter as part of a M.A. thesis. Professor Abdallahi Mohammed of Ahmadu Bello University and Mallam Shehu Umar Abdallahi of Bayero University, also deserve acknowledgement for their useful suggestions. However, only I bear responsibility for the materials presented here.

[1] I have elsewhere defined anti-Sufism simply as those tendencies and movements in Islamic history which have regarded Sufism as a whole, or specific aspects, beliefs and practices of Sufism, as invalid innovations in Islam (*bid'a*), or spurious, superfluous or even totally and fundamentally un-Islamic. See my "Sufism and Anti-Sufism in Nigeria," unpubl. M.A. thesis, Bayero University, Kano, 1988, pp. 38-67.

[2] Umar F. Malumfashi, "The life and ideas of Shaikh 'Uthman Dan Fodio: Being editing, translating and analysis of *Rawd al-jinān* by Gidado b. Laima," unpubl. M.A. thesis, Abdullahi Bayero College, 1973, p. 14.

[3] For example, see: M. Hiskett, "An Islamic tradition of reform in Western Sudan from the sixteenth to the eighteenth century," *Bulletin of the School of Oriental and African Studies,* XXV (3), 1962, p. 596. Cf. M. Hiskett, *The Sword of Truth: The Life and Times of the Shehu Usuman Dan Fodio* (New York, 1973), pp. 40-1; John R. Willis, "*Jihād Fī Sabīl Allāh*: Its doctrinal basis in Islam and some

However, Usman dan Fodio, though by no means an anti-Sufi, did criticize specific instances which he perceived to be corruptive of Sufism in *Iḥyā' al-sunna*[5] and *Kitāb al-bid'a al-shayṭāniyya*.[6] Beyond this, there seems to be no trace of opposition to Sufism throughout the nineteenth century, though it has been suggested that followers of a certain Mallam Ibrahimu were "persons with Wahhabist attitudes" active in Kano circa 1870, and in Lagos by 1920.[7] However, this Mallam Ibrahimu seems to have passed into oblivion, and his followers who were said to have been noticed by British colonial authorities in Lagos could not be categorically linked to anti-Sufism. And even though British colonial authorities were constantly wary of Islamic movements, especially Mahdist ones, British colonial studies on Islam in Nigeria are either silent about a Wahhabi presence in the country,[8] or categorical about its absence. According to one colonial document, "contrary to what is believed in certain French circles, Wahhabism has not spread into Nigeria and does not threaten the doctrinal unity of Islam as it does in certain parts of French territories. Even those quarters which are under the influence of Cairo seem to be impervious to it."[9]

Besides the Wahhabiyya, it has been suggested that the prevalence of legalism, which Marshall Hodgson termed the *shar'i* vision of Islam,[10] might have produced a counterbalance to mysticism.[11]

---

aspects of its evolution in nineteenth-century West Africa," *Journal of African History,* VIII (3), 1967, p. 400.

[4]A. Abubakar, *al-Thaqāfa al-'Arabiyya fī Nījīriyā* (Beirut, 1972), pp. 111-6.

[5]Shaikh Usman dan Fodio, *Iḥyā' al-sunna wa ikhmād al-bid'a* (Sokoto, n.d.), pp. 244-54.

[6]Shaikh Usman dan Fodio, *Majmū' al-kutub al-arba'a al-mufīda* (Kano, n.d.), pp. 26-7.

[7]M. Hiskett, "The 'Community of Grace' and its opponents, the rejectors: a debate about theology and mysticism in Muslim West Africa with special reference to its Hausa expression," *African Language Studies,* XVII, 1980, p. 126.

[8]This is the case with P.H.G. Scott, *A Survey of Islam in Northern Nigeria in 1952* (Kaduna, 1953).

[9]National Archives, Kaduna, "Zaria Province: C 68, Report by M. Mangin, Head of the Department of Muslim Affairs, on his visit to Nigeria in March, 1952," Dakar, Haut Commissariat de la Républic en Afrique Occidentale Française, p. 17. See also "A note on Muslim religious, social and political movements in Nigeria," p. 2, where it was observed: "There have so far been no reports in Nigeria of the heterodox and subversive Wahhabite movement which the French were at pains to disperse at Bamako in the Soudan at the end of 1951." It may be added here that Hiskett assumed that fleeing members of the Bamako Wahhabis might have been the ones who arrived in Nigeria in the 1920s. For further details on the Bamako Wahhabis, see L. Kaba, *The Wahhabiyya: Islamic Reform and Politics in French West Africa* (Evanston, 1974).

[10]Marshall G.S. Hodgson, *The Venture of Islam* (Chicago, 1974), vol. I, pp. 315-58.

However, the possibility that the dichotomy between *haqiqa* and *shari'a* might have materialized into a concrete conflict between Sufis and jurists was vitiated by the fact that most Sufis in Nigeria were also learned jurists, and this combination was nowhere so well blended as in Shaikh Abdullahi dan Fodio, whose contributions to both Sufism and *fiqh* were considerable.[12] It has in fact been observed that before the twentieth century, the *shari'a-haqiqa* divide was not an important one in West Africa, for "many of the most highly respected jurists also enjoyed very large followings as mystics and as *shaikhs* of the Sufi orders."[13] But nowadays, opposition to Sufism, even if not necessarily that of the jurists, has become common in many Muslim communities in West Africa,[14] including Nigeria, of which this chapter is a case-study.

*The rise of anti-Sufism from the 1930s to the 1960s*

In the 1940s and 1950s, Nigeria witnessed the intense popularization of Qadiriyya and Tijaniyya, especially through the publication of booklets by Nigerian authors drawing from the classics of both orders. Prominent among these booklets were: *Kitāb al-su'āl wa'l-jawāb* (*Shurūṭ wird Shaikhinā Abī 'l-Abbās*) by Shaikh Muhammad Salga; *Ifādat al-murīd bi-shurūṭ sharā'iṭ wird Shaikhinā Tijānī* by Shaikh Abubakar al-Atiq; and *al-Nafkhat al-Nāṣiriyya* by Shaikh Nasir Kabara. As this popularization was being brought to a head, other developments were also taking place . In particular, British colonialism had already gone far in transforming Nigeria into a capitalist socio-economic formation. Anti-Sufism first came about as part of the discontent with the colonization process.

---

[11]J.N. Paden, *Religion and Political Culture in Kano* (Berkeley, 1973), p. 65.

[12]For example, see: A.S. Umar, "*al-Takfīr al-ṣūfī 'inda 'l-Shaikh 'Abd Allāh b. Fūdī*," umpubl. M.A. thesis, Bayero University, Kano, 1987; and A.A. Gwandu, "Abdallahi b. Fodio as a Muslim jurist," unpubl. Ph.D. thesis, University of Durham, 1977. See also Muhammad S. Zahraddeen, "Abdullahi Ibn Fudi's contribution to the Fulani jihad in nineteenth-century Hausaland," unpubl. Ph.D. thesis, McGill University, 1976.

[13]C.C. Stewart with E.K. Stewart, *Islam and Social Order in Mauritania: A Case Study from the Nineteenth Century* (Oxford, 1973), pp. 2-3.

[14]In addition to Hiskett and Kaba, *op. cit.*, see Robert Launay, *Traders without Trade: Responses to Change in two Dyula Communities* (Cambridge, 1982), pp. 123-37; Jean-Louis Triaud, "Abd al-Rahman l'Africain (1908-1957) pionnier et précurseur du wahhabisme au Mali," in Olivier Carré and Paul Dumont (eds), *Radicalismes islamiques* (Paris, 1986), vol. II, pp. 162-80; and R.W. Niezen, "The Community of the Helpers of the Sunna: Islamic Reform among the Songhay of Gao (Mali)," *Africa,* 60(3), 1990, pp. 399-423.

Beginning from 1950, and increasingly by the mid-1950s with the introduction of partisan politics and the attainment of self-rule, the new élites from the Kano School of Arabic Studies, Katsina College, Sokoto Arabic Teachers College etc., became more restive in their agitation against colonialism, the emirates, the Native Authority, and the Sufi orders. In particular, graduates of the School of Arabic Studies were so vocal in their condemnation of the Sufi orders that the school came to be regarded as the breeding ground of anti-Sufism in Nigeria. Yet anti-Sufism up to this time was still largely aimed against the perceived extravagances of the mass followings of the Sufi orders, especially due to the popularization of both the Tijaniyya and Qadiriyya which had reached its zenith through the activities of Shaikh Ibrahim Niass and Shaikh Nasiru Kabara respectively.[15]

The articulation of anti-Sufism emerged along with what the new elites perceived as the "virtues" of the social transformations now in progress and the "vices" of the old structures of the society. As it were, the emirates were presented as embodying all the "vices" of the old order; they were thought to be incompatible politically with the democratic spirit of the modern age, and socio-culturally as the bastion of conservatism and reaction. Religiously, the emergent élites found the emirates riddled by a fundamental contradiction, since as Islamic political institutions they should have been protecting and promoting Islam, but were instead seen to have become the repository of ignorance, superstition and syncretism. The gravity of this contradiction was highlighted even more by the fact that the emirates had become subordinated to British colonialism so that the emirs could not hold office without taking an oath on the Qur'an to be loyal to the Christian monarch of Britain. As the colonial order was drawing to an end, the emirates, as the front for colonization through indirect rule, became targets for nationalist agitation politically, socio-culturally and religiously. All of these aspects were clearly expressed by Sa'ad Zungur (1915-58), who can be regarded the father of nationalism in Northern Nigeria. Without going into the details of the nationalist career of Sa'ad Zungur, eventful and inspiring as it was to many,[16] I call attention to the anti-Sufi component of his contribution to the revival of Islam in Nigeria within the larger context of nationalist agitation against colonialism.

Sa'ad Zungur's agenda for the revival of Islam revolved around the call for a return to the pristine Islam believed to have been practised by the Prophet and his companions and caliphs. Zungur was firmly

[15]Paden, *passim*.

[16]For details, see D. Abdulkadir, *The Poetry, Life and Opinions of Sa'ad Zungur* (Zaria, 1974), especially pp. 9-15.

opposed to any "infiltration of superstition into Islam:" polygamy, the seclusion of women in purda, and the denial of education to Muslim women. Sa'ad's agenda for Islamic revival was too radical for the *'ulama* of his time.[17] But he was undaunted, as demonstrated in his *Wakar Bidi'a*[18] (Poem [against] Innovations) in which he inveighed against certain beliefs and practices: attending the shrine of *tsafi*; the practice of divination by some Muslim scholars (*malaman duba*); and the insistence that supplications (*al-du'a*) must be said in Arabic when the supplicant does not understand Arabic at all.

Sa'ad Zungur's opposition to Sufism was specifically against saint veneration which led people to take oaths in the names of Sufi *shaikhs*,[19] whereas Muslim jurists have maintained that oaths should be taken in the name of Allah alone. Yet Sa'ad's opposition was significant, coming when the intensification of *tariqa* affiliation and activities were being brought to a head, and also because his opposition anticipated the all-out opposition to Sufism later articulated by men of his calibre. However, it should be emphasized here that opposition to Sufism by this time was only one component of the general mood of agitation against the unpleasant realities of the colonial situation as sustained through the emirates and the Native Authorities (NA). By the time anti-Sufism became a more broadly-based movement against Sufism in general, rather than against specific aspects of it, there was a reversal in the equation of political protest and the agitation for Islamic revival: those who were radical in their agitation for Islamic revival and very vocal in their opposition to Sufism became politically conservative, while those still in the forefront of political protest became religiously conservative. Shaikh Abubakar Gumi represents the former trend, and Malam Aminu Kano the latter.

Abubakar Gumi, generally regarded as the originator of anti-Sufism in contemporary Nigeria, did not begin his opposition to Sufism by first rejecting its doctrinal basis as a whole. He was in fact initiated into the Qadiriyya at one time, and was also closely associated with the Mahdiyya.[20] Gumi's opposition to Sufism coincided with the

[17]*Ibid.*

[18]S. Zungur, *Wakokin Sa'adu Zungur* (Zaria, 1986).

[19]See lines 64-70 of the *Wakar Bidi'a*, *ibid.*

[20]For details on the life history of Shaikh Abubakar Gumi and the development of his ideas, see M.A. Sanusi Gumbi, *Tarihin Shaikh Abubakar Mahmud Gumi* (no bibliographical data); *Tarihin Wa'azin Shaikh Abubakar Mahmud Gumi* (Kaduna,1988); National Archives Kaduna, *E 14/349 Min of Educ., Mal Abubakar Gumi;* Federal Radio Corporation (Kaduna) Tape No *FRCN/AR 2501 & 72502: Hira da Shaikh Abubakar M. Gumi akan yadda ya ji game da ba shi lambar girma ta King Faisal, Saudi Arabia,* Feb. 1987.

simple beginnings of the emergent élite's opposition to the trio of colonialism, emirate-Native Authority collusion, and perceived religious ignorance and superstition.

Gumi believed that colonialism destroyed Islam in a very subtle way.[21] He argued that Islamic learning was undermined in the schools established by the colonialists, and that the *'ulama* were denied any influence over the emirates. Additional powers were concentrated in the hands of the emirs, although they were not to exercise those powers at will; they became the mere puppets of the colonialists who issued orders for the emirs to carry out (indirect rule). Since the *'ulama* were removed from the process, people had no way of knowing that what the emirs were doing was un-Islamic. Thus Islam was destroyed in the colonial situation by the colonialists' promotion of traditions and customs through the emirs over and above Islam.[22]

As already noted, Gumi's opposition to Sufism was not originally doctrinal, but began within the general context of nationalist agitation. Given his own Islamic background, he was inclined to fight against religious ignorance and superstition, which he perceived as but one acute problem among the many brought by colonialism. Gumi's views before the 1940s contained little anti-Sufism, though by this time he had already renounced his affiliation to the Qadiriyya, since he was sceptical of the Islamic authenticity of Qadiri doctrines. It was in the early 1940s that his anti-Sufi views began to take definite shape.[23] Henceforth, opposition to Sufism in Nigeria started to transcend mere condemnation of the specifics of *tariqa* practices and beliefs, and progressively developed into a sustained critique against the doctrinal foundations of Sufism, championed throughout the 1940s and 1950s by Abubakar Gumi.

Gumi's opposition to Sufism made little progress through the 1950s, because the Sufi orders were then at their peak.[24] Furthermore, his audience was restricted to the circle of his own disciples whose number was quite insignificant compared to the massive following of the Sufi orders. However, a new chapter in the development of anti-Sufism in Nigeria was opened from 1960.

[21]Much of what follows here is from my field interviews with Shaikh Abubakar Gumi in Kaduna, May 1986.

[22]*Ibid.*

[23]Gumbi, *Tarihin wa'azin,* p.3.

[24]Paden, *passim.*

*The popularization of anti-Sufism from the 1960s to the 1980s*

By the close of the 1950s, the fundamental issues in anti-Sufism had already taken shape and they continued to crystallize during the next decade. Gumi's rise to the post of Grand Kadi of Northern Nigeria in 1962 was a watershed in the development of anti-Sufism in Nigeria by placing him in a position from which his anti-Sufi views could influence governmental policies on Islamic matters. Thus, Gumi advised the Sardauna that the activities of Shaikh Ibrahim Niass constituted a repudiation of the great legacy of Shaikh Usman dan Fodio dan Fodio,[25] from which the Sardauna sought to draw inspiration. And since the Sardauna considered himself heir to this legacy, he felt himself responsible to uphold it.[26] Similarly, when rivalry between Tijaniyya and Qadiriyya led to occasional violent clashes, Gumi advised the Sardauna to convene a meeting of the leaders of the two orders with a view to resolving their differences. Consequently, the Sardauna set up the Advisory Committee on Islamic Affairs (*Kwamitin Ba Da Shawara Kan Al'amuran Musulunci*).

The Advisory Committee met three times between 1963 and 1965, but could not achieve much towards resolving the differences between the two conflicting orders. In fact, when the thorny issue of *kabalu* and *sadalu*[27] was brought before the Advisory Committee, and it decided that those who practiced *kabalu* (essentially Tijanis) should not

[25]Interview with Gumi, 1986.

[26]John N. Paden, *Ahmadu Bello the Sardauna of Sokoto: Values and Leadership in Nigeria* (Zaria, 1986), pp. 278 ff.

[27]*Kabalu* (Ar. *qabl*) means crossing the right arm over the left across the the chest while standing in *salat*. *Sadalu* (Ar. *sadl*) means not crossing the arms in this manner but leaving them straight. There are traditions that the Prophet performed *salat* in both ways. In Nigeria *sadalu* used to be more prevalent, but with the intense popularization of Tijaniyya affiliation under Shaikh Ibrahim Niass, *kabalu* became widely practised and almost exclusively associated with Tijani followers of Shaikh Ibrahim Niass since he practised *kabalu*, and was in fact the one who popularized it in Nigeria. *Kabalu-sadalu* became a very vexed problem in Nigeria, sharply dividing the Tijani followers of Shaikh Ibrahim Niass and other Nigerian Muslims. Heated debate, arguments and intellectual controversies led to the production of a very interesting polemical literature which is worth examining in its own right. For example, see Shaikh Nasir Kabara, *Qam' al-fasād fī tafḍīl al-sadāl 'alā 'l-qabd fī hādhihi 'l-bilād*, and the rejoinder to it by Shaikh Sani Kafanga, *Sabīl al-rashād fī radd 'alā mu'allif Qam' al-fasād*. At the level of religious practices, the problem of *kabalu-sadalu* generated a great deal of tension. Those who did not follow Shaikh Ibrahim would not agree to be led in prayers by an *imam* who practiced *kabalu*, and if prayers started and the *imam* was discovered to be doing *kabalu,* his arms would be pulled down, which might start a fight right inside the mosque. It was against this background that the issue became a grave concern for the maintenance of law and order.

be allowed to lead congregational prayers as *imams*, the Committee became divided and could not convene again.[28]

On his arrival in Kaduna, Gumi found another forum in which to popularize his anti-Sufi views: *tafsir* sessions during the month of Ramadan in the Sultan Bello Mosque. During these *tafsir* sessions, which continued until his death,[29] Gumi consciously sought to influence the Sardauna and his ministers, believing that once the political leadership had been influenced, the masses would follow suit. The Sardauna himself did not attend the sessions regularly, though he normally attended the closing session and made donations. But some of the Sardauna's ministers did frequent the *tafsir* sessions. The *tafsir* was not of course meant for high government functionaries only; members of the general public also attended. Thus, an audience larger than that of the circle of his disciples in Kano came to listen to Gumi as he expounded his anti-Sufi views in the course of the *tafsir* sessions. However, while Gumi's views were becoming better known to political leaders and the public at large, certain contradictions were developing to check the speed and extent of the popularization of his ideas. The rivalry between the Tijaniyya and Qadiriyya had acquired extra-religious dimensions, because the associated violence made their disagreements an issue of state security, public peace, and law and order, all of which were of fundamental interest to the government. There were also deliberate attempts by political parties, including the Action Group,[30] to manipulate the Sufi orders by seeking to identify with one order or the other in a bid for the votes of their members. But the Sardauna did not find it politically expedient to identify openly with one particular Sufi order, and as part of his political project of a "United North," he avoided antagonizing the Sufi orders by openly espousing Gumi's anti-Sufism. Instead the Sardauna embarked on the search for "a trans-Sufi order religious community" as a complement to his political project of a Northern Nigeria united on the basis of a common cultural heritage, loyalty and identity. This trans-Sufi order community "emerged during the period 1960-6 and unofficially came to be known as Usmaniyya. The Sardauna of Sokoto, Ahmadu Bello, led the movement until his death in 1966, at which time the momentum slowed to a point where it is not recognized today."[31]

Although the Usmaniyya cannot be strictly considered a Sufi order, its doctrines were those Usman dan Fodio set forth in a number of his treatises on Sufism, especially *Wa lamma balaghtu* and *Uṣūl al-*

[28]Paden , *Ahmadu Bello,* pp. 548-51.
[29]For further details, see Gumbi, *Tarihin wa'azin,* pp. 8-13.
[30]Paden, *Religion...,* pp. 310-12.
[31]*Ibid.*, pp. 146-7.

*wilāya*, both of which the Sardauna caused to be published with Hausa translations. Usmaniyya doctrines were not articulated by the Sardauna but by Abubakar Gumi and the Waziri of Sokoto.[32] Because of the politicization of Sufi affiliation and identity, the Sardauna brought pressure on Gumi to moderate his anti-Sufi doctrines, which led to the contradiction of Gumi preaching against Sufism and attacking both Tijaniyya and Qadiriyya, while at the same time articulating the Sufistic doctrines of the Usmaniyya.

A related issue is the *Jama'atu Nasr Islam* (JNI). The Sardauna established the JNI on the advice of Gumi, and right from its inception Gumi was intimately involved in running it. Given his anti-Sufi disposition, one might have expected Gumi to use the JNI as a platform to further advance anti-Sufism. Yet that was not the case, for the JNI has never really been a platform of anti-Sufism, although there were reservations on that score from the Tijanis and the Qadiris. The JNI strove hard to maintain its character, as originally conceived, as an all-embracing organization for all the Muslims in Nigeria without regard to sectarian, doctrinal or other differences.[33] And perhaps it was as a practical demonstration of its avowed non-sectarianism that the JNI welcomed the courtesy visit to its headquarters by a son of Shaikh Ibrahim Niass when he visited Nigeria in 1969, and caused it to be publicized in its official journal.[34] Nevertheless, the suspicion that the JNI was anti-Sufi continued until the late 1970s when certain developments led to the virtual conversion of the JNI into a platform for counteracting anti-Sufism.

Beginning in 1955, the Sardauna performed *hajj* and '*umra* every year until his assassination in 1966. For him the *hajj* was not a purely religious affair, but also an opportunity for him to establish contact with the Saudis. In this he was largely successful as indicated by the series of visits to Nigeria by religious leaders from Saudi Arabia and also by the Sardauna's election as Vice-President of the Muslim World League, an organization largely created and financed by the Saudis.[35]

The rapport which the Sardauna established with the Saudis yielded donations for the promotion of Islam in Nigeria. Here again he had to depend on Gumi who, as an avowed opponent of Sufism, would have had little problem persuading the Saudis that donations to the cause of

[32]*Ibid.*

[33]A. El-Nafaty, "Meeting of the Supreme Council of the JNI November 3rd, 1968," *Haske: The Light of Islam,* Dec. 1968, p. 11.

[34]Under the caption "Ziyarar Shaikh Muhammad Nasir Niass," *Haske: The Light of Islam,* Mar. 1969, p. 20.

[35]Paden, *Ahmadu Bello,* p. 279.

Islam in Nigeria would not be used for promoting Sufism. Yet we have earlier seen that Gumi's opposition to Sufism at home had had to be muted because of the political issues at stake, which made the Sardauna unwilling openly to antagonize any particular Sufi order, and which also caused him to embark, principally through Gumi, on promoting the Sufi aspects of the legacy of Usman dan Fodio. However, this contradiction was resolved with the death of the Sardauna and the cessation of partisan politics after the fall of the First Republic in 1966. Before examining the further workings of the Wahhabi factor in the development of anti-Sufism in Nigeria during the 1970s and 1980s, one issue which carried forward from the late 1960s remains to be discussed.

Shortly after the death of the Sardauna, Gumi's *tafsir* began to be aired by the Nigeria Broadcasting Corporation (NBC) radio station in Kaduna, thereby creating a national outlet for the dissemination of his anti-Sufism. The exact impact of this development cannot be determined, but clearly Gumi's audience now became virtually unlimited. Furthermore, the restraint which the Sardauna used to exercise on Gumi had disappeared with the former's death. Thus, as the 1970s began, two important aspects of anti-Sufism in Nigeria had already emerged.

First, the popularization of anti-Sufism by the airing of Gumi's *tafsir* over the radio was further widened by the publication of his views in the Kaduna-based Hausa language newspaper, *Gaskiya Ta Fi Kwabo*. It has in fact been noted that "*Gaskiya...* was the first to bring out the writings of Mallam Abubakar Gumi to the world at large starting from 1966, and then other media organs picked them up."[36] As a result of this popularization of Gumi's anti-Sufism through both print and sound mass media, anti-Sufism was transformed into a mass social movement, as will be demonstrated presently.

Secondly, anti-Sufism developed from mere verbal condemnation during the *tafsir* sessions to articulating the critique against Sufism in writing. Here again, Gumi was the pioneer and the inspiration to others. Starting from his articles in *Gaskiya,* his opposition to Sufism led him to produce, in 1972, the first book by a Nigerian author primarily written as a critique of Sufism. As tacitly implied in the title of the book, *al-'Aqīda al-ṣaḥīḥa bi-muwāfaqat al-sharī'a* (Correct Belief in Accordance with the Shari'a), Gumi's critique falls into the *shar'i* side of the *haqiqa-shari'a* polemic. The book starts with an analysis of *kalimat al-shahada:* "There is no god but Allah and Muhammad is the Messenger of Allah." Gumi holds that the first

[36]Gumbi, *Tarihin Shaikh...,* p. 6.

part of this sentence, i.e. "There is no god but Allah," means that nothing deserves to be worshiped in truth except Allah. The second part means that the worship which Allah alone deserves can never be based upon the opinion or the convenience of the worshipper but should be as Allah likes, which is why He sent the Prophet Muhammad as His messenger to teach humans how to worship Him. Thus, whoever worships Allah in any way other than that which He has revealed to the Prophet has not really worshiped Allah at all.[37]

Implicit in this line of reasoning is a rejection of Sufi orders in so far as there were none during the life-time of the Prophet and the immediately succeeding generations, and also because Sufism as a whole, and its orders in particular, involve elements of a personal style of worship. Sufism is rooted in the personal spiritual experience of the individual, and it is the experiences of those individuals who have become accomplished in the Sufi tradition which lead some of them to evolve particular ways (*turuq*) for guiding the spiritual development of less accomplished believers who wished to follow in their footsteps.[38] Gumi is here advancing the argument of a positivistic conception of Islam which admits of no such personal subjectivism, for Gumi holds that "religion is nothing but what God has revealed to His Messenger Muhammad who has duly informed us of the revelation during His life-time and which has also reached us through the standard chains of authorities which can be satisfactorily relied upon."[39]

The above summation provides the essentials of Gumi's critique against Sufism, namely that Sufism is not part of Islam because it emerged long after Islam had been completed. Having established this point clearly, we need not be detained by the details of Gumi's critique, except perhaps for the important concept of *wilaya*, because it has been the most prominent feature in the entire historical development of Sufism in Nigeria[40].

Gumi holds that every believer (*mu'min*) is a *wali*, and that *wilaya* in its essence is one and the same for everyone, although it could be perfected by a truly God-fearing believer (*al-mu'min al-taqiy*). Furthermore, he argues that "*wilaya* belongs to those who believe in and fear God, and these are the ones referred to in Q. 10: 62-4. *Wilaya* is but an expression of following Allah the praiseworthy in what He likes and dislikes, and not by the many *salat* one performs, by constant

[37]Abubakar M. Gumi, *al-'Aqīda al-ṣaḥīḥa bi-muwāfaqat al-sharī'a* (Beirut, 1972), pp. 6ff.

[38]For a detailed study of the historical development of Sufi orders, see J.S. Trimingham, *The Sufi Orders in Islam* (Oxford, 1971), especially pp. 1-30.

[39]Gumi, *al-'Aqīda*, pp. 75-6.

[40]For details, see Umar, "Sufism and Anti-Sufism," pp. 80 ff.

adulation or by religious exercises."[41] Here Gumi rejects the Sufi belief that *wilaya* is attained by constant and various acts of worship. He asserts that the *wali* is the God-fearing believer, and that all the believers are friends *(awliya)* of Allah, as well as of one another in graded categories depending on the strength or weakness of their faith, and the increase or decrease of their God-fearing deeds. Thus, by this simplistic conception of *wilaya* in its literal meaning of friendship, alliance and protection, Gumi disposes of all the sophistication Sufis have blended into the concept of *wilaya*, including *qutbaniyya* and all the graded saintly posts below it.[42]

Throughout the early 1970s, Gumi continued to denounce the Qadiriyya and Tijaniyya as basically un-Islamic; the saint veneration by followers of the two orders he denounced as *shirk*. Gumi's critique of Sufism continued to receive the widest publicity through the three media organs in Kaduna: radio and television services of the then Radio Television Kaduna (RTK); Nigerian Television Authority (NTA) Kaduna; and *Gaskiya*. However, the resulting dissemination of anti-Sufi ideas produced a reaction from the Sufis. The intense rivalry between the followers of Tijaniyya and Qadiriyya, which in the 1950s and 1960s occasionally led to violent clashes, now gave way to a reconciliation in order to prepare a joint defence of Sufism against the sustained onslaught of anti-Sufism. The Tijaniyya-Qadiriyya reconciliation gave birth to collaboration between the Sufi *ulama*, and thus created a front for the joint defence of Sufism. These *'ulama* began to challenge Gumi's critique of Sufism and to advance arguments in its defence in the circles of their disciples. They also wrote books and pamphlets, some specifically prepared as rejoinders to Gumi's *al-'Aqīda al-ṣaḥīḥa*. Similarly, Sufi *'ulama* merged into a block against Gumi in the various Islamic organizations in the country, as well as the semi-governmental organs which relate to Islam such as the JNI, the Supreme Council of Islamic Affairs.[43]

The case of the JNI is particularly interesting. As already indicated, the JNI strove jealously to guard its non-sectarian orientation, yet throughout the 1960s it suffered the suspicion of the *tariqa 'ulama* who regarded it as a front for advancing Wahhabi doctrines in Nigeria. But by the mid-1970s, when the *'ulama* of the

[41] *Ibid.*, p. 10.

[42] *Ibid.*, p. 44, cf. pp. 46 ff.

[43] For example, when a proposal for the appointment of Shaikh Abubakar Gumi as the Grand Mufti of Nigeria was tabled before the Supreme Council of Islamic Affairs, Shaikh Dahiru Usman Bauchi led the *'ulama* of the Sufi orders to reject the proposal. See Shaikh Dahiru's submission to the Council titled, *Taron Majalisar Koli Ta Musulunci Ta Nigeria wanda aka yi ranar Laraba 15/5/1985 (25 ga watan Sha'aban) a Kaduna,* mimeo.

Sufi orders began to collaborate, they saw the JNI as another forum in which to challenge Gumi's anti-Sufism. Thus they "invaded" the JNI and isolated Gumi and made him the lone voice against their block membership. Although the JNI was never really a front for anti-Sufism, this development must have been an unhealthy one for Gumi's continuing campaign against Sufism.

Perhaps the more important result of the reconciliation and collaboration of the leading *'ulama* of the hitherto contending Sufi orders was the emergence of the *Kungiyar Jama'atu Ahlus-Sunnati* and *Kungiyar Dakarun Dan Fodio,* who described themselves, in a 1977 document signed by seventy people, as "*Ahluz-Zikri* – followers of the Tijaniyya and Qadiriyya orders."[44] Basing themselves on the tradition of the Prophet that, "religion is but [giving] counsel," the signatories contended that Abubakar Gumi had erred on several aspects of Islamic teachings, and therefore needed to be counseled. Twenty issues were delineated on which the signatories believed Gumi to have erred.[45] An open letter to Abubakar Gumi was attached to the document, taking up the challenge he was said to have made in the Sultan Bello Mosque on 11 March 1977, to the effect that whoever had any authoritative evidence in support of Sufi orders should come forward with it. The seventy signatories stated in their letter: "We, members of the *Kungiyar Jama'atu Ahlus-Sunnati* of Nigeria, Zaria and Kaduna branches, are hereby requesting that we meet with you in the Conference Hall of the JNI, here in Kaduna, on Saturday, 9 April 1977, at 10.00 a.m. to resolve the problem of *zakat* and some other important issues that touch on the fundamentals of Islam."[46]

The letter further explained that the debate had become necessary because Gumi had already divided the Muslims in Nigeria into his Wahhabi followers and the *Ahlus-Sunna*, followers of the Prophet, by declaring believers to be infidels over the radio.[47] Forty-two issues were listed for the proposed debate, including the *kabalu-sadalu* problem, beliefs and practices of the Sufi orders, and a host of other views expressed by Gumi.[48] Concerning Wahhabism, which he had been extolling in the course of his *tafsir*, the open letter remarked that "all the learned people in Islamic history and sciences say that Wahhabism is a rebellion against Qur'an and *sunna*."[49]

[44]*Hakika nasiha ita ce addini*, mimeo, Kaduna, 1977, p. 5.
[45]*Ibid.*, pp. 2-3.
[46]*Ibid.*, p. 4.
[47]*Ibid.*
[48]*Ibid.*, pp. 5-8.
[49]*Ibid.*, p. 9.

A quick perusal of the issues in the open letter will make it clear that they were too vexed for the quarreling parties to debate amicably, and in fact the debate did not take place. Soon afterwards, the close disciples of Gumi began to realize the need for a new mode of operation against Sufism. The idea was conceived of a formal organization to counteract the activities of the *Kungiyar Dakarun Dan Fodio*. After a year the idea was realised, and on 12 March 1978 *Jama'atu Izalat al-Bid'a* was formally launched in Jos. In his goodwill message to the launching, Gumi advised that the clause *wa Iqamat al-Sunna* be added to the name, and thus was born *Jama'atu Izalat al-Bid'a wa Iqamat al-Sunna (Izala)*. The subsequent history of *Izala* has been too eventful to be even outlined here. Suffice it to note that it has already become widespread everywhere in Nigeria. According to the report of the executive secretary of the movement to its National Symposium in November 1986:

> It has now become imperative to mention the achievements of the movement [i.e. *Izala*] as of today. In the beginning [1978], we had only one mosque for *'Id* prayers which was located in Jos. And then in 1979 we got a Friday mosque. But today [1986] we have, without doubt, these places of religious worship nearly everywhere in this country. It is either that we have constructed new ones for ourselves, or the *imams* in the old ones have seen the light [i.e. have accepted *Izala*]. But [our] great achievement has been teaching in modern schools. We have reached the stage whereby in every corner in this country today we have [established] schools for adult classes, primary evening schools, and also schools for married women. Our branches by 1977-78 were only four (4), today we have branches in 99% of the local government areas in the country, in so far as there are Muslim residents there. There is nowhere in this country today where *Izala* is not preached.[50]

The widespread expansion of *Izala* has been brought about through two principal means. First, recording the preaching of *Izala* on audio cassettes and distributing them all over the country. All the preachings of the movement are normally recorded on cassettes, reproduced in large numbers and then widely circulated. Each recorded cassette normally contains information about the date, place and occasion of its recording. And secondly, organizing preaching sessions in various parts of the country. Since the formation of *Izala*, thousands of preaching sessions have been held at different times and places

[50]M. S. Muhammad, *Jawabin babban sakatare kan takaitacciyar tarihin kungiya a taron karawa juna sani na kungiya da aka yi a haidkwatarta,* 14-16 Nov., 1986, mimeo.

Other factors that might have helped in spreading *Izala* include the organizational facilities of the movement, which was registered as a corporate body on 12 December 1985 by the Nigerian Federal Ministry of Internal Affairs under the Land Perpetual Succession Act of 1962. This meant that *Izala* as a legal entity could now avail itself of all the rights and privileges inherent in that status, which would be useful in court cases, of which there have been many. Many individuals have helped in making *Izala* what it is today, most notably the preachers of the movement, especially Mallam Isma'ila Idris who has been chairman of *Izala*'s Council of Preachers since its formation. Others have contributed in carrying out day-to-day administration of *Izala* activities, and provided inspiration and guidance; among these Abubakar Mahmud Gumi stands out as a national patron of the movement.[51] One of the interesting aspects of the development of Sufism and anti-Sufism in Nigeria is that adherence to either the Sufi or the anti-Sufi camps cut across all social strata, for each camp has members in the most diverse sectors of society. This fact defies the standard supposition in most social scientific paradigms that social movements such as *Izala* ought to attract membership from a particular social stratum.[52]

The doctrines of *Izala* are basically identical with Gumi's ideas: each and every Sufi order is not part of Islam but a new religion standing on its own. In fact, we have seen that *Izala* was conceived originally out of the need to create an organized forum for the continuation of Gumi's anti-Sufism in the face of organized opposition by followers of Sufi orders through the *Jama'atu Ahlus-Sunnati* and the *Kunqiyar Dakarun Dan Fodio, Jundullahi, Fityanul Islam*. The doctrines of *Izala* are articulated in a number of booklets, written submissions and memoranda by *Izala* to various governmental organs and committees of inquiry, and in their countless recorded audio cassettes of the preaching of the movement.

Related to the question of doctrine is the militant way in which *Izala* preaches its doctrines. Although both Gumi and *Izala* preach the same ideas, Gumi does so in a rather subtle way, using non-provocative language and sometimes preaching a single doctrine in stages. But *Izala* goes direct to the point by mentioning the personal names of the founders of the Sufi orders and denouncing them in unpalatable words. Their denunciation as *mushrikun* in the *Report of the Committee on Darika and Anti-Darika Movements in Plateau*

[51] *Ibid.*, pp. 4-5.

[52] See for example, Ousmane Kane, "Les mouvements religieux et le champ politique au Nigéria septentrional. Le cas du réformisme musulman à Kano," *Islam et Sociétés au Sud du Sahara*, 4, 1990, pp. 20 ff.

*State*,[53] especially exasperated them. The Report further noted that the sarcasm in *Izala*'s preaching often led to friction and physical confrontation.[54] The escalation of tension into physical confrontation is by no means confined to Plateau State alone. The Aniagolu Tribunal of Inquiry examined the issue and listed the details of some thirty-four clashes between June 1978 and December 1980, and noted that most of these "called for the intervention of the Police and often resulted in loss of life and damage to vehicles or properties. ... The rival groups involved were principally *Izala*, Tijaniyya, and Qadiriyya."[55] Thus, governmental intervention became inevitable for reasons of state and national security, public peace, law and order etc. At the instance of the Federal Military Government, the Supreme Council of Islamic Affairs set up a sub-committee on *tariqu* to work out a consensus among the leaders of the Sufi orders and *Izala*, and to influence their respective followers towards unity and harmony, instead of schism and tension.

The first meeting of the Committee was on 3 May 1978 at the palace of the Sultan of Sokoto, and after a series of meetings in Lagos and Sokoto members of the Committee reached consensus on twelve points and signed a conciliating document in the presence of the Sultan. The document, which came to be known as the *Sokoto Accord*, or *Matsayar Sokoto* in Hausa, was publicized through the mass media. However, it did not produce the desired effect of reconciling *Izala* members and the followers of Tijaniyya and Qadiriyya, which is not surprizing since the conflict involves fundamental doctrinal differences which cannot be erased by an arranged agreement without due cognizance being taken of the differences themselves. Thus, no sooner was the agreement signed than the signatories and their followers began to put ingenious interpretations on the text.

For example, point 2 of the agreement reads:

> The scholars agreed that books written on Sufism are actually meant for the Sufis, and should not be investigated into once their field was not properly known.

Point 7 reads:

> The scholars also unanimously agreed that the *Hadith* in which Angel Jibril came to the Prophet(s) asking for the meanings of Islam, *Iman* and *Ihsan* has covered three things: (a) The meaning of Islam; (b) The

[53] *Report by the Committee on Darika and Anti-Darika Movements in Plateau State: Main Report*, (Jos, 1980), vol. 1, p. 62.

[54] *Ibid.*

[55] *Report of Tribunal of Inquiry on Kano Disturbances* (Lagos, 1981), p. 87.

> meaning of *Iman*; (c) The meaning of *Ihsan*. The field that explains Islam is what is known as *Fikhu* and its *Furu'* [branches]. The field that explains *Iman* is what is known as *'Ilm al-Tawhid wa 'l-Kalam*. The field that investigates *Ihsan* is what is known as *tasawwuf*, and all that was attached to it in the form of meditations (*wuridai*) or ecstasies (*azkaru*) (*sic*) are collectively mysticism.

Point 2 was interpreted by *Izala* members to mean that Sufism and Sufi orders were not part of Islam, and therefore Muslims should abandon them and stick to the Qur'an and the *sunna* of the Prophet. But the followers of the Sufi orders countered this interpretation by emphasizing the fact that point 7 clearly established an Islamic basis for Sufism and Sufi orders. Point 6 is quite problematic in asserting that:

> The scholars also agreed that belonging to a sect (*Darika*) is not compulsory on Muslims, but looking for someone to follow in religion is compulsory as getting a person to be upright on his own is very rare.

It seems that while conceding that affiliation to a Sufi order is not compulsory on Muslims, the point holds that looking for someone to follow in religion is compulsory. This of course sounds like another way of stating the Sufi belief in the necessity of following a *murshid*. In this way, the Sokoto Accord, drawn up ostensibly to solve the dispute between Sufis and anti-Sufis, became part of the problem.

Meanwhile, the continued tension on the ground, which occasionally led to violent clashes, was somewhat neutralized by the politics of the Second Republic (1979-83) when political parties and political rallies competed for loyalty and attention with the religious organizations. Similarly, recorded audio cassettes of preaching were alternated with recorded party songs and speeches. In the event, it was not so easy for political parties to manipulate the various religious organizations, especially since the question of casting votes became a delicate one. The problem here was whether members of *Izala* and followers of the Tijaniyya and Qadiriyya should vote on a party or individual basis. Although there was no clear stand on this, the consensus appeared to be that voting should not be on a party basis; members of *Izala* were expected to vote for fellow *Izala* members while members of the Sufi orders were expected to vote for their fellow members. Where there were *Izala* and non-Muslim candidates only, then Sufis should vote for the non-Muslim candidate. Similarly, where there were Sufi and non-Muslim candidates only, *Izala* members should vote for the non-Muslim candidate. This position presented a real dilemma for political parties, and led to considerable confusion within the respective religious organizations. None of the political parties could afford openly to associate with one particular religious organization, if only because of the simple fact that all the political parties had in their membership non-Muslims and Muslims who might be of Sufi or anti-Sufi persuasion. Yet Sufi and anti-Sufi considerations were quite relevant among the Muslim electorate when it came to voting. But then not all the Muslim electorate were prepared to place sectarian considerations of Sufism versus anti-Sufism over religious considerations of Islam versus Christianity. With this ambivalence, factionalism within the religious organizations became inevitable, and resignation, dismissal and counter-dismissal became part of the internal workings of the religious organizations, especially *Izala*.

As the 1983 general elections approached amidst these developments, there was widespread apathy resulting from a general loss of confidence in the country in the ability of the federal government, which was controlled by the National Party of Nigeria (NPN), to conduct free and fair elections. In an attempt to galvanize voters, Shaikh Abubakar Gumi declared in May 1983 that voting in the forthcoming elections was more important than *salat*,[56] a declaration that generated heated controversies, and followers of the Sufi orders had a field-day denouncing Gumi. He and his close disciples strove to arrest the damage the declaration had caused, but it was too late; there was no way of avoiding the charge that Gumi was a spokesman for the discredited NPN-controlled federal government, even among some *Izala* members!

Another issue bearing on the conflict between *Izala* and the Sufi orders during the Second Republic and long after was the series of violent disturbances connected with the Maitatsine affair. As nobody wanted to be associated with these events, *Izala* and the Sufi orders found it tempting to accuse each other of involvement with Maitatsine. However, despite all the allegations, there is no concrete evidence linking either *Izala* or the Sufi orders to the Maitatsine disturbances.[57]

The colossal destruction of life and property which resulted from these disturbances forced a reconsideration of questions of religious differences and tolerance, unity and peaceful co-existence, national and state security, and the maintenance of law and order. The state security apparatus became more meticulous in monitoring the activities of the religious organizations. Open-air preaching, which regained vigor after the collapse of the Second Republic, often had to be banned. Such bans have tended to affect *Izala* more than other religious organizations

[56]Gumbi, *Tarihin Shaikh*, p. 11; *Tarihin Wa'azin*, pp. 17-23.
[57]For a discussion of these events, see the chapter by Bawuro Barkindo.

because open-air preaching has been one of its principal modes of operation. Because of this, *Izala* has tended to view such bans as being primarily aimed at checking its own activities, often alluding to an alleged conspiracy between the Sufi orders and certain sympathetic individuals who might be in control of the state security apparatus and the law enforcement agencies. This partly explains why *Izala* fell out with the Shagari regime.

Similarly, when the Buhari government (1984-5) placed a blanket ban on religious activism, and especially on open-air preaching, *Izala* became particularly discontented. Little wonder, then, that both the Shagari and the Buhari regimes – of course, only after their respective falls – came in for special castigation in one of the sermons of Mallam Isma'ila Idris:

> There are two regimes in Nigeria which Allah will not forgive forever: the Shagari and the Buhari regimes ... because these two regimes were always practicing tyranny and oppression and blocking the way of Allah.[58]

However, many Nigerians regarded the Buhari regime as patriotic, and not all *Izala* members agreed with this statement by Mallam Isma'ila Idris, thus escalating dissension and factionalization, and in turn affecting the *Izala* position in its conflict with the Sufi orders.

Another dimension was added to the general conflict during the 1980s with the introduction of Shi'ite doctrines into Nigeria. Since the Iranian Revolution in 1979, Shi'ite literature had been finding its way into Nigeria, disseminating both Shi'ite doctrines and the views of the Islamic Revolutionary regime in Iran. Nigerian Muslims who were attracted to the ideals of the Islamic Revolution in Iran have also become acquainted with Shi'ite doctrines, some of them for the first time. However, *Izala* condemns the Shi'a, just as it does the Sufi orders, as a new religion standing on its own outside the pale of Islam. Nigerian Muslims attracted to the ideals of the Iranian Revolution find this *Izala* condemnation difficult to reconcile with what they read about Shi'a in the Iranian literature. Consequently, they began to part ways with *Izala*.

The advent of Shi'ite doctrines into Nigeria influenced the relationship between *Izala* and the Sufi orders. Whereas *Izala* condemned Shi'a as a new religion, Shaikh Dahiru Usman Bauchi, a prominent Tijani *muqaddam* and a vocal spokesman of the Sufi orders, took pains to explain that there exist sub-branches within Shi'a, and that only the extremist sub-branches (the *Ghulat al-Shi'a*) could be

[58] From a public sermon recorded on audio cassette in Keffi, Plateau State, 13 Oct. 1985.

considered as having gone out of Islam. According to Shaikh Dahiru Bauchi, "the Shi'a we have today, the followers of Ayatollah Khomeini, are Muslims because Khomeini has preached to them and reformed them. They have abandoned many things that used to be associated with the Shi'a."[59] It was then that an amicable relationship came to exist between the Sufi orders in Nigeria and the Islamic Revolutionary regime in Iran. Shaikh Dahiru Bauchi was one of the special guests invited to the eighth anniversary celebrations of the Islamic Revolution in Iran and was granted an interview by the Iranian Hausa magazine *Sakon Islama,*[60] in which he reiterated some of the issues in the quarrel between *Izala* and the Sufi orders.

Some of the major developments during the 1980s which have thus far been discussed combined to lessen the tensions between Sufi and anti-Sufi factions. These include the politics of voting on a party or an individual basis, with or without consideration to the Sufi or anti-Sufi orientation of the candidate, and the internal dissension and factionalization arising from it; the Maitatsine debacle and the banning of religious activism; and the advent and development of Shi'a in Nigeria. However, the tensions were being sustained at the same time by other parallel developments.

First, the efforts of the Sufi *'ulama* to break Gumi's monopoly of religious broadcasting in Kaduna began to yield results by the early 1980s. Shaikh Dahiru Usman Bauchi began to feature in some of the religious programmes of the Federal Radio Corporation of Nigeria (Kaduna), and his own *tafsir* began to be broadcast along with that of Abubakar Gumi during the month of Ramadan. Thus Sufism and anti-Sufism came to share the vast audience of the Federal Radio Corporation of Nigeria (Kaduna). Just as Gumi used his *tafsir* broadcast to preach anti-Sufism, Dahiru Bauchi now did the same on behalf of Sufism, seizing every opportunity to provide Qur'anic bases for Sufism and Sufi orders. This point comes out quite clearly in Shaikh Dahiru's *tafsir* of the eighteenth chapter of the Holy Qu'ran, *Surat al-Kahf,* which he declared to be the Qur'anic chapter on Sufism in which details could be found about: "*shaikhs* and their *murids*; *tariqa*, *tarbiya*, *al-wusul, al-dhikr,* who the *shaikhs* follow, and how they are to be followed, etc."[61] Shaikh Dahiru Bauchi does not restrict

[59]Shaikh Dahiru Bauchi, "*Manufa da matsayinmu akan ibada,*" *Mujallar Amana,* 15 Jan. 1988, p. 17.

[60]"*Mu tattauna: Shehu Dahiru Bauchi Nijeriya,*" *Sakon Islama,* no. 4, Rabi'ul-Awwal 1408 A.H. (1987), pp. 30-3.

[61]FRCN(Kaduna), Tape no. 23: *Tafsir Daga Masallacin Juma'a na Tudun Wada, Kaduna, Shaikh Dahiru Usman Bauchi da Mallam Muhammadu Mai Kaulasan, Suratul Kahf,* Chapter 18, verses 58-73, 30 May 1986.

himself simply to defending Sufism; he often launches aggressive aṭtacks on anti-Sufism and its proponents, as he did in his commentary on Qur'an 18:102-5, by extending the reproach in these verses directly to the anti-Sufis, with clear allusions to Gumi's utterances about voting being more important than *salat*.[62]

Another factor which has sustained the conflict is the separation of mosques, with *Izala* and the Sufi orders each maintaining their own mosques. The mosque has historically been a forum for the communal manifestation of Islam through which identity, solidarity and social cohesion were constantly enhanced. However, *Izala* insists that it has become imperative to establish separate mosques in Nigeria today because of fundamental doctrinal differences. It should be recalled that *Izala* regards the Sufi orders as new religions standing on their own, while the followers of the Sufi orders are condemned by *Izala* as *mushrikun*. The logical consequence of this position is that *Izala* members cannot accept that the followers of the Sufi orders should lead them in prayer. Hence their insistence on separate mosques for their members, whom they claim to be followers of the *sunna* of the Prophet, and separate ones for the followers of the Sufi orders, whom *Izala* condemned as practitioners of *shirk*.[63] We have earlier seen in the report of *Izala*'s executive secretary that establishing separate mosques for the daily, Friday and *'Id* prayers was regarded as one of *Izala*'s major achievements. However, separating mosques has been one of the sources of friction which has continued to keep tension high, attracting criticism against *Izala* even from non-Sufis.

Since the publication of Gumi's *al-'Aqīda al-ṣaḥīḥa* in 1972, other books have continued to appear representing each side of the conflict. In 1978, Abd al-Samad al-Kashini published his *Risālat al-dā'ī ilā 'l-sunna al-zājir 'an al-bid'a* (The Epistle of the Caller to the Sunna and Warner against Innovation). In the same year Isma'ila Idris published a booklet entitled *A Gane Bambancin Gaskiya da Karya* (Understand the Difference between Truth and Falsehood). By 1981, the research of Dahiru Maigari on the life-history of Shaikh Ibrahim Niass – his contribution to the Tijaniyya, especially on doctrinal issues, his appearance, followers and influence in Nigeria – was published as *al-Shaikh Ibrāhīm Niass al-Singhālī, ḥayātuh wa ārā'uh wa ta'ālīmuh* (Shaikh Ibrahim Niass the Senegalese: His Life, his Views and his Teachings). This book is a voluminous exposé of the Tijaniyya under

[62]FRCN(Kaduna), Tape no. 26: *Tafsir Daga Masallacin Juma'a Na Tudun Wada, Shaikh Dahiru Usman Bauchi da Mallam Muhammadu Mai Kaulasan, Suratul Kahf*, Chapter 18, verses 102-110, 1 June 1986.

[63]See what Shaikh Isma'ila Idris has to say on separation of mosques in his interview with *Mujallar Amana*, 15 Mar. 1988, pp. 18-19.

the leadership of Niass, and contains disparaging remarks about him. In a rejoinder to the book titled *Indhār wa ifāda ilā bā'ī' dīnihi bi-shihāda* (A Warning and Admonishing to him who has sold his Religion to Obtain a Certificate),[64] a Tijani enthusiast from Mauritania sought to impeach the motives of Dahiru Maigari and to cast serious aspersions on his personal integrity. This in turn provoked Maigari to publish *al-Tuḥfat al-saniyya bi-tawḍīḥ al-ṭarīqa Tijāniyya* (A Valuable Present to Explain the Tijaniyya Order), where the vehemence of his denunciations made all the previous critiques of Sufism in Nigeria pale into insignificance. The national headquarters of *Izala* published some of its doctrines in a 1986 booklet, *Hasm al-tardīd fī 'ilm al-tawḥīd* (Discontinuance of Doubt in the Science of *tawhid*). This contains sophisticated arguments on complicated aspects of Islamic theology by which the authors seek to expose some Sufi doctrines as incompatible with *tawhid.* A related development has been the introduction into Nigeria of Wahhabi classics from Saudi Arabia, which became more wide-spread during the 1980s. Most popular among such classics has been the *Kitāb al-tawhīd* of Shaikh Muhammad b. 'Abd al-Wahhab, as well as a number of Ibn Taymiyya's works. Through these publications another dimension is added to the intellectual aspect of the confrontation between Sufism and anti-Sufism.

Among the many factors which have continued to generate tension and sustain the conflict, the three discussed here – the *tafsir* broadcasts, the separation of mosques, and the intensification of polemics – have been most significant. Further efforts at reconciliation were attempted; for example, during the 1985 *hajj,* an agreement was reached in Mecca under which Gumi prayed behind some of the Sufi *'ulama*, and they in turn were led in prayer by Gumi.[65] However, this in itself did not produce any tangible unity or reconciliation among their followers in Nigeria.[66] A second attempt was made in 1988, when the Sokoto Accord was reaffirmed by all its signatories as a valid basis for unity among the Nigerian Muslims.[67] It remains to be seen what this reaffirmation of the Accord can achieve in concrete terms.

[64]The certificate here refers to the fact that the research findings of Maigari were first submitted as an M.A. thesis to Bayero University.

[65]See the front page lead story, "*Gayra Sabanin Malamai,*" in *Amana* of 7 Oct. 1985.

[66]*Ibid.*

[67]ee the *New Nigerian,* 19 Jan. 1988 and 21 Jan. 1988.

*Conclusion*

It was suggested at the beginning of this chapter that the rise of anti-Sufism in Nigeria can be traced to the imposition of British colonialism with all its attendant political, social and economic changes. The colonization of Nigeria between 1900 and 1960 brought with it the forceful imposition of capitalism in the country, a process which led to severe disruptions of all aspects of life. Having become deeply entrenched in Nigeria by the time of "flag independence" in 1960, capitalism continued to expand subsequently.

Within the first decade after independence, the Nigerian economy continued to experience transformations from small-scale and largely communal, rural and peasant agriculture toward an increasingly large-scale urban commercial activity with so-called cash crops as the principal commodity. In addition, there were the little industrial ventures which sixty years of colonialism had bequeathed to Nigeria. But the decade of the 1970s saw tremendous expansion in the Nigerian economy arising from the oil boom. The agricultural sector was marginalized as the oil sector came to dominate. The huge financial returns generated by the oil boom, as well as the affluence and the extravagance which accompanied it, produced grave repercussions within Nigerian society at large.

First, competition for the affluence offered by the oil boom gave birth to a rugged individualism, and the affluence itself put stress on the moral fabric of the society, since it undermined the religious consciousness of many Nigerians. There was also a process of mass drift of people from the rural areas into urban centers. This in turn put strong pressure on the limited facilities of the urban centers, which in the first instance were rooted in capitalist fashion to maintain unequal access. Consequently, the process of rapid urbanization was traumatic for many Nigerians, creating inflated expectations and consumerist wants which could not possibly be met given the unequal capitalist distribution of wealth, goods and services. The grievances so created could not but generate protests. Anti-Sufism is one such protest from a segment of Nigerian Muslims.

Second, these transformations within the economy of the oil boom re-echoed at the political level. There was a general shift in the locus of political power and the basis of authority. Before the attainment of flag independence, colonialism had already eroded the legitimacy of the emirates, although they still remained effective political instruments in the hands of the British. However, the first decade of independence saw the further progressive erosion of whatever residual political power the colonialists might have left in the hands of the emirates. All the emirs, including the Sultan of Sokoto, increasingly found themselves prostrating before the Northern Region government in Kaduna. The creation of twelve states in 1967 curtailed more of their residual powers, and in the same year the Area Court Edict abolished the emir's courts, thereby removing the emirs from the administration of the *shari'a*. The beginning of the 1970s saw the emergent bureaucratic élites concentrating more power in their hands through state organs, made even more effective by their tight control over the huge financial resources of the oil boom. Their rise to power may be regarded as a major cause of the decline in the power of the emirs. The process culminated in the Local Government Reform of 1976 whereby the emirs were brought under the control of the bureaucratic machine of the newly-created Local Government Councils. Thus, having lost political power and control over resources, the emirs have now submitted meekly to the hegemony of the new locus of power: the secular national state of Nigeria and its various agencies and organs. This has had damaging consequences for the status of the emirates as Islamic political institutions.

One must emphasize that the political transformation from the emirates to the national state of Nigeria has not created a polity without its own peculiar problems. In fact, the national state has produced a political culture in which the control of state power has become a most lucrative business. The concentration of that power in the hands of a tiny group has necessarily marginalized the multitude of Nigerians, who can only voice their legitimate grievances in the form of protest.

It was amidst the affluence of the oil boom, the rat-race of rugged individualism, the trauma of rapid urbanization, perceived moral and religious lapses, the shift in the locus of political power from the emirates to the national state, the concentration of political power in the hands of a tiny minority and the political marginalization of the multitude of Nigerians, all taking place between the 1960s and the 1980s, that anti-Sufism took definite shape and became popularized. In what ways have all these developments and anti-Sufism acted and reacted upon each other?

First, it should be acknowledged that anti-Sufism is a protest – specifically against Sufism but more generally against many other things: traditional non-capitalist values, the religious authority of Sufi orders, and perceived corruption of religious beliefs and practices. Anti-Sufism as a protest is directly linked with all the aspects of those developments which engender the need to protest. Second, anti-Sufism should be looked at as part of the general transformation of all aspects of life in Nigeria during the period under review. Just as the economy, polity and society underwent transformations, so did religious life.

The shift from Sufism to anti-Sufism entails a reorientation from a communal to an individualistic mode of religiosity, and seems to be more in tune with the rugged individualism of capitalist social relations. Finally, the combined effects of these transformations engender a great deal of tension and discontent within Nigerian society at large, whereas the marginalization of the majority of Nigerians in the political process means that they have no means to obtain the resolution of their many grievances. In such a frustrating situation, a strong tendency can emerge to seek a catharsis through religion or to articulate political issues in religious terms, a tendency which is increased under military regimes when religious organizations and activism become forums for pursuing political objectives in the absence of other political outlets. Anti-Sufism is one such catharsis for some Muslims among the mass of marginalized Nigerians.

# ISLAMIC LEARNING AND ITS INTERACTION WITH "WESTERN" EDUCATION IN ILORIN, NIGERIA

*Stefan Reichmuth*

The remarkable growth of Islamic learning and its institutions in Nigeria has been a phenomenon noticed by many observers during recent years. This process was all the more remarkable because it occurred during a period when the public education system also expanded tremendously and was brought more and more under direct government control. After the introduction of the Universal Primary Education (UPE) scheme in 1976, Islamic schooling increased rather than decreased following the spread of public education in Muslim communities in Nigeria. In several states of the Federation, the two educational systems have been linked at different levels, a development which started during the 1950s and 1960s but gained in importance after the introduction of UPE. The Islamiyya school sector in particular has expanded considerably; it has a much larger percentage of female students than the old *'ilm* schools and continues to provide students for public institutions. On the other hand, Islamic subjects as well as Arabic were established on different levels within the public educational system. Contrary to many fears and apprehensions, there has been a continuous interaction of the different forms of "Western" and Islamic education in Nigeria. This interaction no longer corresponds to the usual distinction between "traditional" and "modern" forms of learning, which was still used by Brown and Hiskett[1] in their approach to the educational situation in Africa. It calls rather for a model whereby educational systems are seen as resulting from conflict and interaction within a given society.[2] Even educational institutions introduced by foreign, colonial intervention have developed in response to internal forces and pressures which led to considerable alterations to the original set-up. The role of Muslim communities and organizations has become more and more significant for the shaping of a national education system in Nigeria.

Ilorin, one of the largest Muslim cities in Nigeria, provides a particularly good example of this interaction of different forms of education. As the centre of one of the Nigerian Muslim emirates,

[1]G. Brown and M. Hiskett (eds), *Conflict and Harmony in Education in Tropical Africa* (London, 1975), especially pp.91-103, 273-7.

[2]For such a model and its macro-sociological implications, see M.S. Archer, *Social Origins of Educational Systems* (London, 1984).

which subsequently became the capital of Kwara State in 1967, it has developed into one of the important educational cities of Nigeria, in terms of both Islamic and "Western" institutions of learning. There are at present three systems of education which can be distinguished in Ilorin: Qur'anic and *'ilm* schools, modernized Arabic schools (*ibtida'i-i'dadi-thanawi*), and public and private "Western" institutions from primary school to university. These systems influence one another, because most children as well as teachers in Ilorin are exposed to or trained in more than one of them. Although for some time now "Western" education has come to be widely accepted, the Islamic sector has also expanded considerably, and several public colleges and departments for Arabic and Islamic studies have been created in the State. Islamic educational societies and youth organizations have become crucial factors in both cultural and political life, articulating, and sometimes also struggling for, Muslim interests in a city which is developing more and more into a multi-religious metropolis.

The following overview of the different systems of learning in Ilorin and their cultural as well as political significance is based on research conducted in the period 1984-9. Apart from many informal interviews and personal observations, it is based on a survey of Islamic schools in the town which was first conducted in 1985 and expanded in the following years.[3] Although this survey is far from comprehensive it nevertheless attempts to give a representative picture of what is going on in the field of Islamic learning and education in the town, in a sector of intense private activity and enterprise which has been aptly described as an "industry."

Islamic scholars and Islamic learning played a crucial role in the emergence of a Muslim emirate in Ilorin after 1800.[4] The internal

[3]The survey was planned and organized in cooperation with Prof. Razaq D. Abubakre, Department of Religions, University of Ilorin. It was conducted by Rasheed Bello and Elias A. Irawosan, graduates of the department. Most further interviews were assisted by Mr. Isa Oke, Kwara State Council for Arts and Culture. The late Emir of Ilorin, Alhaji Zulkarnaini Gambari, and the Madawaki of Ilorin, Alh. Dr. Yahaya Madawaki, provided crucial support in different stages of the research. For detailed documentation of the following summary statements see S. Reichmuth, *'Ilm und Adab. Islamische Bildung und soziale Integration in Ilorin, Nigeria, seit ca. 1800,* forthcoming.

[4]For the history of Ilorin within the framework of both the Oyo Empire and the Sokoto Caliphate see especially S.A. Balogun, "Gwandu Emirates in the Nineteenth Century with special reference to Political Relations, 1817-1903," unpubl. Ph.D. thesis, University of Ibadan, 1970; H.O.A. Danmole, "The Frontier Emirate: A History of Islam in Ilorin," unpubl. Ph.D. thesis, University of Birmingham 1980; Reichmuth, forthcoming.

structure of the town was characterized by a dual hierarchy of warlords and religious dignitaries, with the Emir as the head of both. Alimi, the Fulani preacher who had been the father of the first emirs, came to be regarded as a kind of founding saint, and up to the present day his "rank" (Ar. *jah,* Yor. *olá*)[5] is invoked in prayers by the *alufas* of Ilorin. Like the warlords with their large households, scholars and *imams* became part of the ethno-political system of Ilorin which was designed to keep the political balance in this multi-ethnic and cosmopolitan city. Fulbe, Hausa, Nupe, Kanuri and Yoruba, people from Borgu and Mali and even Arabs belonged to this group. Religious authority was partly attached to the offices of the leading *imams* (Imam Fulani, Imam Imale, Imam Gambari) as religious heads of their quarters, with the Imam Fulani as the Chief Imam of the city. Apart from these and other *imam* offices, teaching and scholarship remained free professions involving a considerable degree of competition and diversification. Significantly, written authorizations (*ijazat*) never played a role in the town; any scholar who was attracted to Ilorin had to obtain the recognition of the Emir and the scholar community, or become a student of one of the established teachers, before he could hope to build up his own position.

In this booming city, which until around 1870 was the second largest town in the Caliphate after Kano and the major trading and manufacturing centre south of the Niger, the Islamic scholars (Yor. *alùfá*) developed into a status group which cut across the different layers of the society. A growing network of Islamic schools reflected the official recognition of Islamic learning in the town. Children from about 7-10 years of age were sent to Qur'anic schools, and the end of schooling very often coincided with the first marriage. The percentage of female students seems to have been much higher than in most other parts of northern Nigeria, perhaps due to the prominent role of women in the economic life of the town and to the absence of early marriage practices among the Yoruba. Adults, especially non-indigenes, also constituted an important proportion of the Qur'anic students. Ilorin attracted large numbers of foreigners. Qur'anic and *'ilm* studies became part of what could be called an educational "package" which the town had to offer and which contained religious instruction and professional training in different crafts, as well as horsemanship and warfare. Qur'anic schooling served as an important way of initiation and integration into the urban society. The "marriage by charity" (Yor. *sàráà*) played an important role here. A poor student of good religious

[5]For these notions, see P. Ryan, *Imale: Yoruba Participation in the Muslim Tradition* (Missoula, 1978), pp.188ff.

reputation was often given a wife by the teacher himself or by another man in the neighbourhood as *sàráà*, which saved him the costs of an otherwise rather expensive marriage, and which also secured him the support of the bride's family.

The initiatory function of the Qur'anic school is still reflected in the *walima* celebrations which are held at the student's completion of certain Suras of the Qur'an. Several schools follow a pattern of these celebrations which seems to be quite old and common in the town and which conveys certain symbolic messages connected with the completed Suras. The celebrations start with Sura 105 (*al-Fil*), followed by Suras 87 (*al-A'la*) and 36 (*Yasin*). All these are important protective texts which convey God's blessing and promise for the believer. Sura 9 (*at-Tauba*) comes next, calling for a clear break with unbelief and paganism, as well as for unflinching support of the cause of God. Finally, the great *walima* celebration which is held for the completion of the whole Qur'an, and which in Ilorin usually takes place on the day before the wedding, involves the recitation of Sura 2:1-5, verses which define the ideal of the active believer committed to God's word and to his religious duties. This transition from a more or less passive acceptance of God's blessing and promise to an active membership in the Muslim community seems to be unique to Ilorin and for some areas closely connected with it. In southern Yorubaland as well as in the north these celebrations follow different patterns. The symbolic and therapeutic use of Qur'anic texts for different situations in social and personal life remains a basic element in Nigerian Muslim culture up to today.[6] Despite the early entrance age to the Qur'anic school, which since the colonial period has become fairly general in the town (3-4 years as against 7-10 years in former times), the *walima* is still postponed until the wedding, which again shows the strong initiatory character of this religious ceremony.

For a good number of the students, the study of other religious texts and disciplines, the *'ilm* stage of Islamic studies, followed the completion of the first recitation of the Holy Book. Many Qur'anic teachers also teach elementary *'ilm* texts, and most *'ilm* scholars maintain a Qur'anic school within their family which serves as the main "feeder" for their *'ilm* classes. Lessons are given individually or in groups. *'Ilm* studies in Ilorin and Yorubaland begin with a number of short Arabic texts and poems of only a few pages, which are commonly read before the longer textbooks in the different religious

[6]For Kano, see J.A. McIntyre, "Context and Register in Qur'anic Education: Words and their Meaning in the Register of Kano Malams," *Sprache, Geschichte und Kultur in Afrika*. Vorträge gehalten auf dem III. Afrikanistentag, 14/15 Oktober 1982, Hamburg, 1983, pp. 362ff.

and literary disciplines. This programme of elementary studies contains basic statements of ritual and dogma as well as some symbolic interpretation of them. The main element consists of moral exhortations (*wa'z*) and poems in praise of the Prophet, combined with some introductory Arabic grammar. From these short elementary texts a tendency towards an Islamic mass education becomes clearly recognizable, and up to the present day they are quite common even in modernized Arabic schools.[7]

Beside this elementary programme, all the *'ilm* disciplines were well represented in Ilorin, and it seems remarkable how fast a new centre of Islamic learning could be created and high standards achieved in this town. A rather intricate combination of legal and theological doctrine with Arabic language and literature as well as with moral and ethical wisdom and magico-therapeutic devices gave Islamic knowledge in Ilorin its particular character. It provided the basis for the reputation of the *alufas* who held offices as *imams* and judges and who also served as teachers, preachers, advisers, and healers. Their role as religious authorities finds an eschatological expression in the intercession (*shafa'a*) which is attributed to them and which they will be allowed to exercise in favour of their disciples and followers at the time of the Last Judgement.[8]

Right from the nineteenth century the *alufas* were not only connected with Emirate authority but also with the particular interests of the ethno-political groups in the different quarters of the town. There were outbreaks of unrest in the Yoruba quarters around 1865 in which some of the leading *imams* and scholars were fully involved, as well as a clash between Emir Aliyu and a leading preacher of the town who also came from that area (probably around 1870). This opposition role continued during the early colonial period with the tax riots of 1913 in which *imams* and *alufas*, again mainly from the Yoruba quarters, were leading elements. During the 1950s many *alufas* supported the opposition party founded in 1954, the *Ilorin Talaka Parapo (ITP)*. Significantly, this party used a Qur'anic slate as its emblem: by this, it obviously tried to generate broad support in the town, and Qur'anic learning, shared by so many as their basic form of education, served as a common expression of opposition against the

[7]Many of them were published by Adam 'Abdullah al-Iluri in his collections *Qāla ash-shaikh* and *al-Fawākih as-sāqiṭa*, both Cairo (n.d.), which are widely used in Ilorin as well as in other parts of Yorubaland.

[8]This goes back to classical Islamic doctrine, see e.g. al-Baijuri's commentary on al-Laqqani, *Tuḥfat al-murīd 'alā Jawharat at-tawḥīd,* Cairo, 1357/1939, pp.116ff. Judging from some very widespread Arabic *wa'z* poems, this still seems to be an important aspect of the position and authority of Islamic scholars in Ilorin, and presumably also in other parts of Nigeria.

rule of the new emirate élite connected with the ruling party in the north, the Northern Peoples Congress (NPC), and with the government of the Northern Region in Kaduna.

The political and economic changes which were brought about by colonial rule also affected the *alufas*. The gradual economic decline of Ilorin and the economic prosperity in the south led to a continuous process of migration. The reputation of Ilorin as a centre of Islamic learning frequently helped *alufas* from this town to establish themselves as teachers, preachers or *imams* in Muslim communities in the south. As in other parts of Nigeria, Sufi brotherhoods gained influence due to growing contacts with other Islamic centres inside and outside Nigeria. Even more significant for Ilorin, and the Yoruba Muslims in general, was a growing veneration of the Arabic language and a marked interest in Arabic rhetoric, presumably in connection with the practice of preaching. Scholars from Ilorin played an important role in spreading this discipline. Another factor was the presence of Arab immigrants in the cities of the south, especially in Lagos and Abeokuta. They gained influence as teachers and through their contacts with Arab countries introduced the trade in Arabic printed books to southern Nigeria.

One of the most influential religious movements in Ilorin, the *Adabiyya,* combined these two orientations, towards mysticism and Arabic language and rhetoric, with a new attitude towards the youth. Their founding figure was Shaikh Muhammad al-Labib Taju 'l-Adab (1885-1923), a son of the *imam* of the Yoruba quarters (Imam Imale). He became one of the famous itinerant preachers and teachers in the south. In the town itself he was at first controversial; he is said to have received his Qur'anic and Islamic education largely without teachers, by direct inspiration. He formed an independent circle of students in Ilorin and in the south. In a letter written by one of his students in 1917 he is even addressed as *Mahdi*, which indicates eschatological beliefs connected with him. Later, too, his students believed in his direct inspirational access to the secrets of Arabic and Islamic learning and in his ability to communicate his knowledge by mystical inspiration. He gave them his own *wird* and formed them into a movement which he called *az-Zumra al-adabiyya.* As can be seen from some of his poems, his understanding of *adab* combined mystical and ethical elements with a strong identification with Arabic.

His youngest student, Kamalu 'd-Din (b. 1907), became his greatest success. He started preaching at the extraordinary age of thirteen and was regarded as a child prodigy. Using him as an example Taju 'l-Adab was able to attract many children to his school for Arabic studies. Until that time Arabic language and literature had been subjects mostly for adults. Taju 'l-Adab is said to have undertaken the first steps towards a reform of Islamic learning which was later continued by Kamalu 'd-Din. When his teacher died Kamal took up his preaching both in Ilorin and in Yorubaland. He managed to secure the support of several other members of the *Adabiyya* in Ilorin and also won a great number of admirers and supporters in Lagos where he has had his own school since 1926. He was the first to import Arabic printed books on a large scale to Ilorin. There, too, he established a school which was run by the *Adabiyya* group.

For Kamalu 'd-Din, like so many other West African scholars during this period, the pilgrimage which he undertook in 1937/8 became a turning point in his activities. He took the opportunity to become acquainted with the education systems in Arab countries, and after his return began to reorganize his own schools along those lines. His new school in Lagos was perhaps the first formal Arabic school founded in Nigeria by an indigenous Nigerian scholar. The school in Ilorin followed around 1943. As happened later in Kano, the new type of Arabic school was at first controversial because it exposed children to the full range of Islamic subjects, especially to *tafsir* which was regarded as a serious matter not suitable for children. The emphasis on Arabic language also remained controversial because, in the view of some scholars, this led away from the genuinely religious subjects. Kamalu 'd-Din, however, had the full support of the Emir Abdulkadiri (1919-59) who even appointed one of Kamal's students as his personal Islamic teacher. Being less than twenty years of age, this student was very young for such a prominent position; it meant a significant breakthrough for the religious status of the youth in the town. During the 1940s Kamalu 'd-Din was able to send some of his students as Arabic teachers to other parts of Yorubaland, where they later founded their own Arabic schools.

Due to their experiences in the south, Kamalu 'd-Din and his followers and supporters also saw the necessity to add "western" subjects to their Islamic teaching. Following the model of Muslim educational societies among the Yoruba, especially the *Ansaru 'd-Din* Society in Lagos, they decided to organize their own society, which was founded in 1943 as the *Adabiyya* Moslem Society. In 1947 their Arabic school in Ilorin was transformed into a fully-fledged primary school combining "western" and Arabic subjects. In the same year the society changed its name to *Ansaru 'l-Islam* Society. It was one of the first voluntary associations founded by Muslims in northern Nigeria. After their school was recognized by the government in 1956, the society became more and more engaged in the "western" type of education. This twofold educational activity gave the *Ansaru 'l-Islam* great influence in the town, and the society became an important factor in public life. Gradually its members gained access to key positions, in the educational administration as well as in the civil service in general. Like the educational societies in the south, it was also able to mobilize the support of Muslim women in Ilorin who organized their own groups and sections within the society. This had a great impact on Islamic learning among women in Ilorin.

The government of the Northern Region under the Sardauna Ahmadu Bello showed great interest in the *Ansaru 'l-Islam* and its educational activities. The *Ansaru 'l-Islam* school in Ilorin was among the first schools in the north which got public grants. The Sardauna visited the school in 1961, and Kamal and his closest assistant accompanied him on his visit to Egypt and other Arab countries. Leading members of the *Ansaru 'l-Islam* even claim that the formation of the *Jama'atu Nasril Islam* (JNI) (1962), as a quasi-official Muslim organization for the northern region, was inspired by what Ahmadu Bello saw in Ilorin. The General Secretary of the *Ansaru 'l-Islam* (Alhaji Labbaika Bello) in fact became the first Administrative Secretary of the JNI in Kaduna and organized its secretariat.

The official recognition which Ahmadu Bello gave to Islamiyya schools served as a great stimulus for the foundation of such schools, which gradually developed into an educational sector of their own. Kamalu 'd-Din himself renewed his contacts with al-Azhar University in Cairo. In 1962 he reached an agreement with the rector of al-Azhar, Muhammad Shaltut, to establish a branch institute (*ma'had*) of al-Azhar in Ilorin. This al-Azhar Arabic and Islamic Higher Institute (*Ma'had Ilurin ad-dini al-Azhari*) started in 1963 with Egyptian teachers as an intermediary Arabic school (*i'dadi* ). It was expanded in 1977 to include a secondary level (*thanawi*). A whole network of "feeder" schools is maintained by scholars who belong to the *Ansaru 'l-Islam* in Ilorin. The *Ma'had* has trained students from the whole of Yorubaland, a good number of whom went to al-Azhar and other Arab universities for further studies. By now the *Ansaru 'l-Islam* maintains six higher Arabic schools in Ilorin and elsewhere which are affiliated to al-Azhar. This seems to be a unique extension of this university to West Africa. When the Shaikh al-Azhar, Jad al-Haqq 'Ali Jad al-Haqq, visited Ilorin in 1983, he was given an enthusiastic reception, which showed the popularity of al-Azhar as well as the symbolic significance it had gained for the Muslim community in Ilorin.[9]

[9]For this perception of al-Azhar as guardian of Islamic identity see especially the book written by one of the early students of al-Azhar from Ilorin, Muhammad al-Busiri Salman al-Aluri, *Dhikrayāt fī l-Azhar baina l-māḍī wa 'l-ḥāḍir*, (Cairo, 1964).

The most important group of schools and scholars beside Kamalu 'd-Din's society is connected with Shaikh Adam al-Iluri (1916-92), another highly reputed scholar-preacher from Ilorin who, with his school, the Arabic and Islamic Training Centre (*Markaz at-ta'lim al-arabi al-islami*) in Agege near Lagos, as well as by his Arabic writings, won great influence among Muslims in all parts of Yorubaland.[10] Of his group, two schools have gained special importance in Ilorin. These are *Daru 'l-'ulum* founded in 1963, and the Islamic Welfare Centre (*al-Markaz al-islami al-khairi*), established in 1973 in the old central mosque. The latter offers instruction in Arabic and Islamic subjects for adults, mainly *alufas* who want to improve their knowledge and to develop their own schools. In this way, the welfare centre has become instrumental in the expansion of the Arabic school sector in the town. Many *alufa* families have by now started to reorganize their family schools, either by adding an Arabic section to their Qur'anic and *'ilm* classes or by transforming them entirely into Arabic schools. A great number of these families also mobilized their former students and clients within and outside Ilorin and founded their own Islamic societies for the support of their schools.

The curricula of the new Arabic schools are a combination of old *'ilm* subjects with modernized Arabic teaching. The subjects taught include geography, elementary arithmetic, physical and health education, and sometimes even English. Some have managed to get their curriculum recognized by the Saudi embassy in order to qualify for Saudi grants and scholarships. Others receive some support from Iraq, Egypt or Libya. Maintained mainly by school fees, the schools also rely on fund-raising activities for their finance. The teachers' salaries are often quite small, and the bonds of loyalty between the founder and his student graduates are his main capital to build upon. Apart from teaching in the school of their master, many young scholars start their own Qur'anic or Arabic schools to support

[10]For Adam al-Iluri, his biography and writings and his *Markaz* in Agege, see R.D. Abubakre, "The contribution of the Yorubas to Arabic Literature," unpubl. Ph.D. thesis, University of London, 1980; J.O. Hunwick, "Neo-Hanbalism in southern Nigeria: the reformist ideas of al-Ḥājj Ādam al-Ilūrī of Agege," *Islam et Sociétés au Sud du Sahara*, 1, 1987, pp. 18-26; P.F .de M. Farias, "'Yoruba Origins' Revisited by Muslims. An interview with the Arokin of Oyo and a reading of the Al-Qabā'il Yūrubā of al-Ḥājj Ādam al-Ilūrī," in P.F. de Moraes Farias and K. Barber (eds.), *Self-Assertion and Brokerage: Early Cultural Nationalism in West Africa* (Birmingham 1990), pp. 109-47; S. Reichmuth, "New Trends in Islamic Education in Nigeria: a Preliminary Account," *Die Welt des Islams*, 29, 1989, pp. 55ff; and "Islamische Bildung und Emanzipation der Muslime: Shaikh Ādam al-Ilūrī, Nigeria, und seine Schriften," *Die Welt des Islams*, 30, 1990, pp. 201-10.

themselves; these schools also serve as "feeders" for their master's enterprise.

This "formal" sector of Islamic schools in Ilorin expanded extensively during the 1970s and 1980s. The present situation can be seen in the table illustrated in Figure 1, which is based on the survey data mentioned above.

| Type | No. | % | No. of students | % | No. of schools respon-ding | Ave. | Min. | Max. |
|---|---|---|---|---|---|---|---|---|
| Qur'anic schools | 110 | 46.0 | 11,167 | 38.8 | 105 | 106.35 | 25 | 320 |
| 'Ilm schools, Qur'anic/'Ilm schools | 68 | 28.5 | 8,717 | 30.3 | 56 | 155.66 | 16 | 500 |
| Ibtida'iyya | 14 | 5.9 | 1,647 | 5.7 | 13 | 126.69 | 35 | 200 |
| I'dadiyya/Thanawiyya (mostly with Ibtida'iyya) | 38 | 15.9 | 7,281 | 25.3 | 36 | 202.25 | 50 | 560 |
| Without indications | 9 | 3.8 | | | | | | |
| Total | 239 | 100.1 | 28,812 | 100.1 | 210 | 137.20 | | |

Fig. 1. SURVEY DATA ON ISLAMIC SCHOOLS IN ILORIN

In addition to the rising number of Arabic schools, these figures show a remarkable strength in the Qur'anic and *'ilm* sector. The 239 schools covered by the survey (containing also data from a government report on religious education published in 1980) certainly represent more than half of the Islamic schools in the town, which can perhaps be estimated at about 350. Based on an average of 137.2 students per school this would mean that the Islamic sector accounts for more than 48,000 students in Ilorin. A comparison with data for primary, secondary and teacher training institutions in Ilorin shows that this number possibly reaches 75% of the number of students in the public sector.[11] There is considerable overlapping here which could not be figured out with any certainty. Many Arabic schools formerly accepted students only after six years of primary education; this is no longer the case. Nevertheless many students attend both public and Arabic schools. As mentioned earlier, Qur'anic education is still the norm for

[11]Estimate based on Kwara State, Ministry of Finance and Economic Development, Statistics Division: *Returns from Ministry of Education,* Ilorin, 1979-80. Number for Ilorin Local Government Area 1985/6: 137,349 students. Since Ilorin Town has half of the primary schools of this Local Government Area and about a third of the secondary institutions, the number of students for the town is estimated to reach about 64,000. It should be noted that the number of students in the public sector has in fact fallen in recent years: for 1988 it is given as 116,587.

most children of Ilorin indigenes; usually they start two years before primary school and continue for some more years along with it.

The growing importance of the Arabic sector, as well as the continuing growth of the Qur'anic and *'ilm* sector during the last decades is clearly shown in the diagram in Figure 2.

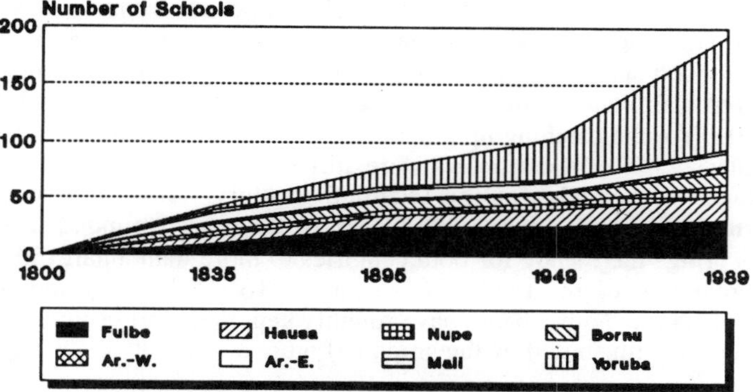


Fig. 2. ISLAMIC SCHOOLS FOUNDED IN THE 20TH CENTURY

In addition to this remarkable growth of the Arabic sector, there is the influence of graduates from Arabic schools within the Qur'anic sector itself. Here, too, 25% (29/116) of the present proprietors had received a "formal" Islamic education. The Qur'anic sector, however, has maintained its share among the founders of Arabic schools in recent years (since 1980: 5/14, more than one third!). This is a clear indication of the expanding "market" and the close interaction of the two systems of Islamic learning in Ilorin.

The high percentage of female students in the Arabic and Islamiyya schools in Nigeria has been noted above. Ilorin is no exception to this, although there were considerable differences between the schools. Some proprietors gave a rather low number of girls, others quoted over 50%. The general impression is of a rising percentage of girls. In one of the schools founded as late as 1979 it had even reached 67% (300/450); the proprietor of this school was very proud of the successes of some of his female students in the national Qur'anic competitions since 1987.

A most remarkable development for Ilorin is the change in the ethnic composition of the *alufa* group since the nineteenth century. Out of a number of 193 families of school founders with available information about their ethnic background, 77 could be traced back to the nineteenth century, 42 of these even to the earliest period of the town (before 1836). There were marked differences between the nineteenth and twentieth centuries, but also between the two first periods. The group of founding families before 1836 shows a composition which is truly cosmopolitan, with Fulbe, Hausa, Gobirawa, Nupe, but also Kanuri, Malians, people from Agades, and even Arabs; only very few of the founders at this time were Yoruba. The second stage reflects the growing incorporation of Ilorin into the Sokoto Caliphate, with the Fulbe as the dominating group (42.9%), but the Yoruba catching up gradually. For the nineteenth century as a whole, 77.9% of the scholars were still from the north. This picture changes completely for the twentieth century: from now on, the Yoruba start to dominate, with 69.8% of the newly-founded schools. This brings their share for both centuries to more than a half (50.8%), whereas that of the Fulbe has shrunk to 16.1%. Hausa and Nupe families, on the other hand, have roughly kept their early share. These changes are illustrated by the graph in Figure 3.

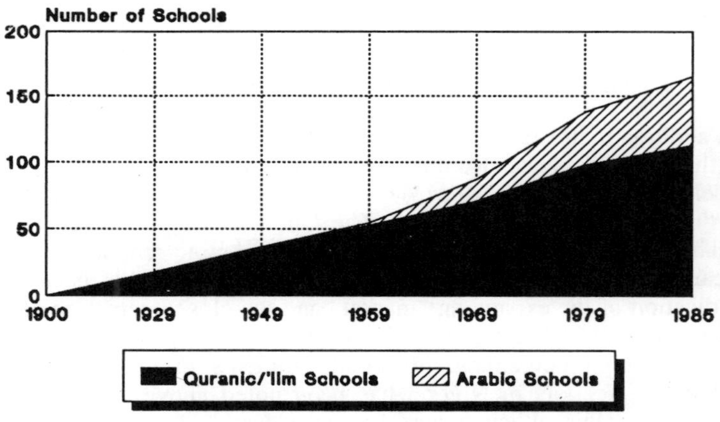


Fig. 3. ETHNIC BACKGROUNDS OF ISLAMIC SCHOOL FOUNDERS

This process of increasing Yoruba participation within the sphere of Islamic schools fits into the general development of Ilorin since the nineteenth century, and seems to be a crucial aspect of the social and cultural integration of the town. It is also remarkable that this process should be connected with a growing emphasis on Arabic within the Islamic school sector itself. That the Arabic language is a unifying force and a means to achieve equality among the Muslims is a view frequently expressed in the writings of Shaikh Adam al-Iluri. With this view he seems to have articulated a fairly general attitude among Yoruba Muslims.

Whereas by 1900 Islamic learning had become part of the social structure of the whole town, "western" education was introduced by the British for administrative purposes and gained wider acceptance as a result of the growing contacts of the Ilorin people with the south. The first Provincial school started in 1915 and was upgraded to a Middle school in 1930. This school, the present Government Secondary School in Ilorin, became the main educational centre for the whole province. Most higher Native Authority staff and even many older members of the present administrative élite of Kwara State (also the late Emir of Ilorin) were among its students. Several elementary schools were also established in the province for the recruitment of staff for the lower ranks of the administrative personnel. However, in the southern and eastern areas of Ilorin Emirate, which were opposed to Ilorin rule and where Christian missions were active, western education as provided by those missions was regarded as a way of emancipation from Ilorin and from the restrictions of colonial rule. These areas maintained the closest contacts to Lagos and to the south. Therefore, even in towns like Ofa which during the colonial period gained a strong Muslim majority, Western schools were quite numerous. After the Second World War the number of schools established by missions or communities had risen to ninety, whereas the Native Authority was running only twelve. The south-eastern part of Ilorin Province, as well as Kabba Province to the east where Christianity was particularly strong, later became educationally the most developed areas of the northern region. They profited considerably from the education policy of the Sardauna who was striving to create a self-sufficient education system for the region. When the first university of the north, Ahmadu Bello University in Zaria, was founded in 1962, a large number of students came from south-eastern Ilorin and from Kabba.

In Ilorin itself, apart from the Christian missions which also founded primary schools for a growing number of Christian migrants to the town, the first private schools founded by indigenes were established by a voluntary association, the Ilorin Progressive Union (Unity School, 1944) and by Kamalu 'd-Din's Islamic society (El-Adabiyya Moslem School, 1947, later *Ansaru 'l-Islam* Primary School). Between 1950 and 1965, twenty-one primary schools were founded in Ilorin, nine by the government, nine by Christian missions, and three by the *Ansaru 'l-Islam* Society which by now was firmly established in the field of "western" education. Ilorin even became the place where the first girls' secondary school for the whole Northern Region, the Queen Elizabeth School, was established in 1956. The number of students from Ilorin town itself, however, was at that stage insignificant (two from about fifty).

Early in the 1970s, the *Ansaru 'l-Islam* started their first secondary schools; the second one was established in Ilorin in 1971. At the present time, they run eight higher institutions in Kwara State. In contrast to states in the south like Oyo, the government of Kwara State did not fully take over the schools founded by communities and religious agencies which still have control over the appointments of principals, the admission of students and other important decisions. This gave both the Christian agencies and the *Ansaru 'l-Islam* a strong position in the educational sector in this state. Members of Kamalu 'd-Din's society were represented in the Local Schools Management Board and in the Kwara State Schools Board which were responsible for the running of the schools in the State. A son of Kamalu 'd-Din, A.O. Kamal, became principal of the old Government Secondary School in 1979. In 1984 he was appointed Permanent Secretary in the Kwara State Ministry of Education, an office which he kept until 1989. Other leading members of the *Ansaru 'l-Islam* (like the late B.L. Yusuf) also held high positions in this ministry.

The national programme of Universal Primary Education (UPE)[12] which was introduced in 1976 in all states of the Federation nearly doubled the number of primary schools in Kwara within one year.[13] For Ilorin Town itself it had quite paradoxical results. UPE coincided with a major local government reform which also took place in 1976. Whereas the number of schools jumped from 88 to 230 in the Local Government Areas which were formed out of the old Ilorin Division, there were apparently at first no new schools in the town itself.[14] In the context of this local government reform, UPE became part of the growing independence of the surrounding rural areas from the town, which since the nineteenth century had exercised a firm control over them. On the other hand the UPE programme led to the employment of many new teachers (1,722, which almost doubled the number of the existing primary school teachers in the State). The statistical data for these years show a new category of "Religious Teachers" without the

[12]For UPE and its results in a state of the former Northern Region, see M. Bray, *Universal Primary Education in Nigeria: A Study of Kano State* (London, 1981).

[13]Kwara State Statistical Digest 1975-6, p. 62: 545; Kwara State Statistical Year Book 1976-7, p. 66: 1,021.

[14]*Loc.cit.*; for the list of Ilorin Town's 30 primary schools in 1977, see A.G. Onokerhoraye, *Public Services in Nigerian Urban areas: A Case Study of Ilorin* (Ibadan, 1981), p. 84. This list shows that all of them were founded before 1971.

usual qualifications (Grade II, Grade III, WASC, GCE). Those teaching Islamic Religious Knowledge (529, almost a third of the whole number of new appointments) most probably were graduates from the private Arabic schools. The same seems to be the case for the secondary sector where a group of "Arabists/Religious Teachers" has emerged from 1974/5 onwards with rising numbers.[15] Thus, contrary to what would be expected, the educational expansion of the mid-1970s seems to have benefited the private Arabic schools in the town perhaps more than the public sector itself, creating considerable job opportunities for their students.

These religious teachers received very low salaries, which led to the emergence of two interest groups founded to promote the interest of teachers from the private Arabic sector. The first was the Islamic Missionaries Association of Nigeria (IMAN) founded in 1975 by the Grand Kadi of Kwara, Justice Abdulkadir Orire, in cooperation with the *Ansaru 'l-Islam* and other Islamic organizations. The other, the Kwara State Joint Association of Arabic and Islamic Schools (JAAIS), *Jam'iyyat ittihad al-madaris al-islamiyya wa 'l-'arabiyya*), founded in 1976, was an association of proprietors of different Arabic schools, with the principal of the Islamic Welfare Centre (Fazazi Ahmad Imam) as its general secretary. Both associations negotiated with the military government to regularize the salaries of Arabic teachers in the public sector. They succeeded in 1979 when the government issued a circular which fixed certain Grade Levels (GL) of the Civil Service for Arabic teachers with different qualifications. Although the pay was still regarded as too low by the Muslim associations, this circular was significant as it represented the first official recognition of the private Islamic sector by the government. After this success the JAAIS tried to work out a unified curriculum for Arabic schools and to get governmental recognition for it. This process, however, still seems to be going on. IMAN, on the other hand, took a different approach as it tried to coordinate the activities of Muslim organizations within the State and to provide Islamic programmes for the public. IMAN has more or less gained control over the Islamic programmes in the State media. It has established its own *Da'wa* Centre. The Association founded its own commercial company (IMAN Industrial Enterprises) to provide a secure financial base for its projects. With all these activities, IMAN closely resembles the Islamic Education Trust in

[15]See the data for primary and secondary schools in Kwara State Statistical Digest/Year Book 1974-5, p. 84; 1975-6, pp. 68ff; 1976-7, pp. 71ff; 1978-81, pp. 138ff.

Minna, which is today one of the most influential Islamic educational organizations in Nigeria.[16]

The educational growth in Ilorin itself started around 1979 with the foundation of new primary and secondary schools in the town. It led to a growing number of students from Ilorin in higher institutions which until then were mainly frequented by the educationally more advanced groups within Kwara. Ilorin University and the Kwara State College of Technology, both founded during the expansionary 1970s, were typical cases, with at first only few students from Ilorin town itself and a rising number after 1980. Around that time, too, public secondary schools like Government Secondary School and Queen Elizabeth School for the first time attracted large numbers of students from Ilorin and produced Muslim majorities. Also in this period the Muslim Students' Society became active within those schools. Mosques were established in all of them, mostly sponsored by wealthy people in the town. Apart from Ilorin, other groups like the Ebira of Okene became active in the educational field, and all this led to a fierce competition between the educational "newcomers" and groups which until then had virtually monopolized the educational institutions and the civil service within Kwara, like the Igbomina, Ekiti and Kabba people. This situation still persists. Since the "newcomers" are largely Muslims and the others Christians, tensions among them often took on a religious flavour.

Educational development and political pressure also led to the emergence of an Islamic sector within the public educational system itself, a development already mentioned above. In 1980 the NPN governor Ibrahim Atta appointed a Religious Education Committee which was assigned to examine the state of Arabic and Islamic Religious Knowledge in Kwara. This committee, headed by the Grand Kadi, Abdul Kadir Orire, toured all the Local Government Areas and conducted investigations and interviews with education officers and leading Islamic scholars. It called for the submission of memoranda, and the public response (as documented in their report) was impressive. Many proprietors of Arabic schools as well as Muslim organizations submitted memoranda, describing their schools and activities, making suggestions and calling for public assistance.[17] The Committee itself issued a list of suggestions mainly designed to improve the situation of Arabic and Islamic Studies within the secondary school sector where

[16]For the IET, see P. Clarke and I. Linden, *Islam in Modern Nigeria. A Study of a Muslim Community in a Post-Independence State 1960-1983* (Mainz/München, 1984), pp. 53ff; S. Reichmuth, 1989, pp. 57ff.

[17]See *Report of the Religious Education Committee on Arabic and Islamic Religious Knowledge*, Vols I-II, (Ilorin, 1980).

until then these subjects had been only of marginal importance. This led to the establishment of three Colleges of Arabic and Islamic Studies in Kwara State in 1981 (Ilorin, Babana/Borgu) and 1982 (Okene). A teachers college in Jebba was also changed to an Arabic Teachers' College. Apart from the usual qualifications, these colleges also accept students from the private Arabic schools for a programme of Higher Muslim Studies comparable to that of the School of Arabic Studies in Kano and similar institutions in other States of the former Northern Region.

The links between the Arabic schools and the public sector were further strengthened by the development of programmes of Arabic and Islamic Studies at the State Colleges of Education (Ilorin and Oro). Apart from graduates from public institutions, students from higher Arabic schools who have reached a certain level of competence in English are also accepted for this programme which leads to the National Certificate of Education (NCE). With this qualification students from the private Arabic school sector now have a better opportunity to join the university for a B.A. course in Arabic or Islamic Studies. Another programme at the College of Education in Ilorin offers courses for a professional diploma in Arabic and Islamic Studies which serves to improve the position of teachers in junior secondary schools from the Arabic school sector. The University of Ilorin also recently introduced a diploma course in Arabic which qualifies a student for higher studies. This shows that in Kwara State, as in other northern states, there are now several links on different levels between the private Islamic and public educational systems.

The arrangement of religious subjects at the University of Ilorin shows a peculiar form of compromise between the different religious groups in Kwara State. It was established in 1976 as a Department of Arabic and Islamic Studies but, following representations to the University authority from Christian groups within Kwara State, it was expanded into a Department of Religions which also includes Christian studies and comparative religious studies.[18] This arrangement was also found at other universities in areas of Nigeria with a mixed population of different religious affiliations (e.g. Jos and Ife, but also Nsukka). As the University of Ilorin started as a college of Ibadan University, most of its first academic and administrative staff came from Ibadan and other universities in the south. Even now most of the academic teachers for Arabic and Islamic Studies come from different states in the south; only two are from Ilorin town. Almost all of them,

[18]For the history of this department see the article written by its former Head, I.A.B. Balogun, "A Decade of Religious Studies experiment," *Journal of Arabic & Religious Studies* (Univ. of Ilorin), vol. 2, December 1985, pp. 1-32.

however, passed in the course of their educational career through Arabic schools which belong either to the *Ansaru 'l-Islam* or to Adam al-Iluri's *Markaz* group. This shows that in the academic field too there is a clear influence of the two most prominent Islamic scholars from Ilorin and their school networks.

Every student of the Department of Religions with a major subject in Arabic, Islamic or Christian Studies has to attend courses in the other religion as well as in African Traditional Religion. This has led to a close interaction of the religious subjects at this university. Whereas the graduates in Christian Studies formed a clear majority in the beginning, this has started to change since 1985, presumably because of the growing number of Muslim students from Ilorin town and from other Muslim areas of Kwara State. Although many people in Ilorin as well as most Muslim staff members of the Department itself are not satisfied with the present arrangement and would prefer a separate Islamic Department, it is a fact that religious tensions at Ilorin University were always remarkably low in comparison to other Nigerian universities, which seems to be due at least partly to the special relationship between the religious subjects and their teachers in this institution. The influence of the Department on the Islamic youth organizations in the town has been considerable, and the Friday prayer held by the *imam* of the University who is a member of this Department has become very popular among the younger "educated" people in Ilorin.

The growth of the Muslim Students' Society (MSS) since the 1960s and other Islamic youth organizations in Ilorin since 1979 cannot be described here in any detail. In all of them, however, members of the Islamic organizations and former students of Arabic schools linked with Kamalu 'd-Din or Adam al-Iluri have played prominent roles, locally as well as regionally and even nationally. Several of their former leaders are now Shari'a Court judges or hold prominent positions in the civil service. Some also became leading functionaries of Muslim bodies like IMAN and the National Council of Muslim Youth Organizations (NACOMYO).

An attempt has been made here to highlight the social and cultural significance of the different forms of Islamic and "western" education in Ilorin, and we have tried to make clear that there are now many links between them which have developed mainly within the last fifteen years. Arabic schools have contributed in no small way to the communal mobilization of the Ilorin people, in a period of rapid expansion and transformation of the town which is now a State capital with a growing non-Muslim population. As the example of Kamalu 'd-Din shows, the establishment of such schools even prepared the way for the widespread acceptance of other forms of school education in Ilorin. Muslim organizations like the *Ansaru 'l-Islam* not only run "western" as well as Arabic schools but also provide crucial links for Ilorin people to other areas of the civil service. The emergence of a public sector of Islamic education also goes back mainly to the influence of Muslim organizations, which are supported by the private sector of Arabic schools and which also from time to time receive the patronage of the Grand Kadi, who has become a central figure in the coordination of their activities. The Islamic organizations in Ilorin have raised the religious status of the youth as well as that of women who play an important role in them. Literary works in Arabic have gained in number and significance, a development due largely to Adam al-Iluri and his writings, and to the discussions which his books and public lectures stimulated. All this shows the key role of the *alufas* in social and cultural developments, even in recent years. They have been instrumental in bringing about a most significant transformation of public life in Ilorin.

# RURAL *MADRASAS* OF THE SOUTHERN KENYA COAST, 1971-92

*David C. Sperling*

The past two decades in Kenya have witnessed the opening of a large number of new Muslim educational institutions (*madrasas*), in rural as well as urban areas, in places where Muslim communities predominate and in places where they are a minority. In spite of sectarian differences, the *madrasas* display marked similarities of style and structure. Nevertheless, they address a wide range of particular problems and goals. Nowhere are specific needs and objectives more apparent than in rural village *madrasas*. Though village *madrasas* possess many of the characteristics of their urban counterparts, they have distinct features that set them apart. This essay examines some aspects of *madrasa* education among rural Muslim communities of the southern coast of Kenya.[1]

### *Urban and rural Islam*

For centuries Islam was an urban religion confined to the Swahili towns of the Kenya coast. The Swahili lived mainly in Mombasa and in the urban centres of the Lamu archipelago, and in a handful of smaller towns to the north and south of Mombasa (Mambrui, Malindi, Takaungu, Gasi and Vanga). Together with the Swahili lived Arab and Indian Muslim immigrants and their descendants, who more often than not had integrated, at least to some degree, into urban Swahili society.

Though established in the coastal towns, the religion of Islam had almost no impact on the Mijikenda peoples of the rural coastal hinterland north and south of Mombasa until the last decades of the nineteenth century. Even then its influence was restricted to certain areas: a few Mijikenda villages in the northern hinterland and to the south of Mombasa among the Digo, the Mijikenda people who came under the strongest Muslim influence.[2] The Digo took to Islam slowly, however, and by the end of the nineteenth century only a small minority were Muslim. Thus, at the end of the nineteenth century

[1]The essay is based largely on fieldwork done in the Coast Province of Kenya in 1990-1. I am indebted to Khamis Omar Mwandaro and Hamisi Tsumo for their help in procuring data in the field.

[2]The Digo are one of nine Mijikenda peoples. They occupy the coastal area south of Mombasa in Kenya and northeastern Tanga Region in Tanzania. The Digo are the only Mijikenda people, and the only Bantu-speaking people of Kenya, to adopt Islam on a large scale.

Islam was unevenly spread; the urban centres of the Kenya coast were Muslim, while the rural hinterland was largely non-Muslim. A few Swahili resided in rural areas and some Mijikenda lived in urban centres; commercial and trading relations abounded between the two peoples, but cultural and religious differences distinguished the urban Swahili from the rural Mijikenda.

The influences attracting the Digo (and other Mijikenda) to adopt Islam emanated from the Swahili towns, and so Muslim Digo converts and their descendants came gradually to share in many of the Islamic traditions which had characterized the Swahili peoples for centuries. As the twentieth century progressed, more and more Digo became Muslim. By the 1940s, except for a few isolated pockets of Christians and some persons living in remote areas, the Digo had become Muslim.[3] Notwithstanding this common Muslim faith, major differences continued to exist between Swahili and the Islamized Digo. For example, the Swahili were literate and had a long tradition of Islamic scholarship and learning, while the Digo were largely illiterate and had no tradition of Islamic education. Urbanized Swahili society was relatively cosmopolitan; rural Digo society was strongly committed to traditional village life. These differences coloured the attitudes of the Swahili and the Digo towards colonial rule, and towards the new educational opportunities offered by the colonial state.

## *Colonial rule and western education*

The beginning of colonial rule in 1895 facilitated the spread of western education (in both its secular and Christian missionary forms). In providing education for the African peoples of the coastal region, British colonial officials first turned their attention to the Muslims. As early as 1897, Sir Arthur Hardinge, the first Commissioner of the East Africa Protectorate, proposed that *waqf* funds should be used to provide a school in Mombasa "at which young Arabs and Swahili...could receive side by side with their ordinary religious instruction elements of history, geography and science...so as to qualify them for posts in the native political and administrative services."[4] By contrast, it was not until some twenty years later that consideration was given to locating a government educational

[3]Details about the spread of Islam on the southern Kenya coast can be found in David Sperling, "The growth of Islam among the Mijikenda of the Kenya coast, 1826-1933," unpubl. Ph.D. thesis, University of London, 1988.

[4]"Report by Sir A Hardinge on the Condition and Progress of the East Africa Protectorate from its Establishment to the 20th July, 1897," *Accounts and Papers* (Parliamentary Papers), LX (1898), p. 25.

institution among the Digo, and when the colonial government opened the Coast Technical Institute in 1921 at Waa, south of Mombasa, its declared purpose was "to educate young Africans in crafts and trades."[5]

Though Hardinge left East Africa in 1900, and nothing came of his proposal until 1912, when the Arab School was opened in Mombasa, his intentions reflected early colonial concern that some form of secular education should be provided for young Muslim children in urban areas as soon as possible. Hardinge had envisaged a school which combined secular and Islamic religious education. As it turned out, religious instruction was not offered at the Arab School in the first instance, and was only added to the curriculum in the 1920s in response to requests from the Muslim community of Mombasa.

In 1919, members of the Arab-Swahili community testified before the Commission of Enquiry into Education in the Colony and Protectorate of Kenya.[6] Their testimony indicated general concurrence on several issues. Most persons who gave evidence were in favour of secular education, provided it was combined with religious instruction; they urged that religious instruction and Arabic be included in the curriculum of the Arab school, and recommended that English instead of Kiswahili should be the medium of instruction. Many Muslim parents were no longer satisfied with the traditional Qur'an school system which they considered inadequate. Some even went so far as to advocate the discontinuation of the Qur'an schools[7] and the compulsory integration of secular and religious education for all young boys.[8]

## *Qur'an schools and the Digo*

The concerns and priorities of Digo Muslims were quite distinct from those of the Arabs and Swahili of Mombasa. In 1919, when the Arab-Swahili community was expressing general dissatisfaction with Qur'an schools and a desire for secular education in English, the number of

[5]Kenya National Archives, 1921 Annual Report, Vanga District, DC/KWL/1/7.

[6]The hearings of the Commission of enquiry were, of course, not restricted to the coast. The findings of the Commission of Enquiry are published in two volumes: *Evidence of the Education Commission of the East Africa Protectorate 1919* and *Report of the Education Commission of the East Africa Protectorate 1919* (Nairobi).

[7]Colonial records show that in 1925 there were 23 Qur'an schools in Mombasa with a total of 548 pupils (Kenya National Archives, Coast Province, Deposit 32/466, Inspection of Private Schools).

[8]Several of those who testified before the Commission of Enquiry felt that training in domestic science, together with religious instruction, should be given to girls, and some persons recommended establishing a girls' school staffed by women teachers, but most agreed that the Muslim community was not ready for the general formal education of girls.

Qur'an schools among the Digo was increasing, in response to their desire for literacy and basic instruction in Islamic doctrine.

The Qur'an school (Kiswahili. *chuo*[9]) was among the Islamic institutions borrowed by the Digo from the Swahili. Before the first Qur'an schools were introduced among the Digo, children of early converts to Islam were taught the rudiments of their faith by visiting teachers from Mombasa or near-by Muslim towns. These first "rural teachers" were usually engaged as personal tutors for the children of a single family in a village, though children of other Muslim converts in the village might attend classes as well. Some Digo Muslim converts also sent their children to study at a Qur'an school in Mombasa or in other towns centres.

As the number of Digo Muslims increased towards the end of the nineteenth century, so did the need and demand for religious education in rural Digo villages. The first rural *chuo* on the southern Kenya coast opened in the 1890s in the Digo village of Tiwi, some 13 miles south of Mombasa. The school attracted Muslim children from Tiwi and various neighbouring villages. By 1900, there were two Qur'an schools in Tiwi. By 1910, Qur'an schools had been established in several other Digo villages, and religious education entered a period of steady growth, closely paralleling the spread of rural Islam. In the early twentieth century the majority of religious teachers were from outside Digoland, but as more Digo acquired religious training, the situation gradually changed until most Qur'an school teachers came to be Digo.[10]

Closely patterned on the Swahili model, the Digo *chuo* was a single-teacher institution designed to provide instruction in the basic tenets of Islam and in the recitation of the Qur'an. The pace of teaching was determined by the teacher, considering the progress and needs of the pupils. By virtue of having only one teacher, the *chuo* was also a single-class institution.[11] The pupils, whatever their age,

[9]The Swahili word *chuo* (pl. *vyuo*) literally means a religious book or text, but has come to have the derived meaning of a school where one learns to read and recite the Qur'an.

[10]Certain landmarks of learning are remembered by Digo Muslim teachers. For instance, the first Digo to study *tajwid* (the art of reciting the Qur'an in accordance with established rules of pronunciation and intonation) was Mwinyihamisi bin Abdallah Mwavyema of Ng'ombeni village. In 1916 as a young adolescent boy he was taken to Mombasa where he studied under the Kilindini teacher Ahmad Matano. When Mwinyihamisi finished his studies in Mombasa, he returned to open a *chuo* in Ng'ombeni.

[11]Whithin the basic single-class pattern, older more advanced pupils could assume the role of assistant teachers or "teacher-students" (Kiswahili, *mkurufunzi*; pl. *wakurufunzi*) and teach groups of younger pupils apart, or help the teacher maintain order and discipline in the larger single class. The *mkurufunzi* had the

would sit around the teacher in a broad open semi-circle, girls on one side, boys on the other, with the oldest at the back. Progress was slow, if for no other reason than that older pupils had to sit through the recitation of known passages by younger pupils.

The teacher usually received a small gift (Kiswahili, *ada* [12]) from the parents of the children on Thursdays (before the Friday holiday) and on the day the *chuo* closed for longer holiday periods. A larger *ada* was offered when a child completed a certain section of the Qur'an or finished his or her studies. Teachers also received remuneration by requiring their pupils to perform various chores; girls would fetch water and firewood or clean around the compound, and boys might help clear a field for planting.

### *Western education and the beginning of rural village madrasas*

During the colonial period, western education had little impact on the majority of rural Muslims in the coastal region. Few missionary or government schools were started in the Coast Province, and the schools that existed catered mainly for non-Muslim children. At the time of independence (1963), there was only one government secondary school, and no missionary schools (primary or secondary) among the Digo south of Mombasa. The absence of schools among the Digo can be attributed, at least in part, to their own negative attitude towards western education. Apprehension about the secular influence of government institutions was expressed by Digo Muslims as early as 1921, when the Coast Technical School was opened at Waa; in that year, the District Officer noted in his Annual Report that there was a "poor local response" to the school, and that the Digo could be induced to send their children to the school "only by constant exhortation."[13] At the end of the next year, the District Officer wrote:

> The establishment of an industrial school at Waa is not appreciated. This in part may be due to the Mohammedan element who fear that their children will receive religious instruction; even the pagans are

---

authority to punish younger pupils, and was usually given due respect by them. Though not paid directly, he was remunerated by being exempted from customary payments and was occasionally allowed to keep gifts given to the teacher by parents of the pupils he taught.

[12]The Kiswahili word *ada*, derived from the Arabic word *adā'*, is not easily translated by a single English word. Though the *ada* is a kind of customary payment, the word "payment" implies too commercial a relationship between family and teacher. In giving the *ada*, parents would periodically express their appreciation to a teacher for his work, but the *ada* could vary in amount or kind and was not a fixed fee.

[13]Kenya National Archives, 1921 Annual Report, Vanga District, DC/KWL/1/7.

holding back for the same reason, as they are naturally imbued with Islamic ideas.[14]

By 1924, less than one-quarter of the 134 pupils enrolled at the Technical School at Waa were Digo.[15] Two years later, at a meeting of the Joint Chiefs' Council, the District Commissioner tried to persuade the chiefs to encourage parents to send more children to the school, but the President of the Council, a Digo headman, openly opposed the suggestion. Eventually the school was closed down and relocated to a site north of Mombasa. The negative stance of the Digo towards western education coincided with their favourable disposition towards Islamic schooling, the demand for which increased steadily throughout the 1930s and 1940s. The number of Qur'an schools proliferated, and eventually Qur'an schools came to exist in nearly all Digo villages.

The Qur'an school system of education continued basically unchanged among Digo Muslims until the 1960s. Beginning in 1964, however, the government of newly independent Kenya embarked on a massive programme to expand education throughout the country. In the Coast Province, primary schools were started in rural villages where previously no school had existed, and large numbers of young Muslim pupils found themselves in government schools, learning secular subjects for the first time. Since few Kenyan Muslims had completed secondary education or teacher training courses by the 1960s, most of the classes in these new government schools were taught by Christian Africans.

With the rapid expansion of the government school-system, Muslim parents began to feel that their children needed a deeper, more comprehensive training in Islam to counteract the secularizing Christian influence of government schools. In the early 1970s, the first rural village *madrasas* began to appear. Though outside influences played an initial role in this new development,[16] the building of rural *madrasas* became a grass-roots movement promoted by village communities.[17] Parents and village elders were quick to recognize the benefits of having their own *madrasa*. A sense of village identity and

[14]Kenya National Archives, 1922 Annual Report, Vanga District, DC/KWL/1/8.

[15]Kenya National Archives, 1924 Annual Report, Digo District, DC/KWL/1/10.

[16]One model for rural *madrasa* education was brought into Kenya in 1973 by Mwalim Muhammad Ali Mwamboga from Tanga, Tanzania. Influences from the Tanga region were also important for the initial spread of Islam in southeastern Kenya.

[17]New village *madrasas* continue to be built in the area and existing ones to be expanded, and the trend shows no sign of abating. Indeed, the expansion of *madrasa* education is one of the more dynamic features of current rural development in the area.

competition contributed to the movement as well. The opening of a new *madrasa* in one village encouraged neighbouring villages to take steps towards starting their own *madrasas*.[18]

*The curriculum and activities of the new madrasas*

During the 1970s, most parents viewed the new village *madrasas* as religious-training institutions complementary to government schools, and few opted out of the government system of education in order to send their children to a *madrasa* for full-time instruction.[19] More recently a number of *madrasas* have added nursery classes (government nursery schools do not exist in the area), and some have introduced the study of secular and technical subjects in higher classes. This latter development is still in the experimental stage and is the subject of debate. Some parents feel that their children will benefit by studying religious and secular subjects together in a Muslim environment, for in theory they will then no longer need to attend government or Christian institutions to gain the knowledge and skills required to compete in the modern world. Other parents argue that due to lack of materials and qualified teachers, most *madrasas* are unable to offer as high a standard of secular education as is available in government schools.

The curriculum of the village *madrasa* is more structured and more advanced than that of the *chuo*. Pupils are grouped into classes according to age and academic progress, and are thus introduced to a variety of subjects (such as *tarikh, sira, hadith, fiqh, nahau, akhlaq, qasida, tajwid, and tawhid*) in a systematic way. In order to offer a range of subjects to different classes, the *madrasas* employ several teachers. The daily time-table resembles that of a government school, with fixed class-periods, breaks for recreation etc.[20]

One of the more important subjects is Arabic language. Pupils learn Arabic from their first day in school. Arabic is also used as the language of instruction throughout the *madrasa*. In the lower classes,

[18]A similar spirit of village rivalry (often based on clan lineages) fostered the construction of rural Digo mosques in the 1920s. See Sperling, "The Growth of Islam," pp. 125, 130.

[19]The role of Muslim parents in determining the kind and amount of religious education their children follow is well documented by a recent study in the Philippines: Abdulrahim-Tamano M. Pandapatan, "Factors Related to Muslim Students' Decision to enroll in Madrasah or Other Schools, "in *Muslim Education Quarterly*, Vol. 7, no.3 (1990), pp. 47-64.

[20]For a study of the impact of western methods on *madrasa* education, see Thomas Owen Eisemon and Ali Wasi, "Koranic Schooling and its Transformation in Coastal Kenya," *International Journal of Educational Development*, Vol. 7, no. 2 (1987), pp. 89-98.

where pupils have not yet acquired enough Arabic to understand what the teacher is saying, the teacher will nevertheless still speak to the class in Arabic and then repeat what was said in Kiswahili. In this way the importance of Arabic is stressed from the beginning, pupils are motivated to learn it and are helped to do so in a practical way.

Some village *madrasas* have adopted modern teaching methods and other western-style activities such as prize days and parents' days, including a kind of graduation ceremony complete with certificates signed by the Chief Qadi of Kenya. Several *madrasas* have introduced extra-curricular activities such as games, choir and drama; a few provide boarding accommodation, thereby offering educational opportunities to Muslims from more remote areas who might otherwise not have access to higher Muslim education. One *madrasa* has recently begun an adult studies programme through evening classes.

### *The categorization of rural madrasas*

Rural *madrasas* can be classified in several ways, for example as day or boarding schools, or on the basis of curriculum in order to distinguish those which offer only religious education from those offering secular or technical subjects as well. Another distinction can be made between *madrasas* which have evolved out of a pre-existing *chuo* and those which have been built as entirely new institutions. In practice, as might be expected, there is a mixing of these categories, and one finds various combinations ranging from the day *madrasa*, which offers only religious education, to the boarding *madrasa* which offers religious, secular and technical education. In general, the more funding available to a *madrasa*, the more facilities and options it is likely to have introduced.

However, it is the nature of management and control which best characterizes the essential differences among rural *madrasas*: some are self-governing village institutions and others are controlled by outside sponsors. Whereas the self-governing village *madrasas* are rural in origin and ethos, those controlled by outsiders tend to be rural only in location. In fact, the largest foreign-sponsored rural *madrasa* on the southern Kenya coast is not located in a village.

*The management of madrasas: the village committee*

Most rural *madrasas* are of the self-governing type, and are managed or supervised by village committees. Even when a village *madrasa* has been founded mainly through the initiative of a single individual, that person almost always calls together other villagers to gain broader community support for his efforts. Thus, from the outset a village committee is usually involved in the establishment of a new *madrasa*, and in recruiting teachers and marshalling the financial and material means with which to begin.

Such a committee may approach the head-teacher of an existing *madrasa* for help in identifying a possible head-teacher for the new *madrasa*. At the same time, the committee must discuss the siting of the *madrasa* (the promoter of the project or a leading member of the committee may offer land) and assess the resources at its disposal.

The village *madrasas* have many possible sources of finance, none of which is sufficient in itself. All member of the committee pledge help in one way or another, and all villagers are expected to contribute in some way, with their labour, with materials etc. The *madrasa* committee may also ask a prominent local trader to donate expensive items such as building blocks or tin roof-sheeting. And they may approach prosperous Arab or Indian businessmen in Mombasa or other towns who are known for their religious philanthropy.

The committee works out not only how to build the *madrasa*, but also how to run and sustain it, particularly how to meet the main expense of teachers' salaries. In this regard the committee decides the amount and frequency of fees to be charged, which are usually set quite low so as not to exclude the children of more needy families. Since the fees rarely cover the teachers' salaries, the committee seeks to raise additional funds for this purpose. In one village, for example, the local fishermen's cooperative society meets part of the monthly deficit by paying two-thirds of a teacher's salary. In a number of *madras* teachers work as volunteers without receiving any salary.

*Autonomy and relations with foreign donors*

Very few village *madrasas* receive funds from overseas donors. When asked why this is so, the reply may be that they do not have contacts through which to ask for such funds. On further discussion, however, attitudes emerge that reflect deeper issues.

Foreign donations can have strings attached. In one of the village *madrasas* receiving overseas funds, applicants for teaching positions must go to Mombasa to be interviewed. In another *madrasa*, the donor sends his agent to sit in on class-lessons in order to evaluate the teachers. Thus, the village committee finds itself subject to outside checks and constraints. Not having the authority to appoint the teachers (including the head-teacher), the committee lacks ultimate control over the *madrasa.*

Scepticism exists regarding the motives of urban-based donor agencies. One head-teacher described how some time ago representatives of a donor agency based in Mombasa came to his *madrasa* offering to help by raising overseas funds. They took photographs of the *madrasa,* even a video-tape recording, and went away with grand promises. The head teacher later saw the photographs of his *madrasa* (which was, however, not named) on the notice-board of the donor agency supporting an appeal for funds, but he has not seen or heard from the representatives again. He is now convinced that his *madrasa* was used to raise money that he will never receive.

Suspicions are further raised by the secretiveness with which foreign donations are received and distributed. One of the major boarding *madrasas* of the area is sponsored by an overseas donor. The teachers are paid generous salaries, and the pupils receive monthly allowances, but neither the teachers nor the pupils have been told the name of the sponsor. In view of such occurrences, village *madrasa* communities seem to have little interest in asking for or receiving foreign funds, lest they lose their autonomy and freedom to run their *madrasa* as they wish. They express the view that they would prefer to struggle along on their own without foreign donations.

### *In defense of popular Islam*

Underlying the desire of village committees for autonomy is the fear of outside doctrinal influences which threaten the very nature of rural Digo Islam. This point is best illustrated by reference to *maulid*, a long-standing feature of Islam in the area, and indeed of Swahili Islam. The custom of *maulid* celebrations is seen to be the object of criticism mainly by foreign (or foreign-trained) teachers who preach against it as *bid'a* (religious innovation).[21]

*Maulid* first became popular among the Digo in the 1930s. It is more than just a popular custom, however, for the practice of *maulid* played an important role in the growth and consolidation of Islam. During the decade of the 1930s, many Digo became Muslim during or immediately after attending *maulid* celebrations. Regular *maulid* celebrations now occur throughout the year, with specific villages

[21]Of course, not all foreign or foreign-trained teachers consider *maulid* to be *bid'a*, nor are all foreign-trained teachers opposed to the practice of *maulid*.

having their own set days as part of an annual "*maulid* calendar." The importance of *maulid* is recognized in the curriculum and activities of most village *madrasas*. Students may learn a whole *maulid* text, or learn to recite certain verses and to sing appropriate responses. Village *maulid* performances which were once organized by the *imam* of the local mosque are now organized by the teachers of the *madrasa* with the full participation of the parents and pupils.

*Networks and rural solidarity*

More than fifty per cent of village *madrasas* belong to a formal network of one kind or another, and those which do not tend to cooperate informally with other *madrasas* and thereby gain benefits similar to those of a formal network. Foreign-sponsored rural *madrasas* tend to operate in isolation (though, of course, they may belong to a broader external network of their own), and do not belong to village *madrasa* networks. Formal networks originate in several ways: through the creation of "branch" *madrasas* dependent on a senior *madrasa*, through an "old boys" network (personal bonds between head-teachers who have gone through a course of studies at the same institution), or simply because of geographical proximity.

A good example of a network of branches is the one created by Muhammad Ali Mwanboga, the founder of the Shamsiya Kibarani *madrasa* in Kinondo location.[22] Since founding his original *madrasa* in 1973, Muhammad Ali has created eight other "Shamsiya" *madrasas* in the area, usually at the request of village elders. Most of the teachers of the Shamsiya *madrasas* have been educated by Muhammad Ali. He continues to look after their professional training by making periodic visits to the various Shamsiya *madrasas*, and advising them on teaching and administrative methods.

The *madrasas* of the Shamsiya network help each other in many practical ways: by exchanging ideas about teaching and other problems, by sharing books and teachers of specialized subjects, and by giving each other support during imporant activities such as fund-raising, parents' days and *maulid* celebrations. The Shamsiya *madrasas* also cooperate by exchanging teachers for exam supervision, or by supplying replacements when the teacher of a *madrasa* is sick or absent. The village *madrasas* of other formal (and informal) networks cooperate in ways similar to those of the Shamsiya network. Through such cooperative efforts, of course, village *madrasas* are able to

[22]The Shamsiya *madrasa* movement originated in Tanga (Tanzania) in the 1960s under the impetus of Shaykh Muhammad Ayub, who trained Muhammad Ali Mwamboga.

overcome their difficulties and deficiencies much more effectively than they could ever do on their own. The various networks have not only improved the quality of village *madrasa* education, but have also created a genuine spirit of rural solidarity.

*The significance of village madrasas*

In broad terms the village *madrasa* movement can be viewed as a modernizing attempt to counter Christian influence and to meet the challenge of secularization; at least the village *madrasas* seem to have first emerged in this context. The transformation now taking place, however, appears to be much more than a simple process of modernization. Though only entering its third decade, the *madrasa* movement has already brought about significant change. The rise of *madrasas* has meant the virtual disappearance of the traditional one-teacher Qur'an school. More importantly, the impact of village *madrasas* has gone well beyond the sphere of formal education. All informants agree that by increasing religious knowledge the *madrasas* have brought a greater awareness of the importance of religion to young and old alike. Consequently, more people are practicing Islam than before. More people attend Friday (and daily) prayers, and more women are praying than in the past. Thus, village *madrasas* have more than fulfilled their purpose of providing the younger generation of Muslims with a deeper religious training. By bringing about a general religious renewal, the *madrasa* movement has had a profound influence on daily village life.

The *madrasa* movement also demonstrates the resourcefulness and resilience of rural Islam. Not only can village Muslim communities with limited resources actively fashion their own institutions, but they can do so in a creative and dynamic way, thereby asserting their common cultural and religious identity.

# THE *MUSLIM NEWS* (1960-1986)
## EXPRESSION OF AN ISLAMIC IDENTITY IN SOUTH AFRICA

*Muhammed Haron**

*Introduction*

The Muslims of South Africa, in addition to being a religious minority,[1] form part of the majority oppressed society. But despite this doubly disadvantageous position, they took full advantage of the "religious tolerance"[2] displayed by the British colonialists in the nineteenth and early twentieth centuries and by the Christian Nationalist government since 1948. They were granted the opportunity to build mosques[3] and Muslim educational institutions,[4] which preserved their distinct religious identity for over two centuries.

These institutions, however, were not the only ones to assist in the preservation of an Islamic identity.[5] As a community, they also

* I would like to acknowledge the valuable criticisms of an earlier version of this paper made by Dr. A. K. Tayob, Mr. Y. Mohamed, Mr. E. Salie, Mr. F. Sayyid, Ml. F. Essack and Dr. L. Brenner.

[1]A. Kettani, in *The Muslim Minorities* (Leicester:, 1979), p. 5, defines a Muslim minority as "a group of Muslims living in a political entity in a state of numerical inferiority in comparison to the non-Muslims;" and in his article "The problems of Muslim Minorities and their solutions," in *Muslim Communities in non-Muslim States* (Islamic Council of Europe,1980), p. 92, he stated, "A Muslim minority ... is a part of a population differing in the fact that its members are Muslims and is often subjected to differential treatment." See also, G. Lubbe, "Muslims and Christians in South Africa," *Islamochristiana*, vol. 13 (1987), pp. 113-129.

[2]Although R. C.-H. Shell did not address the issue of "religious tolerance" or "freedom" when he critically assessed the "Islamic conversion at the Cape," it may be assumed that as a "Muslim minority" they were, at best, tolerated. See his, "Rites and Rebellion: Islamic conversion at the Cape, 1808-1915," in *Studies in the History of Cape Town* (Cape Town, 1984), pp. 1-46.

[3]F. R. Bradlow and A. Cairns, *The Early Cape Muslims: A study of mosque, genealogy and origins* (Cape Town, 1978); A. Davids, *Mosques of the Bo-Kaap* (Cape Town, 1980); and S. le Roux, *et al.*, "Mosques of the Western Transvaal Platteland - a pilot study," *Architecturesa*, 1987.

[4]Y. A. Kader, "Islamic Religious Education in Durban and the surrounding areas, 1860-1979," unpubl. M.Ed. thesis, Faculty of Education, University of Durban-Westville, 1981; M. Ajam, "The raison d'être of the Moslem Mission Schools," unpubl. D.Ed. degree, Faculty of Education, University of Cape Town [hereafter UCT], 1986; M Haron, "Muslim Education in South Africa," *Muslim Education Quarterly*, vol. 6, no. 2 (1988), pp. 41-54; and Y. Mohamed, S. E. Dangor, and A. M. Mohamed (eds), *Perspectives of Islamic Education* (Johannesburg, 1991).

[5]Following N. Smart's definition of religion in his *Beyond Ideology: Religion and the future of Western Civilization* (London, 1981), p. 13, one might define "Islamic identity" as "a response of the Muslim individual to his cosmic and

sought channels such as the printed word to express their distinct Islamic identity. During the past two centuries many Muslim theologians produced religious texts.[6] In addition, Muslims also launched periodicals which reported community events and related issues. Even though many of these periodicals have come and gone, each one has, to some degree, contributed towards the Islamic resurgence experienced during the past two decades.

One of the most important publications to emerge was the *Muslim News.* Launched in 1960, it was the first fortnightly Muslim newspaper to appear during a critical period in South African political history.[7] It recorded the views of South African Muslims about socio-political events both within and outside South Africa. Although it went through many changes before its eventual demise in 1986, it came to play a significant role in recording aspects of the Muslim community's history.

The establishment of the paper should be viewed as an important milestone in the history of the Muslims in this region since it helped in shaping a distinct South African Islamic identity, an identity which differs from many other Muslim minorities in the world. Their preparedness to participate actively in South African society, at all levels, has made their contribution all the more significant. Their identity as Muslims has always stood out on the basis of their involvement in the various structures within both right- and left-wing circles.

The purpose of this essay is to provide a socio-historical account of the *Muslim News* which portrays how the newspaper projected an Islamic identity. It includes an analysis of how the *Muslim News*

---

personal surroundings." See also W. A. Bijlefeld, "On Being Muslim: The Faith Dimension of Muslim Identity," in Y.Y. Haddad, B. Haines and E. Findly (eds), *The Islamic Impact* (Syracuse, 1984), pp. 219-39.

[6] A. Davids, *Afrikaans of the Cape Muslim Community from various lithographs books and manuscripts between 1968-1910* (Islamic Studies Seminar: Dept. of Religious Studies, UCT), 1991; and his "The Word Cape slaves made," *South African Journal of Linguistics* (Pretoria), 1989, pp. 1-35.

[7] S. Zwemer, in "Islam in Cape Town," *Moslem World*, vol. XV, no. 4 (1925), pp.327-35, mentions that during the early 1920s four newspapers were circulating among the Muslims of the Cape, namely the *Moslem Outlook*, the *Cape India*, the *African Voice*, and *African World*. See also, A. Basit, "Islamic Publications," in *The Voice of Islam* (Karachi), vol. XIV, no. 1 (1965), pp. 29-33; F. Collie, "The economic survival of community newspapers: The *Muslim News*, the *Southern Cross* and the *Cape Herald*," unpubl. B.A. undergraduate paper, Dept. of Economics, UCT, 1982; and Z. Arief, "The *Muslim News* – a Community Newspaper," unpubl. undergraduate B.Soc.Sc. paper, Dept. of Social Anthropology, UCT, 1987.

dealt editorially with two issues which deeply affected this identity: the Ahmadiyyat movement and the Palestinian question.

*Socio-historical background*[8]

The *Muslim News* was launched when Zubayr Sayyid, formerly a peanut distributor in Johannesburg, and Ghulzar Khan, a trained teacher and the former editor of *Al-Habib* (1949-51), decided to publish a community newspaper. It first appeared on 16 December 1960, although it was not formally registered as a newspaper until 24 February 1961. *Muslim News* therefore came into existence at a time when the African Nationalist Congress (est. 1912) and the Pan Africanist Congress (est. 1959) were banned, the Sharpeville massacre had recently taken place, and when South Africans were witnessing the birth of the Republic of South Africa.

The organizational structure of the *Muslim News* consisted of an editorial committee which was directly accountable to the Board of Directors. The first editorial committee consisted of Zubayr Sayyid (a proprietor and businessman), Ghulzar Khan (now a city councillor), Abul Kays (a journalist), Mahmood Mukadam (a businessman) and Imam 'Abdullah Haron (a Muslim theologian and salesman).[9]

Imam Haron was unanimously appointed by the Board of Directors and the editorial committee as editor of the *Muslim News*. This decision may have been based on the fact that the Imam was a member of the Muslim Judicial Council,[10] as well as his knowledge of Arabic and his contact with the society at grassroots level. The Imam translated Arabic news items for publication in the *Muslim News*. Kays, who had been a journalist in Bombay and for a while worked for the Cape Town-based *Golden City Post*, together with Khan, covered the major stories and news. These three individuals were considered the backbone of the *Muslim News* during its early years.

[8]Information in this section of the paper is based upon interviews with three individuals intimately involved with the newspaper: Mr. Rashid Sayyid (19 Jan. 1991), Mr. Faried Sayyid (27 Jan. 1991) and Mr. Ghulzar Khan (3 Feb. 1991).

[9]For Imam Haron, see: M. Haron, "Imam 'Abdullah Haron: Life, Ideas and Impact," unpubl. M.A. thesis, Dept.of Religious Studies, UCT., 1986; N. Monroe, "Imam Haron: a biographical sketch," in *Janus*, Department of History, UCT., 1978; R. Omar, "The political impact of the death of Imam Haron," unpubl. B.A. thesis, Dept. of African Studies, UCT., 1987; and B. Desai and C. Marney, *The Killing of the Imam* (London, 1978).

[10]The Muslim Judicial Council (MJC) was established in 1945 by the Muslim Progressive Society, which was itself founded in 1940 in order to oversee the religious needs of the Muslim community at the Cape. See G. Lubbe, "The Muslim Judicial Council – A Descriptive and Analytical Investigation," unpubl. D.Litt. and Phil. thesis, University of South Africa, 1989, pp. 62-82.

Even though the members of the editorial committee had little or no experience in publishing a newspaper they nonetheless made an invaluable contribution by launching this forthnightly publication, which towards the end of its life appeared only as a monthly. It was indeed a unique effort at the time since no other Muslim newspaper was being printed at the Cape, with the exception of a few community magazines.[11] In their first editorial the board clearly spelt out the aims and policies of the paper. Since there was no other Muslim newspaper they were justified in their claim that this was the Muslim community's "Own Newspaper:"

> "Muslim News" is a non-commercial journal, run by an Editorial Board, and therefore, entirely independent; "Muslim News" will publish material of interest to and for the enlightenment of Muslims without fear or favour; "Muslim News" will seek guidance from the Holy Qur'an, the Sunnah and Islamic Jurisprudence; "Muslim News" will not thrive on public donations but be sold at a price, and will publish advertisements as its source of revenue ... We regard "Muslim News" as a paper of the Muslims ... by the Muslims ... for the Muslims ... and we would like you to join us in making "Muslim News" your OWN PAPER.

These aims and policies gave a clear indication of the relationship between the newspaper and the Muslim community it served. However, even though the editorial committee stated that the paper was to be "of ... by ... and for Muslims," the fact is that it was destined to carve out its own distinctive Islamic identity which at times differed from that of the Muslim community as a whole. This occurred whenever the paper took a stand which was in opposition to prevailing Muslim opinion, on the basis of the editorial committee's understanding of the primary sources of Islam.

The editorial committee operated effectively as a unit for the first few years; however, disagreements existed among them on numerous religious and socio-political issues. These came clearly to the fore in the mid 1960s when Dr. H.F. Verwoerd, the South African Prime Minister and arch-architect of apartheid, was killed. Zubayr Sayyid proposed that they publish an epitaph for Verwoerd, which led to vehement opposition from other members of the editorial committee, and eventually to the resignation of G. Khan who was also serving voluntarily on the Cape Town City Council as a "black" representative. Since Khan's political outlook was markedly at

[11]Some of the magazines printed during that period were *The Light* (Johannesburg), *Islamic Mirror* (Cape), *Al Mujaddid* (Durban) and the *Muslim Digest* (Durban). See M. Haron, "Periodicals on Islam in South Africa," *Bulletin on Islam and Christian Muslim Relations*, vol. 6, no. 2 (1988), pp. 15-26.

variance with that of Sayyid, it was understandable why he took such a firm action. According to Khan, this incident also caused Imam Haron slowly to distance himself from the paper. In another incident which seems to have affected the relationship between Imam Haron and Sayyid, the latter offered support to Tom Swartz as a member of the Coloured Representative Council, a body created by the apartheid state to serve the interest of the "coloureds" only.[12] Khan's resignation and the Imam's withdrawal had no real impact upon the editing and printing of the paper because Zubayr Sayyid's son, Rashid, had taken an active part in administering the paper since its inception.

Although Rashid Sayyid officially took up the post of editor only after Imam Haron was incarcerated in May 1969, he had been acting in that capacity since 1967 owing to the difficulties which had arisen between the Imam and Zubayr Sayyid. At the time of Rashid's appointment, only three members of the original editorial committee were still serving. His appointment also resulted in an ideological shift from a pro-Muslim Judicial Council to a pro-Muslim Assembly stand. The membership of the Muslim Assembly (MA), founded in 1967, consisted primarily of professional people; it was a socio-educational organization which distanced itself from South Africa's *'ulama* bodies. Between 1967 and 1973, when Rashid Sayyid left the country, the cordial relationship which had existed between the *Muslim News* and the Muslim Judicial Council was transformed into one of almost continuous friction as editorial policy became supportive of the Muslim Assembly. In 1968, the paper felt compelled to defend itself against charges that it was a mouthpiece for the Muslim Assembly by explaining that its support was due to the "good work" the organization was doing in the community.[13]

Prior to this period, Imam Haron had apparently been able to contain any undue criticism of the Muslim Judicial Council, of which he was a member. Now, however, the situation began to deteriorate, as several incidents reported in the *Muslim News* attest. In January 1967, the editors felt called upon to defend the paper against charges of bias and failure to publish the truth; the editorial denial was defiant: "We refuse to be influenced by any group or person because we want to keep your paper truly independent."[14] Shortly thereafter, however, accusations were made that the *Muslim News* was a "*fitna*" newspaper because it published extreme criticisms of the MJC. Shaikh Shakier

[12]See R.E. Van Der Ross, *The Rise and Decline of Apartheid* (Cape Town, 1986), ch.. 18, and G. Lewis, *Between the Wire and the Wall* (Cape Town, 1987), ch. 9.

[13]See *MN*, 4 Oct. 1968; M. Haron, "Imam 'Abdullah Haron," pp. 18-19.

[14]*MN*, 6 Jan. 1967.

Gamieldien, president of the MJC, wrote a letter to the paper defending his organization's position.[15]

In October 1968 certain members of the Muslim Judicial Council accused the *Muslim News* of being an "Indian mouthpiece" and of promoting "Indianism." A. Kays, writing under the name of Riter, rejected these charges in a critical piece defending the paper's interpretations of events; he also indicated in his article that Imam Haron was now *persona non grata* in the MJC.[16]

The next year, the administration of the MJC and the Muslim Butchers' Association were subjected to severe criticism by a committee appointed by the *Muslim News*. The committee was chaired by Shaikh Salih Dien, graduate of the American University of Cairo and patron of the Muslim Assembly; following a thorough investigation, it concluded that the local cheese being consumed by Muslims was not *halal*. These charges unleashed a barrage of criticisms by the MJC in response.[17]

Within a month of this incident, Shaikh Abu Bakr Ṇajaar, a key figure in the MJC administration, attacked the *Muslim News* for appointing a non-Muslim as editor, one James Matthews. Zubayr Sayyid defended the appointment of Matthews as a free-lance journalist who neither evidenced hostility towards, nor made any derogatory statements about, Islam.[18]

These incidents demonstrate only one aspect of the editorial influence which the Sayyids exerted on the paper. The apolitical line adopted by the *Muslim News* throughout the 1960s was the result of their uncompromising stand in restricting reporting of events in South Africa solely to socio-religious and cultural events despite the independent position and views of other members of the editorial committee. By contrast, reports about the Muslim heartlands devoted considerable attention to socio-political problems.

Zubayr Sayyid did not deter other members of the editorial committee from engaging in the socio-political affairs of their community so long as this was not done in the name of the *Muslim News* or on behalf of the Board of Directors. He felt that reportage on political matters should be kept to a minimum and should always appear without any direct or indirect editorial commentary. Thus, during the mid-1960s, when three members of the editorial committee were being continuously harassed by the Security Branch because of their political involvement, the *Muslim News* did not utter a word

[15]*MN*, 26 Jan. 1967.
[16]*MN*, 4 Oct. 1968; 18 Oct. 1968.
[17]*MN*, 20 June 1969.
[18]*MN*, 18 July 1969.

against the policies of the state. A. Kays was banned from 1966 until the early 1970s for his critical stance against the apartheid regime; G. Khan, during his term of office as Cape Town city councillor, was occasionally questioned and even warned not to indulge in politics; and Imam Haron was eventually murdered by the Security Branch in September 1969. Because the Security Branch were vicious in their treatment of political prisoners and activists, they struck fear into the hearts of the oppressed masses. It is therefore assumed that Zubayr Sayyid, as the financier of the paper, was affected by that atmosphere and was consequently not prepared to see the paper banned or closed down.

The editorial which Rashid Sayyid wrote at the time of Imam Haron's detention reflects accurately his and his father's perception of Islam as well as their relationship with the Imam.

> Imaam Abdullah Haron's ... detention is not known to "Muslim News." But it is safe to assume that Imaam Haron is not being detained for his religious views, that he is not being detained for spreading the doctrine of Islam. If Imaam Haron is being held because of his political views, then there is nothing "Muslim News" can do about the situation, as Imaam Haron's position was to express the religious aspects of the community. "Muslim News" would not hesitate one moment to register the protest of all Muslims if our Deen is imperilled.[19]

This editorial clearly expressed Sayyid's view that Islam should be perceived as a religion and not as a total way of life encompassing all aspects of community life. This politically reactionary statement enjoyed support at the time from among many members of the Muslim Assembly, the Muslim Judicial Council and the Muslim Progressive Society. Imam Haron, however, held a different view similar to that of *al-Ikhwan al-Muslimun* in Egypt and the *Jama'at al-Islami* of Pakistan. The Imam saw politics as an integral part of Islam and he therefore perceived Islam as a way of life. The division between religion and politics articulated by Rashid Sayyid was well-suited to the interests of a proprietor since it exonerated him from blame for the Imam's actions.

However, following the departure of Rashid in 1973, the newspaper underwent radical changes, brought about by the arrival of his two younger brothers, Abdul Quddus (a Karachi University graduate), and Abdul Qayyum (a printer). The former had been influenced by the ideas of the *Jama'at al-Islami* and of Dr. Fazlur-Rahman al-Ansari, and the latter by the protagonists of the Black

[19] *MN*, 6 June 1969.

Consciousness movement (est. 1970). Many black-controlled institutions, of which the *Muslim News* was one, were influenced by the Black Consciousness movement's ideas and practices.[20] The changing socio-political scenario deeply affected the new members of the editorial committee, who were also members of the Board of Directors, and they introduced changes in editorial policy accordingly.

The paper's new political orientation drew the attention of the Security Branch, which immediately clamped down by detaining Qayyum. Not long thereafter James Matthews was also banned. This harassment continued unabated from 1975 until after 1983, during which time twenty-one issues were banned. The brief detention of Qayyum and the eventual departure of Quddus into the business arena resulted in a cousin, Faried Sayyid, joining the paper in 1975 as a part-time reporter; in 1976 he became a permanent member of the editorial committee. He had legal and journalistic training and was thus quite capable of handling the responsibilities which he took over.

Faried became editor, a position he held until the paper's demise. He and James Matthews were the key members of the editorial board, and together they turned the *Muslim News* into a progressive newspaper. They were joined by a number of enthusiasts who assisted in giving a respectable image to the newspaper among the oppressed masses at the Cape. Among these were Anis Salie, who later became a reporter for the *Cape Herald* and a member of the ANC; Rafiq Rohan, a fine arts graduate and a teacher, who was employed in about 1980 subsequently joined the ANC and is currently sub-editor of *South*, a Cape-based newspaper; Anwar Omar, a graduate and photographer; Adil Bradlow, a graduate and photographer-reporter; and Ajmud-din Ghafoor Chiktey, who studied journalism at Rhodes University and served the paper between 1980 and 1986. The paper gained much respect within community circles for its clear stand against apartheid structures; until 1986, it consistently and without fail voiced its opinion against the discriminatory laws.

Despite the number of journalists and photographers it attracted and the popularity it had gained among community organizations, the paper experienced many financial difficulties. Signs of its slow demise were already visible as early as 1978 when Qayyum departed overseas. Faried Sayyid, although a close relative, found it difficult to obtain the necessary funds for the paper from the proprietor's business; this was because the sons of the proprietor had been experiencing financial problems in their own business which affected their attitude towards

[20]See G.M. Gerhart, *Black Power in South Africa* (Los Angeles, 1978), ch. 8; and T. Lodge, *Black Politics in South Africa since 1945* (Johannesburg, 1983), ch. 13.

the paper. Their problems, which indirectly affected the running of the *Muslim News*, resulted in the reduction of staff. Various avenues that were explored to salvage the paper came to naught. According to Faried Sayyid, "a distinct feeling was [already] conveyed by family members [between 1984 and 1985] that the *Muslim News* had to close down." None of the brothers was prepared to negotiate with any individual or group to sell the rights so that the *Muslim News* might have continued as a community newspaper.[21] It thus ceased publication not long after the closure of five other progressive papers, such as the *Rand Daily Mail*.[22]

Table 1. THE POLITICAL EVOLUTION OF EDITORIAL POLICY

| | *Political Position* |
|---|---|
| 1960-7 | Conservative; pro-Muslim Judicial Council |
| 1967-73 | Liberal; pro-Muslim Assembly |
| 1973-8 | Semi-radical; Black Consciousness inclined; Critical towards Muslim organizations |
| 1978-86 | Radical; pro-Black Consciousness, Pan Africanist Congress, *Qibla*; Neutral towards United Democratic Front and its affiliates, such as the Call of Islam |

There is little doubt that the *Muslim News* played an important role during the last years of its existence, when it was seen and referred to as part of the "alternative" or "progressive press."[23] Other news media, as well as socio-political organizations, made constant reference to it. The *Cape Times*, for example, used to lift editorials from it for publication in its column "Black Viewpoint." These papers were

[21]The Sayyid family attempted to resume publication of the paper as a monthly in 1991, but it has not been as successful as anticipated, appearing only irregularly.

[22]J. Grogan and C. Riddle, "South Africa's Press in the eighties: Darkness descends," in *Gazette: The International Journal for Mass Communication Studies* (Dordrecht), vol. 39, no. 2 (1987), p. 12.

[23]K. G. Tomaselli, "Race, Class and the South African Progressive Press," *International Journal of Intercultural Relations*, vol.10 (1986), p. 53; and C. A. Giffard, "The role of the Media in a changing South Africa," *Gazette*, vol. 46, no. 3 (1990), p. 151.

aware that the *Muslim News*, despite being a Muslim newspaper, was in close contact with a cross-section of the society, particularly at grassroots level. Faried Sayyid mentioned that Gerald Shaw, a *Cape Times* reporter, concluded in an article of his in 1976 that the *Muslim News* reflected the viewpoint of the broader community. Many of the daily newspapers did not have the kind of news network enjoyed by the community newspapers and thus experienced much difficulty in gaining credibility amongst the masses for their reports.

Table 1 provides a broad overview of how the political position of the *Muslim News* evolved during the twenty-six years of its existence. It indicates only the public position the paper projected in its editorial policies, and does not account for differing views among members of the editorial committee.

### *The editorials of the "Muslim News"*

The changing political orientation of the editorial committee was of course reflected in the content of the editorials which appeared in the paper. During the 1960s, reports about anti-apartheid activities within the community were infrequent, and emphasis was placed upon coverage of socio-political conditions in the Muslim heartlands rather than in South Africa itself. Editorials focused on the revolution in Algeria, the Six Day War between Egypt and Israel, and conditions in India and Pakistan. During the 1970s and '80s, the paper continued to cover international issues; attention was given, for example, to the Islamic Revolution in Iran, conditions in Palestine and the war between Iran and Iraq. But now an increasing number of editorials began to focus upon social and political issues within South Africa, as community news media and community-based organizations became more forthright in voicing their opinions against apartheid policies.

The editors began to develop links between Islamic religious institutions, such as fasting and pilgrimage, with the socio-political conditions which prevailed in South Africa, and thus they gave the reader a new and politically relevant understanding of these institutions. For example, when the Muslims were about to enter the period of fasting, focus was placed upon the hunger and poverty in the townships surrounding the major cities. Other themes were also dealt with, such as Christian-Muslim relations, Muslim personalities, and socio-moral issues affecting the Cape Muslims. These kinds of editorials gave character to the *Muslim News*, and exerted considerable influence on its readers, both Muslim and non-Muslim.

*The "Muslim News" and the Ahmadiyyat movement.* Among the many themes addressed in editorials over the years, particular concern was expressed during the mid-1960s and early 1980s about the emergence of new religious movements in the Cape such as the Baha'i and the Ahmadiyyat. The growth of the Ahmadiyyat led to extensive debates within the Muslim community, then under the guidance of the Muslim Judicial Council which attempted to stifle the movement's expanding influence. In May 1965, the MJC declared adherents of the Ahmadiyyat to be apostates, a decision which led to great tension within the Muslim community as many persons were wrongly accused of being "unbelievers."

These tensions were reflected in certain headlines of the period, such as "Faith or love? Young Muslim misled by Ahmadis;" "Unanimous *fatwa*: Cape *'ulama* declare Jassiem as *Murtad*."[24] At a meeting of the MJC in September 1965, the presiding officer Shaikh Najaar stated that: "There are no sects, there is no Catholicism or Protestantism. A Muslim cannot differ with the fundamentals of his faith. If he did so he could not be a Muslim ... No authority ... can ever impose its will upon the Muslims in matters of our faith ... Jassiem cannot perform Islamic ceremonies, nor can any Mirzai ... be allowed burial in our cemeteries."[25]

Although Imam Haron was editor of the *Muslim News* during this period, he does not seem to have been in agreement with the hardline approach on this issue adopted by either the editorial board or the Muslim Judicial Council.[26] He was seemingly of the opinion that the Ahmadis should be approached and convinced, and then if they did not wish to believe, the Qur'anic injunction "To you, your religion and to me, mine" should be implemented.[27] This opinion did not result in the Imam's refusal to subscribe to the MJC's view; on the contrary, he supported it and abided by their decision, and even displayed it at the Claremont Al-Jamia Mosque where he presided as *imam*.[28] However, members of the *'Ibad ur-Rahman* Study Group (1965-9), which was based at Al-Jamia Mosque, vehemently disagreed with the MJC

[24]*MN*, 25 Jan. 1963, and 7 May 1965.

[25]*MN*, 24 Sept. 1965. In 1965 the Muslim Cemetary Board and the MJC were taken to court by a young couple who had been accused of being Ahmadis and whose still-born child was initially refused burial in the Muslim cemetary; *MN*, 27 Aug. 1965.

[26]See M. Haron, "Imam 'Abdullah Haron," p. 73. G. Khan confirmed this interpretation in his interview of 3 Feb. 1991.

[27]Qur'an, 109:6; interview with G. Khan, 3 Feb. 1991.

[28]Claremont is a southern suburb of Greater Cape Town where many "coloureds" resided until 1966 when they were forced by the Group Areas Act to move to areas specifically demarcated for them.

decision and could not see why Imam Haron should comply with it. This disagreement eventually led to the resignation of Isma'il Saban as chairman of the mosque; he was a leading member of *'Ibad ur-Rahman*.[29] On the other hand, former members of the Claremont Muslim Youth Association and the Cape Town Muslim Youth Movement who had now become involved in other community organizations agreed with Imam Haron that no formal action need be taken against the Ahmadiyyat, Qadiyyani or Baha'i movements.[30]

As indicated above, there was a gradual evolution within the editorial board from an apolitical position in the 1960s to a theologically-based political standpoint in the 1980s, by which time Muslims were less willing to become embroiled in theological issues which diverted their attention from more urgent socio-political issues in their midst. It was in this light that Faried Sayyid judged it unwise to incite the community to further internal hostilities.

During the late 1970s and '80s, a new breed of activist Muslim organization appeared on the scene, such as the Muslim Youth Movement of South Africa (est. 1970) and the Call of Islam (est. 1984),[31] which vigorously campaigned with the theological bodies against the heretical ideas espoused by the new religious movements. A recent study illustrates that 70-90 per cent of the Muslims in the Greater Cape Town region – where Muslims have been the most vigilant – strongly disapproved of association with heretics and apostates.[32] Although the attitude of Muslims towards the Ahmadis was politically aggressive during the 1980s, some of the articles were carefully written so that the *Muslim News* would not get drawn into any court cases.[33] There were also politically motivated articles such as "Ahmadism and Imperialism," which played on the many negative connotations of imperialism and demonstrated how the new religious movements were a by-product of it.[34]

[29]*MN*, 22 Mar. 1968.

[30]Y. Larney, "The Establishment of the Cape Muslim Youth Movement (1957) and the reawakening of Islam as an Ideology," unpubl. B.A. thesis, History Department, University of Western Cape, 1989; also interviews with G. Khan, C. Sadan (former CMYA member) and T. Levy (former CMYM member). The CMYA and the CMYM functioned between 1957 and 1963.

[31]S. von Sicard, "Muslims and Apartheid: The Theory and Practice of Muslim Resistance to Apartheid," *Journal Institute of Muslim Minority Affairs*, vol. X, no. 1 (1989), p. 217.

[32]Y. Da Costa, "Islam in Cape Town : A study in the Geography of Religion," unpubl. Ph.D. thesis, Dept. of Geography, University of South Africa, 1989.

[33]*MN*, 2 Aug. 1982; *MN* 18 May 1985; *MN*, 18 July 1986.

[34]*MN*, 1 June 1985.

Despite all the efforts to discredit and marginalize them, the Ahmadis did not allow themselves to be intimidated. They responded boldly; they advertised in a local daily newspaper, the *Cape Argus*, their request to the government for permission "to collect contributions from the public" in order to erect an "Islamic" centre and to distribute "Islamic" literature. The Muslims reacted to this by asserting that the Ahmadis "do not have the right to involve themselves in any activity under the banner of Islam;" they thus clearly defined the position of the Ahmadis and in turn defined their own. The headline of the *Muslim News* captured the reaction of the Muslims succinctly: "Angry reaction over the Ahmadis' claim to be Muslims."[35]

These conflicts centred on the fundamental question of whether the broader Muslim community was going to allow the Ahmadis to share its "Islamic identity." As far as the majority of Muslims was concerned, the Ahmadis had no "right to involve themselves in any activity under the banner of Islam." In this view, integration into the broader community was, and is, dependent upon the rejection of the beliefs of the Ahmadiyyat movement, and so long as the Ahmadis claim an "Islamic identity," the conflict between them and mainstream Muslim society will continue.

*The "Muslim News" and the Palestinian question.* While mainstream Muslims were vehemently opposed to the Ahmadiyyat, they rallied very hastily around the Palestinian question which gave substance to a global Islamic identity. This was one of the most sensitive issues for which the Muslims displayed continuous and unstinting support, via pamphleteering or actual demonstrations. As early as 1948, when the Muslims heard of the occupation of Palestine by the Zionists, they held a protest meeting which was addressed by Imam Haron and others in Faure (Cape).[36] In the early 1980s an anonymous Muslim group printed car-stickers reading "Let my people return – Palestine is crying," which became, and are still, very popular. These methods continued to sow the seeds of anger against the Zionist forces in occupied Palestine. The *Muslim News* played an important role in covering issues relating to the Palestinian situation. Numerous articles were published on the *al-Fatah* movement by Imam Haron who, before his incarceration and murder, had apparently met Yasser Arafat on one of his Middle Eastern trips towards the end of the 1960s.

The anti-Zionist content of some articles in the *Muslim News* led to the banning of certain issues. One article entitled, "Zionist troops

[35]*MN*, 11 June 1982.
[36]Interview with Shaykh Nazeem, 1986.

leave student with broken bones" caused the issue to be immediately banned.[37] The paper was also accused of being anti-Semitic; the *Zionist Record and South African Jewish Chronicle*[38] lashed out at the *Muslim News*' allegedly biased and distorted reporting the of the October War.[39]

The titles of articles listed below illustrate the level of anger of the Muslims towards the Zionists:

"The Zionist Menace" (4 June 1965)
"Zionist Dajjal" (14 July 1967)
"Cold-blooded Acts of Israeli Occupational Forces" (25 Aug. 1967)
"Another Israeli Sacrilege" (27 Mar. 1970)
"Illegal State of Israel - proclaimed by Zionists" (28 May 1971)
"Zionism a Black history of terrorism" (15 Mar. 1974)
"Israeli Genocide" (editorial, 28 May 1976)
"Israeli election Victor: Terror Gang Leader" (27 May 1977)
"Zionism is Racism" (7 Oct. 1977)
"Israel cannot be the protector of Christians" (7 Sept. 1978)
"Israel and South Africa: partners in racism" (19 Oct. 1979)
"Palestinian voices the Zionists try to silence" (6 June 1980)
"Zionists trample Qur'an in raid" (27 Mar. 1981)
"After the massacre ... the Israeli terror continues" (11 Feb. 1983)
"Zionist Apartheid Links" (editorial, 9 Mar. 1984)
"Defeated Zionists reign terror" (29 Mar. 1985)

Here we can appreciate the extent of Muslim identification with the Palestinian cause; this kind of reporting was and still is "geared to appeal to a particular camp,"[40] namely the Muslims and the rest of the oppressed society. The titles in which Muslim symbols are depicted, such as the Qur'an or the mosque, have a great impact upon sensitive Muslim readers. Since they are able to relate the Palestinian conditions to their own, it was not at all difficult for them to demonstrate their sympathies in articles, letters and pamphlets or by the demonstrations that have occurred annually in the Cape since the late 1970s.

The establishment of the Palestine Islamic Solidarity Committee in Durban further illustrated the Muslims' vigilance and concern for what was taking place in Palestine.[41] An editorial entitled "Why we support the Palestinians" clearly expressed the appeal of Islam's global identity:

[37]*MN*, 13 May 1977.
[38]*MN*, 12 Sept. 1975.
[39]*Zionist Record and South African Jewish Chronicle*, 22 Aug. 1975, p. 6.
[40]Aslam 'Abdullah, "Muslim Print Media: Present Status and Future Directions," in M.W. Davies and A.K. Pasha (eds), *Beyond Frontiers* (London,1989).
[41]*MN*, 16 July 1982.

> The response of both the liberal and right wing media towards those who support the just Palestinian cause has, not suprisingly, been identical. Behind their facade of self-righteousness they cry, "The problems of the Middle East must remain there and not be imported into South Africa, as we have enough of our own problems."
>
> The Muslims throughout the world, be they in China or Palestine, see themselves as a single unit, linked by a dynamic force that does not allow themselves to remain silent when people, especially those of the same faith, have their human rights trampled upon. ...
>
> We, as Muslims, identify with the oppressed Palestinians because we experience oppression ourselves under unjust rulers in this country. If we are being accused, as Muslims, of importing the problems of the Middle East into this country we don't deny the fact because the laws of South Africa force us to identify more closely with the oppressed people of Palestine. We are Muslims first and last, therefore, whatever happens to our brethren in the Middle East is of dire importance to us. In the same way that their problems are ours, our problems here in South Africa are theirs.[42]

This editorial not only declared the unambiguous support of South African Muslims for the Palestinians, it also lashed out in criticism against the liberal and right wing media for their short-sightedness and inability to recognize oppression elsewhere. The *Muslim News* saw itself as rectifying the distorted notions which the liberal media had been disseminating. The paper also tried to give its readers a perspective on how Muslims might view their own circumstances in relation to the situation of others who undergo similar experiences. In this way, it projected an "Islamic identity" which was relevant to both the national and international context.

### *Conclusion*

The *Muslim News* was one of the instruments which assisted South African Muslims to "craft a more self-contained Islamic image" by liberating Muslim opinion from the control of the liberal and right-wing media.[43] Despite the many changes of orientation which the paper underwent during the twenty-six years of its existence, due primarily to changing personnel, it nonetheless played a significant and direct role in establishing an Islamic identity for South African Muslims which distinguished them from numerous other cultural,

[42]*MN*, 20 August 1982.

[43]This quotation was paraphrased from G.D. Newby, *The Making of the Last Prophet: A Reconstruction of the Earliest Biography of Muhammad* (Charleston, SC, 1989).

political and social groups in the region. The construction of this identity, and self-image, has assisted the Muslim community of South Africa in avoiding the kind of identity crisis suffered by many Muslims in the rest of the world.[44]

We have seen this process illustrated in the paper's approach to two major, but very different kinds of issues, the Ahmadiyyat movement and the Palestinian question. The Ahmadis put up a tenacious fight to legitimize their claim to be Muslims, to share in the broader-based Islamic identity of the community, but the *Muslim News*, along with other theological bodies, succeeded in marginalizing them. The role of the paper in this long-running debate was to protect the integrity of Islamic doctrine as understood by the broad base of the Muslim community and in the process to draw Muslims together against the threat of an alleged heresy. The *Muslim News* also sought to discredit the forces of Zionism, as well as those liberals in South Africa who were unable to discern the parallels between the struggles for justice waged by the Palestinians and by the oppressed peoples of South Africa against apartheid. The paper's coverage of this issue drew South African Muslims more closely into the international *umma* and at the same time associated them with the struggle in their own country.

[44]A. Ahsan , "The Identity Crisis within the Modern Muslim Nation-States," *Al-Tawhid* (London and Tehran), V, no. 2 (1987), pp. 97-130; and J.J. Donohue and J.L. Esposito, *Islam in Transition: Muslim Perspectives* (Oxford, 1982), ch. 1, "Early Responses: Crisis and the search for Identity."

# THE ROLE OF KISWAHILI IN EAST AFRICAN ISLAM

*Justo Lacunza Balda*

In studying written sources about Islam in the Swahili language (Kiswahili), one encounters two different, though closely related, kinds of research material. The first are the classical texts, especially the *utenzi* literature in the form of long poems written in the *utenzi* metre, which has eight syllables in the line and four lines in the stanza; there are also other forms of poetry such as *ukawafi, kisarambe, takhmis, tawil, shairi, wimbo.*[1] The second constitutes a genre of contemporary literature which takes the form of short pamphlets written mostly, but not exclusively, in prose. Two contemporary Muslim authors, Shaikh Abdallah al-Farsy (1912-82) and Shaikh Said Musa (b.1944), have employed prose and poetry extensively in writing about Islam in Kiswahili.

The *utenzi* tradition continues today not only with Islamic religious poems, but also with political and secular productions.[2] Two contemporary Muslim publications in Swahili, *Sauti ya Umma* and *Mizani*, publish *utenzi* poems and earnestly invite their readers to send in their poetic compositions or their views on Islam.

### "*Sauti ya Umma*"

*Sauti ya Umma* is printed in the Islamic Republic of Iran by the government-controlled *Taasisi ya Fikra za Kiislamu* (The Foundation of Islamic Thought) and sent to East Africa and to other countries in Africa where Kiswahili is spoken, such as Burundi, Malawi, Rwanda, South Africa, Zambia and Zaire. The monthly colour magazine has six main sections: *barua za wasomaji* (readers' letters); *maoni ya wasomaji* (readers' views); *mafundisho ya kidini* (religious teaching); *bustani la watenzi* (the garden of poets); *tafsiri ya Qur'ani*

[1]See S. M. Komba, *Uwanja wa Mashairi* (Dar es Salaam, 1976), pp. 9-72; J. Knappert, *Four Centuries of Swahili Verse* (London, 1979), pp. 33-65; M. H. Abdulaziz, *Muyaka, 19th-Century Swahili Popular Poetry* (Nairobi, 1979), pp. 48-105; R. Ohly, "Literature in Swahili," in B. W. Andrzejewski, S. Pilaszewicz and W. Tyloch (eds), *Literatures in African Languages, theoretical issues and sample surveys* (Cambridge, 1985), pp. 460-92.

[2]R. Mwaruka, *Utenzi wa Jamhuri ya Tanzania* (Arusha, 1968); G. A. Mhina, *Utenzi wa Kumbukumbu za Azimio la Arusha* (Dar es Salaam, 1978); E. M. Machimbi, *Utenzi wa CCM* (Dar es Salaam, 1981); S. A. Kibao, *Utenzi wa Uhuru wa Kenya* (Nairobi, 1987).

(commentary of the Qur'an); *hadithi za Mtume* (traditions of the Prophet).[3]

During the era of Ayatollah Khomeini's leadership (d. 1989), the main trends of his Islamic Revolution were gradually explained in *Sauti ya Umma*. Events such as the eight-year Iraq-Iran war (1980-8), the killing of Muslims in Mecca during the *hajj* (31 July 1987), the use of chemical weapons by the Iraqi regime against the Kurdish population of Halabja (March 1988), and American policy in the Middle East have been commented upon at length both in prose and poetry. There is also great emphasis on cultural relations between Persia (*Uajemi*) and East Africa and the role played by the Persians in the history and development of Islam. *Sauti ya Umma* has published in nine parts (nos. 43-51) one of the longest *utenzi* poems written in modern times entitled *Uhusiano wa Kisiasa, Kitamaduni na Kibiashara baina ya Uajemi na Afrika* ("Political, Cultural and Commercial Relations between Persia and Africa"). The poem was written by A.A. Noordin and has 658 stanzas with a total of 2632 verses. The author is very much aware of the importance of Kiswahili in writing about Islam so that its principles can be understood by both the classically-educated Muslim élite and ordinary believers who know no other language, including Arabic.

*Ndipo kufanya wamuzi*
*kuitungia utenzi*
*Raia na viongozi*
*waweze kujisomea*
(Indeed I have decided
to compose the *utenzi*
so that citizens and leaders
will be able to read it for themselves.)

*Ili isiwe thakili*
*Natunga kwa Kiswahili*
*Wa karibu wa mabali*
*Niwawezeshe kujisomea*
(That it may not be tiresome
I compose in Kiswahili
so that I may empower
those near and those far away
to understand it.)[4]

[3]*Sauti ya Umma* has been published from about 1985. Subscribers are requested to fill in a long questionnaire, and knowledge of Kiswahili is necessary if one is to receive the magazine. In fact it is sent as a gift and cannot be sold; "*Zawadi lisiuzwe*" (gift, must not be sold) is written on the first page.

[4]Stanzas 35-36, *Sauti ya Umma*, no. 43, March/April 1988.

The knowledge and teaching offered by *Sauti ya Umma*, and more particularly the inspiration of Iran's Islamic revolution, have found a welcoming echo among many Muslim leaders and readers in East Africa.

> *Sisi tuko nyuma yenu ingawa tuko baidi na inchi ya Iran, lakini hatuwati kumuomba Mungu ili mupate mafanikio mema na ushindi mkuu.*
> (We are behind you even if we are far away from the country of Iran, but we do not cease to ask God that you may succeed and obtain a great victory.)[5]

> *Mbariki kiongozi wa Iran Imam Khomeini na wafuasi.*
> (Bless Imam Khomeini the leader of Iran together with all his followers.)[6]

> *Mapinduzi ya Islamu ya Iran yanapendeza sana kwa sababu yanatetea Uislamu duniani.....Wanainchi wa Iran muwe macho kuulinda Uislamu kusije kukatokea mapinduzi mengine kinyume ya Uislamu, Mungu ayalinde Mapinduzi ya Iran.*
> (The Islamic revolution of Iran is very much liked because it defends Islam in the world. ... Citizens of Iran, watch carefully in order to protect Islam, that another revolution may not take place against Islam. May God protect the revolution of Iran.)[7]

> *Nami pamoja na Umati Muhammad SAW tumo misikitini kila siku ili kuwaombea wanamapinduzi wa Irani kupigana na kushinda.*
> (I myself together with Muhammad's [peace be upon him] Muslim community are in the mosques every day to pray so that the revolutionaries of Iran may fight and be victorious.)[8]

### "*Mizani*"

*Mizani* is published by UWAMDI, (*Umoja wa Wahubiri wa Kiislamu wa Mlingano wa Dini* (Union of Muslim Preachers of Related Religions).[9] Until 1990 this organization was called *Umoja wa Wahubiri wa Kiislamu*, and it is only since they began the publication of their newspaper that they became known as UWAMDI.

The publication is very much concerned with the quality of Muslim leadership in Tanzania, and right from the start, in early 1990, it came into a bitter confrontation with BAKWATA *(Baraza Kuu la Waislamu wa Tanzania* – Supreme Council of Tanzanian Muslims)

[5]Sh. A. M. Kharusy, Mombasa, Kenya, *Sauti ya Umma*, no. 42.
[6]Sh. H. A. Mgange, Kondoa, Tanzania, *Sauti ya Umma*, no. 42.
[7]Ndg. A. M. Massawe, Himo, Moshi, Tanzania, *Sauti ya Umma*, no. 42.
[8]Ndg. H. H. K. Kazinja, Buyango Katoke, Bukoba, Tanzania, *Sauti ya Umma*, no. 43.
[9]The Secretary General of UWAMDI is Ustadh Swaleh Athumani Ngoy, born in Ujiji.

because it expressed concern about the way BAKWATA was leading the Muslim community. The paper reported the Friday *khutba* of Shaikh Kassim bin Jumaa Khamisi, Imam of the Mtoro mosque in Dar es Salaam, when he called upon Muslims "to remove the national leaders of BAKWATA" (*kuwaondoa viongozi wa Kitaifa wa BAKWATA*). Another report commented that "the Muslims are tired of BAKWATA's leadership" (*Waislam wachoshwa na uongozi wa BAKWATA*).[10]

The *Mizani* newspaper also aims to offer its readers guidelines on matters related to Muslim traditions based on Qur'anic revelation or Prophetic tradition (dress, food, manners, worship etc.) and to Christianity, particularly the person of Jesus as seen by the Qu'ran. The newspaper has five main sections: *maoni ya washairi* (poets' views); *barua zenu* (your letters); *waislamu ulimwenguni* (Muslims of the world); *mafundisho ya Kiislamu* (Islamic teaching); *mafundisho ya Kikristu* (Christian teaching).

The charismatic leader behind the UWAMDI movement is Shaikh Musa Hussein, regarded by his followers as their teacher and mentor. He was born in Ujiji in 1918 and studied in Usagara and Mpwapwa. Later he became an agricultural officer in Bagamoyo until he joined the ranks of TANU (Tanganyika African National Union) in his native Ujiji. He entered politics and became, after independence, chairman of the newly-formed government organization *Umoja wa Vijana* (Youth Union) in Kigoma Region. Sh. Hussein studied Islam under Shaikh Kibaraka Ibrahimu, a famous Muslim leader in Ujiji also known for his relentless opposition to colonial rule in the 1950s. Sh. Ibrahimu travelled extensively as an itinerant Muslim preacher and teacher, visiting Burundi, Rwanda and Zaire, where he was a pioneer in the use of Kiswahili as the language of Muslim religious education. The central idea of his teaching was that Islamic knowledge could not be acquired just through the recitation and memorization of the Qur'an in the Qur'anic schools or by learning the principles of Arabic grammar. For him Islamic teaching needed to come out of the Muslim classroom into public places. Such teaching, moreover, could not be forever monopolized by the Muslim élite who continued to insist upon the systematic memorization of Qur'anic passages as *the way* for the Islamic education of Muslims.[11]

Sh. Hussein also studied under another reputed Ujiji Muslim teacher, Sh. Songoro Marjami Lweno (d.1989), who was well known

[10] *Mizani*, no. 4, 6 April 1990.

[11] Fieldwork, 1970-4, 1980-2 and 1988. Sh. Kibaraka Ibrahimu lived in Mgambazi (Kigoma), in part to distance himself from the pedagogy which prevailed in the Qur'anic schools of Ujiji.

for his controversial views on the Bible.[12] Sh. Marjami was an influential figure in Ujiji and had built a reputation as a teacher among his pupils and followers, who came not only from Tanzania but also from Burundi, Kenya, Uganda, Rwanda and Zaire. Many of the itinerant preachers and teachers who today educate the Muslim communities in these countries were trained under the guidance of Sh. Ibrahimu and Sh. Lweno.[13] Most of the teachers and preachers who belong to UWAMDI , and who go under the name of the "Preachers of Islam," come from Kigoma region and have been trained by Sh. Hussein, especially S. A. Ngoy,[14] N. M. Fundi and M. A. Kawemba.[15]

Two significant developments mark UWAMDI's Muslim action and Islamic outlook nowadays. First of all, *Mizani* proposed a national union in Tanzania of all the groups involved in the Islamic Call (*Da'wa*) movement. Such groups have been influenced by the work of A. H. Deedat (b.1918), a South African Muslim preacher, writer and radio broadcaster, who directs an Islamic Centre in Durban. Deedat has written several works on the relationship between the Qur'an and the Bible: *Is the Bible God's Word?*; *Crucifixion or Crucifiction?*; *Christ in Islam?*; *What the Bible says about Muhammad*; *Al-Qur'an the Ultimate Miracle*.[16] Secondly, the Islamic Revolution of the Islamic

[12]Sh. S. M. Marjami, *Mtume Muhammad s.a.w. katika Biblia* (Lahore, n.d.). At one time Sh. Marjami seemed to take the line of Sh. Amri Abedi (1924-64), who, after training as an Ahmadiyya teacher in Pakistan (1954-6), became a staunch defender of the Ahmadiyya position regarding the Qur'anic revelation. However, Sh. Marjami never became an Ahmadiyya Muslim.

[13]Many Muslim teachers in Burundi, Rwanda and in the Zaire regions of Kasongo, Bukavu, Goma, Bunia and Kisangani were trained in Ujiji. The language of Muslim religious education in these countries is Kiswahili. The study of Kiswahili is compulsory in schools in Rwanda, a country where, in peoples' minds, it is very much linked to the Muslim religion. Fieldwork: Burundi (1982 and 1988), Rwanda (1982 and 1991) and Zaire (1982 and 1991).

[14]His main task in UWAMDI is to answer questions coming from Christian circles, especially from Christian evangelists. See the answers given to evangelist Sylvester Gamanya in *Mizani*, no. 4 (6 April 1990) concerning *uungu wa Bwana Yesu (AS)* (the divinity of the Lord Jesus [peace be upon him]).

[15]Both preachers came from Ujiji, although their grandfathers emigrated from Zaire. They have preached together until recently, but now each has gone his own way. Apparently M. A. Kawemba has left Tanzania for Oman where there is an important and numerous Kiswahili-speaking Muslim community (fieldwork: July-August 1988). They have published together a pamphlet in English entitled *Islam in the Bible* (Zanzibar, 1987). M. A. Kawemba has also written together with O. Matata two other pamphlets in English: *The Message of Jesus and Muhammad (PBUH) in The Bible* (Zanzibar, c.1989) and *The Sons of Abraham* (Zanzibar, c.1990).

[16]A.H. Deedat was born in India and moved to South Africa. *Mizani* has echoed his teachings, for example in fomenting a controversy about the resurrection, one of

Republic of Iran has been increasingly held up as an example to follow and emulate; its particular attraction seems to be the political dimension of Ayatollah Khomeini's teachings. A special feature was published in *Mizani* on the first anniversary of Imam Khomeini's death in June 1990. Because of their highly politicized and confrontational tactics, some public meetings of the "Preachers of Islam" have been cancelled and their licenses to address street rallies withdrawn.[17]

*Continuity and change through the Swahili language*

The writings of three Swahili Muslim authors, Sh. al-Amin b. Aly (1890-1949), Sh. A. S. al-Farsy (1912-82) and Sh. S. Musa (b.1944), demonstrate the historical chain of Muslim scholarship in East Africa and underline the role played by Kiswahili in Islamic education. There has been a progressive departure from a conception of Islam based on the Arabic linguistic legacy towards an ever-increasing use of Kiswahili as the language of Islam in East Africa. The process seems today irreversible, although some Muslim leaders still advocate a return to the glorious past when Arabic was the language of Islam, *par excellence*, in East Africa.[18] The use of Kiswahili has contributed to the popularization of Islam and to its spread in many parts of Africa outside the geographical limits of East Africa. Road-signs written in Kiswahili between Bunia and Kisangani (Zaire) inform drivers where to stop and enjoy *halal* Islamic food. The latest Qur'anic school in Bunia (Zaire) has a sign written in Arabic above the entrance door (*al-madrasa al-islamiyya*), but the only language of instruction in the school is Kiswahili.[19] Muslim refugees from the Sudan and Uganda living in

---

Deedat's favourite themes (*Mizani*, no. 8, 1 June 1990). Similar themes are treated in his books and videos, which are published in London by MHK Productions.

[17]Three Muslim preachers from Tanzania were deported from Mombasa by the Kenyan authorities in November 1987 after violent demonstrations. The three preachers, two of whom were M. F. Ngariba and M. A. Kawemba, intended to hold a public meeting to discuss the "Holy Books." In some towns in Tanzania, like Tanga, Sumbawanga and even Dar es Salaam, the "Preachers of Islam" are not permitted to address public meetings.

[18]See A. A. Mazrui and P. Zirimu, "The Secularisation of an Afro-Islamic Language: Church, State and Market-place in the spread of Kiswahili," *Journal of Islamic Studies*, Vol. 1 (1990), pp. 24-53. In most of the Qur'anic schools in Ujiji and Tabora the basic principles of the Arabic language are taught, however, all teaching is done in Kiswahili. (Fieldwork July-August 1988).

[19]Fieldwork, January 1991.

Ariwara (northeast Zaire) are taught about Islam in Kiswahili, which has become a *lingua franca* in the region.[20]

The nineteenth-century renaissance and Islamic reformist movement greatly influenced the Muslim vision of Sh. al-Amin b. Aly of Mombasa, who was considered one of the leading Muslim scholars and advocates of Islamic reform in East Africa of his time.[21] Sh. al-Amin was not only an accomplished scholar and jurist, he was also "the chief Kathi and the Wakf Commissioner and Visiting Justice in Prison. He has to take part in practically all social services."[22] Sh. al-Amin had great knowledge of the Islamic sources written in Arabic. It was perhaps this aspect of his expertise that prompted him to insist on the necessity of going back to the original languages in which the Qur'an and the *hadith* were recorded and written down. Through his writings and teaching Sh. al-Amin inspired the educational development of Muslims in East Africa and stressed the need of learning Arabic, not as an end in itself, but rather as an essential means for the understanding of the Qur'an. Nevertheless, he realised the significance of Kiswahili for the education and spread of Islam in East Africa, and he was the first Swahili scholar to be aware of the potential impact of Kiswahili for Islamic reform. Through the two papers which he established, *Sahifa* (October 1930) and *al-Islah* (February 1932), he informed his readers about the problems facing Muslims in East Africa, such as European colonial rule, the Christian missionary presence and tendencies towards westernization.

Sh. al-Amin, writing in Kiswahili, drew attention to the role played by the Arabic language in the history of Islam. He feared that cultural, linguistic and economic changes would eventually cause a decrease in Islamic consciousness in East Africa:

> *Kujifunza Kiarabu ni wajibu wa killa mwislamu mume na mke*
> (It is imperative for every Muslim, male or female, to learn Arabic.)
>
> *Ni ujinga ulioje kwa Mwislamu kuwa yeye yuwasali hajui maana ya akisomacho katika Sala yake au akasema Kur'ani kama kasuku.*

[20]Fieldwork January-February 1991. A striking example which illustrates the rapid spread of Kiswahili is its use on posters announcing the official population census in Uganda (January 1991).

[21]See A. S. al-Farsy, *Wanavyuoni Wakubwa wa Mashriki ya Afrika,* pp. 29-33; R. L. Pouwels, "Sh. Al-Amin b. Ali Al-Mazrui and Islamic Modernism in East Africa, 1875-1947," *IGNES*, 13 (1981), pp. 329-45; F. H. Elmasri, "Sheikh Al-Amin bin Ali al-Mazrui. Un réformiste moderne au Kenya," in F. Constantin (ed.), *Les voies de l'Islam en Afrique orientale,* pp. 59-71.

[22]Letter from M. A. Hinawy to W. Hichens (1 July 1937): W. Hichens, "General Correspondence relating to Swahili Literature," MS 253028 (SOAS).

(What sort of a religious ignorance is it for a Muslim who prays and does not know the meaning of what he reads in his prayer or who recites the Qur'an like a parrot?)[23]

Sh. A. S. al-Farsy, who had studied under Sh. al-Amin, adopted a different approach to the use of Arabic when writing about Islam. He argued that Islam itself needed to shake off the yoke of religious colonialism, which had been imposed by the Arabic language:

> *Uislamu hautaki Istiimari (Ukoloni) wa dini. Si lazima lugha ya Kiarabu.*
> (Islam does not want colonialism in religion. Arabic is not at all necessary.)[24]

This comment is not to be understood as a betrayal of Arabic or as a denial of its role both in East African Islam and in its relation to Kiswahili. Rather it should be considered, first of all, as a move towards a greater freedom in the use of Kiswahili as a legitimate African language for writing about Islam without necessarily being forced to accept a foreign language as the sole medium of Islamic expression. Secondly, Sh. al-Farsy's view is an affirmation that Kiswahili had in fact become the dominant language in East Africa and that Muslims in the region no longer need be subjugated to a language they considered to be foreign and imported. These attitudes have contributed to the evolution of what might be described as "Swahili Islam."

Sh. Said Musa, today's most prolific writer and scholar in East Africa, considers the use of Kiswahili as the obvious and natural medium for the publication of Islamic literature in East Africa:

> *Mambo sasa yamekuwa mepesi siyo kama zamani masomo ya dini yalivyokuwa kwa Kiarabu bila Kiswahili. Sasa masomo ya dini kwa Kiswahili.*
> (Things are now easy, not like in the past when lessons on religion were in Arabic without Kiswahili. Now religious lessons are in Kiswahili.)[25]

Sh. Musa, in his biography of Sh. al-Farsy, writes:

> *Alisoma kwake muda mchache lakini alimfungua macho na kumfungua mdomo.*
> (He [Sh. A. S. al-Farsy] studied with him [Sh. al-Amin b. Aly] for a short time, but he [Sh. al-Amin] opened his eyes and his lips.)[26]

[23]Sh. al-Amin, *Uwongozi,* p. 22.

[24]Sh. A. S. al-Farsy, *Tunda la Quran,* pp. 4-5.

[25]Sh. S. Musa in the prologue to Sh. A. S. al-Farsy's *Sayyidna Khalid bin al-Walid.*

[26]Sh. S. Musa, *Maisha ya Al-Imam Sheikh Abdalla Saleh Farsy katika Ulimwengu wa Kiislamu,* p. 30.

This is the kind of metaphorical language which Sh. Said Musa used to explain how the Mombasan "educated Arab"[27] guided the first steps of the Zanzibari. Sh. A. S. al-Farsy was fully aware that Kiswahili was the language most widely spoken in East Africa, and he was convinced that it, and not Arabic, should be used as the linguistic vehicle not only for teaching and propagating Islam, but also as the contemporary means for transmitting and imparting Islamic knowledge. Furthermore, Sh. al-Farsy intended at all costs to avoid any total dependence upon Arabic. He was committed to providing guidance founded on the Qur'an and to formulating principles based on the *hadith*; Sunni orthodoxy had to be preserved against any doctrinal innovations (*mabidaa*) that did not fit with the Qur'anic revelation or were contrary to the *sunna* of the Prophet. But how was this possible if most Muslim believers in East Africa were unable to read Arabic, the language of the Qur'an? He responded by adopting the translation of the Qur'an as his major enterprise. In 1950 he published his own translation into Kiswahili of a selection of Qur'anic verses under the title *Tafsiri ya Baadhi ya Sura za Quran, Yasin, Waqia, Mulk.* The complete translation, *Qurani Takatifu*, appeared in 1969, having been financed by the Kuwaiti Ministry of Endowments and Islamic Affairs. The introduction was meant to have been written by the famous Muslim revivalist Sayyid Abu 'l-A'la Mawdudi (1903-79), but his text was not ready at the time of printing. Mawdudi's introduction appeared in subsequent editions in 1974, 1980, 1984 and 1987 under the title *Msingi wa Kufahamu Qurani* (The foundation for the understanding of the Qur'an).

Sh. al-Farsy wanted to write an orthodox translation of the Qur'an because till then the only complete Kiswahili translation of the Qur'an was an Ahmadiyya version published in 1953 under the title *Kurani Tukufu*. Sh. al-Farsy's initiative was not well received in Sufi-oriented groups in East Africa, especially among the leadership of the Riyadha mosque in Lamu (Kenya). The translation gave rise to major problems of praxis, such as the correctness of the Qur'anic recitation, the danger of putting the divine text in a language understood by the average Muslim believer and thus paving the way to personal interpretations, and the unveiling of the scriptures which until then had been explained only by those with knowledge of Arabic. The Sharifian leaders of the Riyadha mosque expressed their views on *Qurani*

[27]Letter from M. A. Hinawy to W. Hichens (26 Feb. 34) in "General Correspondence relating to Swahili Literature," MS 253028. (SOAS). See also R. L. Pouwels, *Horn and Crescent. Cultural Change and Traditional Islam on the East African Coast, 800-1900* (Cambridge, 1987) pp. 132 and 149-51.

*Takatifu* under the title of *Fimbo ya Musa*, edited by Ahmad Ahmad Badawy. They particularly resented the fact that Sh. al-Farsy had not sought their approval for his translation. However, the fundamental issue remained the question of how any translation of the Qur'an might be justified:

> *Hunu upungufu wa lugha yetu ya kiswahili kwa mnasaba wa kiarabu. Wala si kiswahili tu, bali hapana lugha yoyote ilo kundufu kama lugha ya kiarabu. Kwa hiyo kufasiri quran kwa lugha Ajnabii haina maana yo yote wala faida yo yote wala baraka.*
> (There is a deficiency in Kiswahili, our language, in relation to Arabic. And not only in Kiswahili, however; there is no other language as extensive as the Arabic language. Therefore to translate the Qur'an into a foreign language has no meaning at all.)[28]

The contemporary voices of dissent against the Kiswahili translation of the Qur'an come from Wahhabi-influenced circles whose members want to maintain and reaffirm the Qur'an and the *sunna* in their pristine and original form in Arabic. Translations and interpretations, so it is argued, might dilute or eliminate Qur'anic injunctions or the precedents of the *sunna*. The Wahhabi movement has begun to take root in places like Ujiji where the Muslim brotherhoods played an important role in keeping Islam alive. M. A. Kettani, an adviser on Muslim minorities to the General Secretariat of the Organization of the Islamic Conference (Jeddah, Saudi Arabia), has referred to Sh. al-Farsy's translation as "the Swahili interpretation of the Holy Qur'an by Shaikh Salih Al-Farsi."[29] Manifestations of this kind of influence can also be seen in a return to the reading of the Qur'an and the formation of Qur'an Reading Councils, such as the Tanzania Council of Kor'an Reading. A. H. Mwinyi, President of Tanzania, took a positive stand on this issue by announcing that a special fund should be introduced to encourage Qur'an readings, and he contributed 50,000 shillings for the purpose.[30] The latest edition of *Qurani Takatifu* carries a reassuring note for those who still think that it is merely an interpretation of the Arabic text or simply a translation:

> *Tuliupitia upya Msahafu wote na tukasahihisha makosa tuliyoyagundua.*
> (We have revised the whole copy of the Qur'an and have corrected the mistakes we have found.)[31]

[28]A. A. Badawy, *Fimbo ya Musa Sehemu ya Kwanza,* p. ii.
[29]M. A. Kettani, *Muslim Minorities in the World* (London, 1986), p. 177.
[30]*Daily News* (Dar es Salaam), 15 April 1988.
[31]*Qurani Takatifu*, 5th edn, 1987, *Maelezo juu ya chapa ya tano.*

Sh. Musa is the most prolific contemporary writer of popular Islamic literature in Kiswahili. His steady contribution to the propagation and development of Islam is both significant and important. He does not come from the coast like his predecessors (Sh.al-Amin and Sh. al-Farsy) and cannot be called a "Swahili" in the sense of being born in a town of the interior with a Swahili population; he was born in Kilimanjaro region, a predominantly Christian area and moved to the coast in 1962, where his first mentor and teacher was Sh. al-Farsy. For Sh. Musa religion and politics are closely linked:

> *Mtume Muhammad SAW ni mwanasiasa mkubwa na ndio maana ameweza kueneza dini popote ulimwenguni. Hivyo dini na siasa ni kitu kimoja*
> (The Messenger Muhammad p.b.u.h. was a great politician and because of that he was able to spread religion [Islam] everywhere in the world. Thus, religion [Islam] and politics are the same thing.)[32]

Such a goal obviously cannot be achieved unless Muslims are politically conscious and possess enough knowledge of Islam. Islamic literature therefore needs to be produced in a language Muslims understand, which in the context of East Africa is Kiswahili. Sh. Musa has written about 200 books, of which only about forty have so far been published. In issue no. 32 of *Sauti ya Umma*, he listed the titles of 182 of his works which still await publication, partly because of economic problems. He has also promised a new translation of the Qur'an. In the view of Sh. Musa, Muslims in East Africa must have access to the meaning of the Qur'an, and for them Kiswahili provides the key to that knowledge:

> *Qurani haifasiriwe. Nani alisema maneno haya kuwa Qurani haifasiriwi Bwana? Mungu au Mtume? Hata...mtu asiyejua ndio anaambiwa asifasiri, uwongo.*
> (Who said those words, sir, that the Qur'an is not meant to be translated? God or the Prophet? Absolutely not [neither God nor the Prophet said it]. The person who does not know is told not to translate it [the Qur'an]. This is false [that the Qur'an must not be translated].)[33]

Sh. Musa's Islamic thought finds an echo in the Islamic propagation activities of UWAMDI; he is particularly attuned to the politico-religious orientation of the Islamic Republic of Iran:

> *Mapinduzi haya ya Kiislamu ya Iran na uwongozi wa Imam Khomeini ndio uwongozi mzuri mno.*

[32]Sh. S. Musa in *Sauti ya Umma*, no. 32, p. 30.
[33]Sh. S. Musa, *Saumu na Maelezo Yake*, p. 38.

(This Islamic revolution of Iran and Imam Khomeini's leadership are indeed excellent. Myself, I fully agree with them.)[34]

*Conclusion*

Among the many factors which, in different combinations, are contributing to the evolution of Islam in East Africa, three tendencies are particularly influenced by the use of Kiswahili.

First, there is a relentless desire to present the ideals of Islam and a perfect model of the Islamic faith to the Muslim believer, but a persistent tension prevails among divergent factions each of which insists that its own interpretations are authentically based on divine revelation (Qur'an). This situation results from the fact there is no official hierarchy of Islamic authority in East Africa which is charged with defining and interpreting such sublime principles. There are, for example, ten different translations of *al-Fatiha*, the opening chapter of the Qur'an, currently in print, and their doctrinal implications vary according to the author.[35] There is a clear divergence in the way Muslim religious scholars and teachers exercise their independent authoritative judgement to determine the exact meaning of the Qur'anic text or of the Prophet's traditions. Moreover, the fact that many Muslims can now read the Qur'an in Kiswahili increases the possibility of even more individual interpretations of the texts in the name of Islam.

Secondly, the secular states in East Africa have not gone unchallenged by the Muslim leadership. Tension exists between state and Islam in East Africa, and the new Muslim leadership which has emerged does not accept the *status quo* of the separation of religion and politics demanded by secularism. There is little doubt that in the context of Islam in East Africa the issue of Islamic Swahili politics is a contentious and elusive topic. Groups such as *Ansaar Muslim Youth* (Mombasa), *al-Dawatu ila Sunna* (Kenya and Tanzania), UWAMDI (Tanzania), *Vikundi vya Da'wa* (Tanzania) are determined to bring Islam to the forefront of political life, particularly under the umbrella of an intellectual *jihad* to improve the Islamic knowledge of Muslims. There seems to be a three-dimensional aspect to the Islamic revivalist waves of East Africa: first, individual commitment;

[34]Sh. S. Musa in *Sauti ya Umma*, no. 32, p. 29.

[35]The authors of published translations, in chronological order, are: G. Dale, Al-Amin b. Aly, M. A. Ahmadi, K. Amri Abedi, A. S. al-Farsy, M. A. Mohammed, S. Musa, M. A. Ridai, A. Mbarak and one who is anonymous. Other oral translations are also in use, which are not yet in print.

secondly, community involvement; and thirdly, political action. Kiswahili literature is playing a significant role in this process.

Thirdly, the arrival and presence of Christian communities in East Africa continues to challenge the expansion, growth and identity of Muslims. Christians have been regarded as enemies of Islam and of Muslims. Although Muslims have generally favoured secular education and the school system brought to East Africa by missionaries, they were warned of the dangers of following an educational system other than the one provided by the Muslim *madrasas*. The most outspoken defender of Islam against the threat of Christianity was Sh. al-Amin b. Aly, who saw relations between Islam and Christianity in terms not only of categories of faith, but also of open competition to win new followers in East Africa.[36] The problem of Muslim-Christian relations continues to cause as much concern to church leaders as to Muslim leaders and politicians. The crusading attitude of some Christian communities in Kenya against Islam and the open attacks of the *Wahubiri wa Kiislamu* (UWAMDI) against Christianity do not help to create an atmosphere of understanding and respect among communities which use Kiswahili for the development, growth and propagation of their respective faiths.

[36]See Sh. al-Amin b. Aly, *Faida ya Zaka Katika Kuwatengeza Islamu na Kukuza Dini*, p. 7; *Dini ya Islamu*, p. 58; *Uwongozi*, p. 46.

# INDEX